THINKING AND PLAYING MUSIC

THINKING AND PLAYING MUSIC

Intentional Strategies for Optimal Practice and Performance

Sheryl Iott

ROWMAN & LITTLEFIELD
Lanham • Boulder • New York • London

Published by Rowman & Littlefield
An imprint of The Rowman & Littlefield Publishing Group, Inc.
4501 Forbes Boulevard, Suite 200, Lanham, Maryland 20706
www.rowman.com

6 Tinworth Street, London SE11 5AL, United Kingdom

Copyright © 2021 by The Rowman & Littlefield Publishing Group, Inc.

All rights reserved. No part of this book may be reproduced in any form or by any electronic or mechanical means, including information storage and retrieval systems, without written permission from the publisher, except by a reviewer who may quote passages in a review.

British Library Cataloguing in Publication Information Available

Library of Congress Cataloging-in-Publication Data

Names: Iott, Sheryl, 1964- author.
Title: Thinking and playing music : intentional strategies for optimal practice and performance / Sheryl Iott.
Description: Lanham : Rowman & Littlefield Publishers, 2021. | Includes bibliographical references and index.
Identifiers: LCCN 2021011757 (print) | LCCN 2021011758 (ebook) | ISBN 9781538155301 (cloth) | ISBN 9781538155318 (paperback) | ISBN 9781538155325 (epub)
Subjects: LCSH: Practicing (Music)—Psychological aspects. | Music—Performance—Psychological aspects. | Music memorizing. | Music—Instruction and study—Psychological aspects. | Piano—Instruction and study.
Classification: LCC ML3838 .I67 2021 (print) | LCC ML3838 (ebook) | DDC 781.1/1—dc23
LC record available at https://lccn.loc.gov/2021011757
LC ebook record available at https://lccn.loc.gov/2021011758

To my parents, who taught me to work hard;

To my teachers, who taught me to work well;

To my husband, who taught me all the things for which there are no words.

CONTENTS

Acknowledgments	xi
List of Figures	xiii
Introduction	xix

PART 1

1 The Beginning Musician: Practice Is Play — 3
Music and the Brain — 5
   Aural Cognition, Language Acquisition, and Musical Processing — 8
Music Perception and Preparatory Audiation — 15
Optimal Teaching Strategies for the Young Beginner — 16
   Whole-Part-Whole — 26
Aptitude — 27

PART 2

2 The Intermediate Musician: Fluent Music Reading and Early Problem Solving — 35
From "Beginner" to "Intermediate" — 35
Visual Processing — 36
Beginning Music Reading: Bringing Meaning to the Score — 38
   [Long-Term] Working Memory, Chunking, and Template Theories — 43
Execution, and Benefits, of Mental Practice — 51
"Theory"—When, How, and Why — 52
More Relevant than Learning Styles: Personality, Character, and Motivation — 54

3 Practice Strategies for Musicians of Burgeoning Independence — 59
- If You're Not Thinking, You're Not Practicing — 63
- Don't Do It Again Until You Know Why — 64
- Audiation Pause = Learning Pause — 65
- Hands Together! — 66
- Patterns and Mental "Chunking" — 67

4 Specific Practice Strategies for the Intermediate Musician — 69
- Preparatory Practice Strategies — 69
- Chunking Strategies — 72
- Tempo and Rhythm — 75
- Facility — 76
- Think It Then Play It — 77
- Structural Lines — 78
- Contrapuntal Music — 79
- Benefits and Challenges of These Types of Practice Strategies for the Intermediate Musician — 85

PART 3

5 The Advanced Musician: The Cognition of Expertise — 91
- Toward "Expertise" — 92
- Mindful Practice and Avoidance of Excessive Automatization — 96
- Knowledge Representation, Working Memory, and Skilled Visual Processing — 97
- Long-Term Memory: Retention and Retrieval — 104
- Multiple Intelligences and Rule Learning — 108
- (Creative) Problem Solving — 114
  - Impact of Mood on Problem Solving and Success — 117
- Motor Control and Development, and the Risks of Excessive Automaticity — 122
- Multimodal Imagery and Musical Memorization — 126
- Deliberate, Distributed, Interleaved Practice — 129
- Self-Monitoring and Self-Evaluation — 135

6 Conceptual Solutions to Technical Problems (They Are All Technical Problems) — 143
- Practice Tools and Strategies for More Challenging Problems — 143
- Layers — 146
- What to Think About When — 151
- Think It Then Play It — 155
- Scaffolding and Hypermeter — 162
- Mental Practice, Mapping, and Memorization — 171

7 Practice Strategies for Solving Physical Problems — 183
- Physical Practice: Chunking, Gestures, *The Chart*, and Fingerings — 183
- Chunking » Gesture — 183

Gesture » Detail	187
To the Thumbs	193
The Chart	194
Hands Alone	199
Fingerings and How They Help Form Meaningful Units	200
Above Strategies in Sequence and Combination	207

PART 4

8 How Intentional Practice Benefits Performance — 215

APPENDICES

Appendix A: Sample Lesson Plan and Practice Sheet: Beginning Musician	221
Appendix B: Sample Practice Assignments: Intermediate Musician	225
Appendix C: The Integrated Lesson	233
Appendix D: Practice Strategies by Category and Figure Numbers	237
Appendix E: Areas of the Brain Involved in Language and Music Production and Comprehension	239
Appendix F: Workshop Templates	243
Bibliography	245
Index	255
About the Author	261

ACKNOWLEDGMENTS

Where to begin.

I'll start by thanking my readers: John D. Lee, Emerson Electric professor, Department of Industrial and Systems Engineering, University of Wisconsin–Madison; Alex Wilson, assistant professor of trumpet at Grand Valley State University; Linda Jones, pianist and studio teacher; Gayle Kowalchyk, lecturer and piano faculty, California State University–Northridge; and Jeff Swinkin, associate professor of music (theory) and head of theory/composition/technology at the University of Oklahoma: for their insights, suggested resources, ideas, nudges, questions, and some very detailed observations that only made this book better. I'd also like to thank Michael Tan and Naomi Minkoff, "my" editors at Rowman and Littlefield, for their persistence, enthusiasm, professionalism, and patience. This book would not be what it is now without their priceless contribution.

To my teachers: Deborah Belcher, who put up with my practicing-not-practicing and who never seemed to tire of repeating herself over and over and over; Joseph Evans, who infused every lesson with warmth, affection, and the joy of making music; Albertine Votapek, who taught me the musicality present in *Every. Single. Note.* And who invested so much time and belief in me and what I might accomplish; Ian Hobson, who taught me how to take what I wanted and figure out how to actually, physically, do it; and Ralph Votapek, who would present paradoxical challenges like, "I want to hear all of *Tombeau de Couperin* next week, and don't neglect Hannah" (my daughter, who was three at the time), prompting the pursuit of better practice so as to accomplish more in less time.

To my students, who seem persistently amused and enlightened by my bizarre metaphors, and who never seem to mind when I interrupt a lesson, shouting something like, "OOooooh! That's a really good idea!" and then jump up to grab my iPad for a quick snapshot and jot down a few notes. Many of those moments have turned up in this book—I hope you recognize them. I sometimes wonder if I've learned as much from you as you've learned from me.

To my friends and colleagues, with whom I've had countless conversations about all of this, and who still don't turn and run in the other direction when they see me coming. Especially Jackie Bartsch Fisher, the best friend a person could have, and the best teacher I've ever met.

To my children, who grew up listening to me practice endlessly and having their home taken over by countless students, and who had to learn how, if, and when to interrupt Mom so she could get out of her head long enough to answer. Claims they may make of my "bashing around at the piano" are specious rumors, and/or reflect their own lack of understanding of the messy nature of truly beneficial practice. I learned so much from watching you learn. That's all in here, in no small way.

And finally, to my husband, Gordon Sly, who sets the bar high through his innate intelligence and exemplary prose, and who inspires me in how he imbues everything he teaches with the music itself. You believe in me, always, and even despite our widely disparate writing styles. I'm exceedingly grateful for your frequent and ready replies to emails sent from the next room with "Can you help me fix this sentence?" in the subject line and for your careful last look. The idea for this book was formed with you on a train in Italy, with you as excited about it as I was as it first began to take shape. You've listened to me go on and on and on and on (and on) about all of this for nine years now. Thank you for listening, and for keeping the house from burning down around me on all the days I wouldn't have noticed.

FIGURES

Figure 1.1	ABC	7
Figure 1.2	Comparing ease of reading handwriting in English and Portuguese	7
Figure 1.3	Tonality-establishing tonal patterns	14
Figure 1.4	The "rhythm tree"	20
Figure 1.5	Rhythms as patterns	20
Figure 1.6	Simple tonal patterns	21
Figure 1.7	Similar function tonal patterns for musicians with higher audiation ability	21
Figure 1.8	B-flat major patterns in graphic notation	23
Figure 1.9	Rhythm patterns in 6/8 time	23
Figure 1.10	"May Song" sequence	25
Figure 2.1	Clementi, "Sonatina in C major," Op. 36 No. 1, mm. 1–4, showing simplicity	36
Figure 2.2	Bach, "Musette in D major," mm. 1–8, showing similarity	37
Figure 2.3	Bach, "Prelude in C major," *WTC I*, mm. 1–2, showing continuation	37
Figure 2.4	Bach, "Prelude in C major," *WTC I*, mm. 1–2, showing proximity	37
Figure 2.5	Thought-to-motor command	41
Figure 2.6	Audiation loop	42
Figure 2.7	Visual processing loop	43
Figure 2.8	Unbeamed vs. beamed rhythms	48
Figure 2.9	Mozart, "Sonata in G major," K. 283, I., meaningful units	48
Figure 2.10	"Broken Record Boogie" first "notation"	49
Figure 2.11	"Broken Record Boogie" landmarks and keys	50

Figure 4.1	Burgmüller, "Arabesque," sequence of preparatory and practice strategies	70
Figure 4.2	Burgmüller, "Arabesque," two-measures-to-the-next-downbeat groups	71
Figure 4.3	Expected: i-iv-V^7 vs. altered: i-iv-V^7/A	71
Figure 4.4	Major, Dorian, and Phrygian scales in C and G major key signatures	73
Figure 4.5	Clementi, "Sonatina," Op. 36 No. 1, mm. 1–19, showing chord blocks	73
Figure 4.6	Clementi, "Sonatina," Op. 36 No. 1, mm. 1–19, scales and scale fragments	74
Figure 4.7	Clementi, "Sonatina," Op. 36 No. 1, mm. 1–4, 13–19, rhythm chanting	76
Figure 4.8	Clementi, "Sonatina," Op. 36 No. 1, mm. 7–8, evolution of structural line	77
Figure 4.9	Clementi "Sonatina," Op. 36 No. 1, mm. 12–15, three-beat groups, then measure + 1	77
Figure 4.10	Gossec, "Tambourin," mm. 21–24, comparing similarities	78
Figure 4.11	Clementi, "Sonatina," Op. 36 No. 1, mm. 7–12, structural line	78
Figure 4.12	Clementi, "Sonatina," Op. 36 No. 1, mm. 7–12, execution of *Urlinie*	79
Figure 4.13	Attributed to J. S. Bach, "Minuet in G," BWV Anh. 116, essential rhythms	79
Figure 4.14	"Minuet in G," BWV Anh. 116, showing analysis markup	80
Figure 4.15	"Minuet in G," BWV Anh 116, blocks and practicing the seam	81
Figure 4.16	Bach, J. S., "Musette," from *English Suite in G minor*, arrg. for cello, technical patterns and recurring melodic material	82
Figure 4.17	Bach, "Musette," from *English Suite in G minor*, arrg. for cello; *Urlinie*	83
Figure 4.18	Bach, "Musette," from *English Suite in G minor*, arrg. for cello; 3-beat patterns.	83
Figure 4.19	Bach, "Invention No. 1," showing long-term melodic structures	84
Figure 4.20	Bach, "Prelude No. 1," *Well-Tempered Clavier*, Book I, opening measures, reduction with horizontal voicing indicated	84
Figure 4.21	Exponential vs. linear learning	86
Figure 5.1	Water cycle model showing extraction of information from long-term memory by working memory, resulting in (subsequent) cognitive states	100

FIGURES

Figure 5.2	Cognitive model including retrieval, comparison, action, and storage	101
Figure 5.3	Mozart, "Sonata," K. 283, I., and Chopin, "Nocturne in E minor," Op posth., I., meaningful units	103
Figure 5.4	Iott, sight-reading excerpt	110
Figure 5.5	Sight-reading tonal patterns	110
Figure 5.6	"C fingering" hands (scales), showing 5–4	111
Figure 5.7	"Fingers together" hands (scales) for B, D-flat, and F-sharp major and B-flat and D-sharp minor	112
Figure 5.8	"Thumb rule," note and fingering groups for F-sharp minor scale, natural form, left hand	113
Figure 5.9	Note and fingering groups F-sharp minor, natural form, right hand	113
Figure 5.10	Expert's problem-solving process	119
Figure 5.11	Impact of mood on problem-solving efforts	120
Figure 5.12	Hindemith, "Sonata for viola and piano," Op. 11 No. 4	126
Figure 5.13	Bach, "Goldberg Variations," Aria, mm. 6–8 and 25–26	131
Figure 5.14	Leitner's boxes	133
Figure 6.1	Bach, "Fugue in B-flat major," *WTC I*, BWV 866, mm. 1–12, by voice	147
Figure 6.2	Bach, "Fugue in B-flat major," *WTC I*, BWV 866, mm. 1–12, by subject, countersubjects	147
Figure 6.3	Bach, "Invention No. 1," structural realization	149
Figure 6.4	Bach, "Vier Duetten," Duet 1, first subject statement	149
Figure 6.5	Mozart, "Piano Sonata in B-flat major," K. 333, mm. 71–80, Alberti bass in chunked chord patterns, common tones tied	149
Figure 6.6	Brahms, "Romance," Op. 118 No. 5, mm. 1–4 and 9–13, open score, showing parallelisms and invertible counterpoint	150
Figure 6.7	Brahms, "Romance," Op. 118 No. 2, mm. 49–56, melody/countermelody canon	151
Figure 6.8	Schumann, "Kreisleriana," Op. 16, I., mm. 1–5, layering	152
Figure 6.9	Dussek, "Sonatina in E-flat major," Op. 19/20, mm. 19–23, conceptual chunking	153
Figure 6.10	Kuhlau, "Sonatina in C major," Op. 20, No 1, III., mm. 14–35, conceptual chunking	153
Figure 6.11	Schumann, "Kreisleriana," I. structural points and layering	154
Figure 6.12	Schumann, "Kreisleriana," I. "think-it-then-play-it," one- and two-beat groups	155
Figure 6.13	Think-it-then-play-it-loop	156
Figure 6.14	Liszt, "Un Sospiro," from *Three Concert Etudes*, mm. 63–65, think-it-then-play-it, two-beat groups	159

Figure 6.15	Liszt, "Un Sospiro," mm. 63–64, think-it-then-play-it, by the beat	159
Figure 6.16	Liszt, "Un Sospiro," mm. 63–67, think-it-then-play-it, by the measure	160
Figure 6.17	Brahms, "Trio for clarinet, cello, and piano," Op. 114, III., mm. 114–142, clarinet part, meaningful unit and short similar patterns	161
Figure 6.18	Brahms, "Trio for clarinet, cello, and piano," III., mm. 114–134, clarinet part, longer similar patterns and slur-to-slur	162
Figure 6.19	Bach, "Prelude in B-flat major," *Well Tempered Clavier* I, mm. 1–8, harmonic structure and first two steps of scaffolding	163
Figure 6.20	Bach, "Prelude in B-flat major," mm. 1–3, expansions	164
Figure 6.21	Bach, "Prelude in B-flat major," mm. 1–4, harmonic scaffolding	164
Figure 6.22	Haydn, "Sonata in C major," Hob. XVI/50, II., beats, and beats and "ands"	165
Figure 6.23	Beethoven, "Sonata in E major," Op 14 No 1, II., mm. 1–16, downbeats and hypermeter	166
Figure 6.24	Beethoven, "Sonata in E major," II., mm. 1–8	167
Figure 6.25	Kennan, "Sonata for trumpet and piano," III., mm. 92–100 comparing 1st and 2nd editions	168
Figure 6.26	Kennan, "Sonata for trumpet and piano," III., m. 92–100, comparing counting systems	169
Figure 6.27	Enesco, "Légende," trumpet and piano, mm. 20–25, scaffolding	170
Figure 6.28	Hook, "Minuetto," basic analysis	173
Figure 6.29	Dickinson, reductionist map of Bach's "Minuet in G minor," mm. 1–8	174
Figure 6.30	Brahms, "Intermezzo," Op. 118 No. 1, general "map"	174
Figure 6.31	Shockley, map of Brahms's "Cappriccio in G minor," Op. 116, No. 3	175
Figure 6.32	Iott, map of Schumann, "Kreisleriana," VIII.	175
Figure 6.33	Iott, map of Schumann, "Kreisleriana," VIII., comparing melodic material and bass line entrances	176
Figure 6.34	Student K. R.'s first map of first subject statements, Bach's "Fugue in B-flat major," *WTC I*	177
Figure 6.35	Iott, map of bassline and harmonic progression for Bach's "Prelude No. 1," *WTC I*	178
Figure 7.1	Debussy, "Arabesque No. 2," mm. 1–4, chunking	184
Figure 7.2	Debussy, "Arabesque No. 2," mm. 1–2–3–5*, chunk-to-gesture	184

FIGURES

Figure 7.3	Debussy, "Arabesque No. 2," mm. 1–3, comparing similar gestures	184
Figure 7.4	Debussy, "Arabesque No. 2," mm. 1–3, compared to mm. 9–10	185
Figure 7.5	Debussy, "Prélude," from *Pour le Piano*, mm. 6–12, right-hand blocks	186
Figure 7.6	Debussy, "Prélude," from *Pour le Piano*, mm. 41–42, blocks » gesture	186
Figure 7.7	Debussy, "Prélude," from *Pour le Piano*, mm. 64–69, chunking	188
Figure 7.8	Debussy, "Prélude," from *Pour le Piano*, mm. 76, 85–86, group » gesture, triplets	188
Figure 7.9	Debussy, "Prélude," from *Pour le Piano*, mm. 124–132, 157–165	189
Figure 7.10	Debussy, "Prélude," from *Pour le Piano*, mm. 128–131, 159–161, evolution from simplified structure to gestural realization	190
Figure 7.11	Debussy, "Prélude," from *Pour le Piano*, cadenza planning	191
Figure 7.12	Schumann, "Fantasy," Op. 16, II., final eleven measures, think-it-then-play-it	191
Figure 7.13	Schumann, "Fantasy," Op. 16, II., rhythms reversed	192
Figure 7.14	Debussy, "Prélude," from *Pour le Piano*, mm. 115–126, ghosting	194
Figure 7.15	Hand anatomy diagram	195
Figure 7.16	Bach, "Prelude in B-flat major," *WTC I*, mm. 10–15, "to the thumbs"	195
Figure 7.17	Liszt, "Un Sospiro," mm. 34–35, "to the thumbs"	195
Figure 7.18	Chopin, "Nocturne in E minor," Op. posth., mm. 33–36, "to the thumbs"	196
Figure 7.19	Shifting groups of four	196
Figure 7.20	The Chart	197
Figure 7.21	Chopin, "Sonata in B minor," II., mm. 1–11, realization of "The Chart"	198
Figure 7.22	Two against three, three against two	200
Figure 7.23	C major, but not exactly	201
Figure 7.24	Beethoven, "Sonata in D minor," Op. 31 No. 2, *The Tempest*, mm. 67–77, fingerings	202
Figure 7.25	Beethoven, "Sonata in E-flat major," Op. 81a, *Les Adieux*, III., mm. 4–8, fingerings	202
Figure 7.26	Beethoven, Op. 81a, III., mm. 29–30, Schenker edition	203
Figure 7.27	Beethoven, Op. 81a, III., mm. 29–30, conceptual chunking	203

Figure 7.28	Beethoven, "Sonata in G major," Op. 14 No. 2, III., mm. 225–228, alternating 3rds	204
Figure 7.29	Schubert, "Impromptu in E-flat major," Op. 90 No. 2, mm. 1–19	204
Figure 7.30	Chord inversion fingerings	205
Figure 7.31	Beethoven, Op. 31 No. 2, I., mm. 1–17, gesture building and fingerings	206
Figure 7.32	Schubert, "Impromptu in A-flat major," Op. 90 No. 4, mm. 1–3, fingerings	207
Figure 7.33	Liszt, "Un Sospiro," mm. 30–35, melody, "to the thumbs" » gesture	208
Figure 7.34	Liszt, "Un Sospiro," think-it-then-play-it	209
Figure 8.1	Mindful practicing loop	216
Figure App.1a	"Peter, Peter Pumpkin Eater"	222
Figure App.1b	"Falling Leaves"	223
Figure App.1c	"Cotton Candy"	223
Figure App.1d	Sample lesson assignment	224
Figure App.2	Triads and inversions	225
Figure App.3	Cadence pattern	225
Figure App.4	Telemann, "Gigue a l'Angloise"	227
Figure App.5	Burgmüller, "Ballade," from *100 Easy Etudes*, mm. 1–46	228
Figure App.6	Bartok, "Dance," from *For Children*, vol. 2	230
Figure App.7	Bartok, "Dance," chord progression map	231
Figure App.8	Map of Sonata-Allegro form, major key movement	234
Figures App.9	Maps of the brain	239–241

INTRODUCTION

This is the book I wish I had read thirty years ago—or even forty—at the beginning of my recognition that I needed to practice *better*, but without an inkling of what that might look like.

The thing is, an awful lot of us have spent an awful lot of time toiling away at our chosen instrument(s). If we were lucky, those hours were somewhat structured, probably by a teacher, and by sheer virtue of accumulated time and repetition, varyingly productive.

As a youngster, I was not a good practicer. Rather, I played, over and over and over again, until my timer dinged and I was released from the piano as from a prison cell. Even as a college undergraduate, as I put in more and more time, I still spent most of that time doing what I now call "poking around in the dark with a stick." I would start my piece at the beginning, play until I made a mistake, go back and play the spot over and over again, hoping not to make the same mistake. Once successful, maybe a few times in a row (not always; once was sometimes—often?—enough), I would continue to the next snag. Seems deliberate, disciplined, doesn't it? But how I avoided that mistake was not always coherent, and even if I did manage to play a passage or piece well, it wouldn't necessarily go any better the next day because I often *didn't know how I was doing what I was doing while I was doing it*.

Sound familiar?

In fact, I believe many musicians experience this. Eventually, you may even have developed a sense of which practice strategies work well for which types of passages or challenges, and have the discipline (some might even call it a personality disorder) to spend hours and hours a day trying them all out, over and over and over again. But even when you recognize *what* works, you might not always understand *why*.

As a developing pianist, I gradually recognized that, as a result of a lot of time and repetition, certain things seemed to happen. I (gradually) knew (somewhat) better where I was and what was next, I could hear and see much of the music in my head as I played it (usually 80 percent right hand/melody, aided by perfect pitch—which was really helpful for knowing that the next melody note was a D, but not so helpful when it came time to know what harmony was supporting it or where it was going), and I had enough muscle memory that I had some mental "space" to express myself musically. Adjusting for changes in acoustics, the instrument, other vagaries of performance, was not as available to me as I would have liked it to be, partially because even when I was *thinking* I wasn't necessarily *listening*. I was also aware of the fact that a lot of these improvements seemed to take a *lot* of time, and were a bit hit or miss. This distressed me, and certainly contributed to some pretty powerful performance anxiety that persisted for years.

What was most interesting to me is that no one else seemed to realize how clueless I was, nor how unmindful my approach—a testimony to the long hours I put in, I suppose.

My road to an interest in researching and codifying efficient practice strategies was a long one, with a few notable moments of incrementally powerful influence. The first was my work with Ian Hobson as a master's student at the University of Illinois, where I was introduced to the concept that I played the piano with more than my fingers—crazy, right?—and that what I did with my shoulder, arm, elbow, wrist, hand, etc. could facilitate, or interfere with, whatever I was trying to get out of the instrument. It also seemed important to recognize and remember what I was doing so that I could do it again, and this physical awareness certainly facilitated that. The second was as a result of teaching, telling my students how to work on solving a problem, and recognizing various pitfalls of less structured approaches, many of which were common practice for me and many of my friends and colleagues. Finally, when working on a doctorate with three young children at home, there was no opportunity for the previous system of masses of accumulated time and excessive repetition. There was literally no time to waste, so poking around in the dark with a stick was just not going to cut it anymore. And while there are certainly benefits to repetition in and of itself—if we want our body to respond reflexively to our mind, some, maybe even a lot, of it is necessary—*mindful* repetition seems to be the key to security and efficiency.

I found a better way. And it seemed that I learned a lot more, a lot faster, and performed with a lot more security as I paid a lot more attention in my practice sessions to what I was doing, why and how I was doing it, and what the acoustic result was.

I must also give credit here to William Westney and his extremely influential book *The Perfect Wrong Note: Learning to Trust Your Musical Self*. The element of trust is really an important one, one I had not really considered before, and perhaps has the strongest influence on our ability to perform at our best. To paraphrase: we *will* question ourselves onstage, and we simply aren't prepared until we've practiced in such a way that we have asked and answered those same questions, and rehearsed the solutions, creating the sort of solid musical memory that will stand up well under serious pressure (Westney, 2003, p. 146). His approaches worked well for me, inspiring further investigation. I wanted to know more about *how* we learn when learning music, so that I could structure my practice to be both more efficient and more effective, and provide more help to my students. Of course this was all many years and thousands of pages of research ago.

Perhaps the most important thing I have realized as a result of this change of focus and approach, and as a result of my many years teaching students of all ages and levels of ability, is that *every single person* can benefit from better structured practice, practice that works in parallel with the way our minds want to work anyway, and maximizes our productivity so we can learn more, faster, with more security, leaving room for more secure, flexible, and expressive performance.

I've taught four-year-old beginners, incredibly talented pianists at Interlochen Arts Camp, retired music teachers, students at the beginning of their music study at community college, students preparing to audition for some of the best conservatories in the country, and everything in-between. I've worked with students in various places on the autism spectrum, students with severe learning disabilities, others with amazing ears and photographic memory. My observation of musicians across this entire spectrum shows that musicians learn more, progress faster, and perform with more confidence and security, *if they practice well*. Effective practice strategies are as useful, important, and relevant to advanced, uniquely talented individuals as they are to intermediate, beginner, or what we might call "remedial" ones. It is my hope that the information herein is helpful to musicians of all ages and levels, and to their teachers and parents.

But how to practice well? Cognitive science holds some answers. There are shelves and shelves of books and articles out there about how we learn, and how we learn music. These include seminal books such as *Make it Stick* (Brown, Roediger, & McDaniel, 2014), *Psychology of Problem Solving* (Davidson & Sternberg, eds., 2003), *Oxford Handbook of Cognitive Engineering* (Lee & Kirlik, eds., 2013), and many published works authored by Dowling, Ericsson, and Sloboda, among others. You can also find many books on practicing. What you will not find, however, are any that put the two topics together, cognition + practice, in a *practical* way, and this seems like an important connection to make.

This book explains how to practice well, and efficiently, using supporting cognition research to try to explain why those processes work. My goal here is to show how we learn, how we learn music, and how to create and structure musical and practice experiences that capitalize on the brain's natural tendencies so that we learn as efficiently as possible and benefit from the added security of a foundationally-sound and multilayered approach.

I will also link relevant cognitive elements to specific approaches, including discussion of when to learn what, what to pay attention to, and to the level and type of awareness and mindfulness that is crucial to efficient and secure learning.

This book will make frequent reference to K. Anders Ericsson; he not only coined the term *deliberate practice* but practically founded the whole field of study on expertise. There is a wealth of additional resources and examples that I hope will both inform and inspire.

Ericsson et al., in "The Role of Deliberate Practice in the Acquisition of Expert Performance" (1993) define deliberate practice as "a regimen of effortful activities designed to optimize improvement" (p. 363). But what constitutes an "effortful activity"? And is "effortful" enough? There are many who practice very conscientiously, for hours and hours and hours, but who are often heading down quite the wrong paths. Effort is clearly being expended, but may actually be making the route to performance security more arduous rather than less. I hope this book will help conscientious musicians avoid misplaced effort.

To start, I would like to expand his definition, adding a few specifics that will form the basis of much of the discussion to follow.

Deliberate practice is "a regimen of effortful activities designed to optimize improvement" (Ericsson et al., 1993) *by being age- and level-appropriate, structured in alignment with the processes by which we learn music, and reflective of the thought and physical processes we will want to draw on in performance.*

The working title for this book was *Practice Makes Perfect and Other Lies My Piano Teacher Told Me*. I hate to be the bearer of bad news, although many of you probably know this already—but practice doesn't make perfect. Perfect practice doesn't even make perfect—we're not machines! What beneficial intentional practice *does*, beyond the mere physical training that is certainly an important element of good practice, is to train us to remember whatever it is we want to pay attention to (what to think about, when), and increase the odds that we will be able to do it again whenever we want.

The book is divided into four sections. The first addresses the young beginning instrumentalist, focusing on language development, development of audiation,[1] and an exploratory, playful approach to practicing for the young musician. The next addresses the "intermediate" musician—one who reads music, can understand concepts in some abstraction, and plays pieces that are a little bit longer and more challenging, requiring better working memory, more independent problem solving, and a gradually, incrementally more structured approach to practice. This section will also compare some of the cognitive theories that relate to important components of music learning, especially chunking and template theories. The third section of the book focuses on the advancing musician, moving toward what we might call *expertise*. This stage requires better knowledge representations and more information stored in and accessible from long-term memory, and makes more demands on the musician in terms of motor control and development, creative problem solving, and independence in practice and decision-making. As early music-practice experiences for young children are more exploratory, and gradually become more complex, so must the cognition discussion as well as the description of the best practice strategies. The book could possibly be read out of order, although one will find references to previously discussed topics that would hopefully stimulate curiosity about

INTRODUCTION

the foundations that are laid in the book, and that are so important to our music learning.

I wrap things up in the fourth section with a short explanation of how cognitively-sound, intentional, effective practice contributes to secure, flexible, convincing performance as well as some sample lesson plans, practice plans, and other supplementary material.

My goal is to express some very scientific concepts in accessible language and link them to the corresponding level of musical and intellectual development through outlining and describing the best teaching and learning practices for each stage. I tried at all times to connect the discussion of the cognitive topics with the appropriate level of musicianship, and to avoid going off on too long or too many tangents. Many of the cognitive theories could fill a chapter of their own, but the line must be drawn somewhere, so I tried to include as much as necessary to summarize the various theories and models and to support the various practice strategies without straying too far afield. The extensive bibliography should help point anyone interested in further information in appropriate and myriad directions.

While I believe this book can benefit teachers, teachers of pedagogy, even parents of developing musicians, the primary audience, especially of the later chapters, is musicians themselves—anyone interested in making better use of their time at the instrument, and in performing with more ease, security, and joy.

As a pianist myself, and as pianists deal with the distinctive requirements of playing a lot of notes at the same time, most of the examples will be from the piano repertoire. I do include examples for instrumentalists at each of the levels, and believe that a great many of the approaches described for piano excerpts work just as well for musicians learning single-line instruments (except perhaps for the chord chunking strategies, although even some of this is relevant to string players). The examples also are mostly drawn from the traditional Western canon.[2] While I recognize the important goal of diversity and inclusion of multiple repertoires and stylistic influences, I also wanted to focus on accessibility, making music in the public domain the preferred choice as much as possible. If the examples are not readily and legally available on https://imslp.org, they are, briefly and therefore within the context of fair use, excerpted within the book. There is no reason that the practice strategies herein wouldn't work just as well for the learning of more contemporary repertoire.

My belief in the importance and impact of some basic understanding of cognition in teaching and learning is supported by the cognitive scientists themselves:

> [E]ducation is based on decisions that are grounded in value judgments that deal with the "what" and "why" of teaching, but findings in neurobiology may indicate new ways of "how" to teach. Teaching interacts with the disposition and potential of each individual. Although neurobiological findings can't tell us why to teach music of a particular culture and what to select from the broad variety of musical traditions, empirical findings can advise us on how and when to teach so that mind, memory, perception, and cognition can be developed most effectively. (Gruhn & Rauscher, 2006, p. 61)

My intention is not to try to recount the details of every cognitive theory known to man—I am not a cognitive psychologist, and that book would be far too long—but to explain those relevant to practice at each stage and then link them to specific approaches. I am addressing the book to "you" the musician, but it can be read as a parent or teacher as well. Ideally, I will succeed in deconstructing some complicated theories and presenting useful strategies that can be applied by musicianship at every level.

In *The Last of the Metrozoids*, Adam Gopnik (May 2004) demystifies the advantageous alchemy of optimal teaching and learning:

> It is said sometimes that the great teachers and mentors, the rabbis and gurus, achieve their ends by inducting the disciple into a kind of secret circle of knowledge and belief, make of their charisma a kind of gift. The more I think about it, though, the more I suspect that the best teachers . . . do something else. They don't mystify the work and offer themselves as a model of rabbinical authority, a practice that nearly always lapses into a history of acolytes and excommunications. The real teachers and coaches may offer a charismatic model—they probably have to—but then they insist that all the magic they have to offer is a commitment to repetition and perseverance. The great oracles may enthrall, but the really great teachers demystify. They make particle physics into a series of diagrams that anyone can follow, football into a series of steps that anyone can master, and art into a series of slides that anyone can see. A guru gives us himself and then his system; a teacher gives us his subject, and then ourselves.

NOTES

1. The ability to hear *and understand* music while listening to, performing, reading, or in memory.
2. Therefore, works of composers who are mostly white and male.

PART I

1

THE BEGINNING MUSICIAN

Practice Is Play

The most important teacher a musician will ever have is his/her first one.

This concept is recognized by many in the field of general education, and we can see the effect of it on our own children. This is when they learn to read, work in groups and get along with each other, not to run with scissors.

In music it is when the foundation is laid of what will become a tall, intricate, and comprehensive structure.

And even if you, like me, recognize the importance of developing sight-reading skill and of a disciplined, systematic approach to practice for advancing musicians, this does not mean that beginning music students must be sat in front of a music book at their first lesson and taught to read from the grand staff, nor should they be subject to arduous practice regimens and intimidating expectations. We also don't need to wait for them to demonstrate some kind of innate talent set, although a bit of interest does help.

Sloboda (2005) reports the results of a study by Sosniak that showed no particular signs of exceptional ability in the early years of training for twenty-four highly accomplished pianists. What they did all seem to share were quality relationships with parents and teachers, and early lessons that were *fun*, taught by teachers who shared their love of music and with whom they shared strong mutual affection. On the other hand, critical, strict, achievement-oriented approaches were shown not to be successful in establishing musical interest that stood the tests of time and effort. Pleasurable experiences prove to support the development of intrinsic motivation, which encourages learners to persist for the joy of learning and/or expressing themselves musically. Contrastingly, focus on achievement causes learners to be more concerned about what others are thinking of them or their performance than on expression or exploration (Sloboda, 2005, pp. 269–271). One can see how this could be extremely detrimental.

Sloboda (2005) also observes that many elite musicians have parents who are encouraging, supportive, and capable of providing opportunities for appropriate instruction and practice, suggesting that admiration, pleasure, and lack of extrinsic pressures go a long way toward allowing musicians to develop on their own without the need of pressure to excel or "prove" anything (p. 270). This is perhaps the most important kind of help parents can provide—that, and making sure that there is an instrument in the home in good condition, enthusiasm over the student's participation in musical study, and encouragement of routine time spent at that instrument in focused yet playful practice activities.

For the early months or even years of lessons, a generally exploratory approach is most appropriate.

This may seem like an odd statement to make at the start of a book about practicing, but a discussion of how young beginning instrumental learners should practice is in some ways inappropriate.[1] Considering the research referenced above, paired with the commonly held belief that children learn best through *play*, I would argue a child's first experiences with learning a musical instrument should feel just like that. Play. In both senses of the word.

Westney (2003) writes about the adverse effect of focus on "correctness" in the early years and how it can lead to a sacrifice of originality and spirit. What would happen if, rather, we focus on what he calls the "juiciest" traits of musical performance: energy, individuality, communication, zest, imagination, sensitivity, rhythmic vitality, and last but certainly not least, a *healthy physical connection with the instrument* (pp. 32–34)?

In his article "The Acquisition of Expert Performance as Problem Solving," Ericsson (2003) observes that "future experts are often introduced to their domain in a playful manner at an early age without any objective evidence that their ultimate performance will be outstanding" (p. 65).

Research tells us that how a person feels emotionally during a particular learning experience directly impacts not only how s/he feels about the topic itself, but also *his/her aptitude*, meaning his/her *ability to learn* the associated topic or material (Schwarz & Skurnik, 2003). Some believe that these emotional experiences potentially affect the learner's ability in that domain *for the rest of their lives*. In later sections I will discuss the impact of both a positive and negative mood on things like problem solving and successful recall, but for beginners, always, a positive mood/experience should be stressed.

Consider, perhaps, adopting the Montessori philosophy of educating through the fostering and enhancement of the child's natural sense of joy, wonder, and discovery, and consider yourself the doorkeeper, guide, and fellow traveler to the magical world of music and piano (or violin, or flute, or didgeridoo) playing.

Don't get me wrong. I am certainly not claiming that young beginning instrumental students should not "practice." I *am* claiming that the practice should pretty much mostly feel like fun, and be set up by the teacher/doorkeeper/guide/fellow traveler to be successful, effective, and relatively low "risk." Think: exploration, discovery, experimentation, and observation, rather than "right" versus "wrong."

(Although corrections can certainly be made. I usually opt for comparisons: "This is what you played" or "I loved your variation of that melody!" and then "This is what the composer wrote; can you play it that way?")

I would say that these are the most important aspects of early lessons on any instrument. Beyond specifically structured improvisation experiences or using experimentation to compose or find a song by ear—both excellent activities to pursue with the young beginner—this approach can be extended to when a student is able to play a number of rote songs, and is encouraged to experiment with different interpretations. I keep a bowl of poker chips on a shelf near my piano with various "feeling" words written on each chip: angry, in a hurry, sad, happy, excited, tired, etc. and some just with "?" where the student gets to come up with their own. The student selects a chip at random and is then asked to play whatever rote song they just played in that particular mood. The more experienced/sophisticated ones will transpose from major to minor, or even Dorian or Phrygian; some might change the meter or rhythm; quite often various registers, articulations, and dynamics are *intuitively* chosen. The fun part is when they start to play something in a particular way, and then stop themselves, and say, "No, not that—" and try it somewhere else or in a different way.[2]

This reminds me of when my daughter was five or six years old, learning violin with a Suzuki teacher. She had clambered her tiny self up onto the piano bench and was trying to play "Twinkle" on the piano by ear, using a single finger, and only playing white keys. As you can imagine, some of these sounded varyingly bizarre (Lydian!). I was in the other room, trying to decide whether I should go and show her how to play them all in white-key major, or just leave her alone to explore. As I was still contemplating these options, she played it starting on B—I knew it was coming—*Locrian*. I came to the doorway and peered in, and she said, "I know that one sounds weird, Mommy, but I *like* it." I decided that, as long as she realized that it sounded "weird," no audiational damage was occurring, and I went back about my business.

How beginners learn must be the foundation of how they are taught, and how they are introduced to the ideas and execution of "practice" is of crucial and everlasting importance. Therefore, I would like to spend the next few pages talking about how children learn; how they learn music; how they can be taught so as to foster and encourage joy, wonder, and discovery; and how best to prepare these young musicians for subsequent stages of instrumental learning and the rigors of the more disciplined, focused practice strategies that advanced playing will require at some point in the future.

MUSIC AND THE BRAIN

It is only when the body provides the brain with meaningful information to process, then, that we can give new meaning back to all that we experience. (Gordon, 1997, p. 33)

> *By using the term* embodied *we mean to highlight two points: first that cognition depends upon the kinds of experience that come from having a body with various sensorimotor capacities, and second, that these individual sensorimotor capacities are themselves embedded in a more encompassing biological, psychological and cultural context. By using the term* action *we mean to emphasize once again that sensory and motor processes, perception and action, are fundamentally inseparable in lived cognition. Indeed, the two are not merely contingently linked in individuals; they have also evolved together.* (Varela et al., 2017, Loc. 4579 of 7672 Kindle eBook)

Many cognitive scientists and music educators have concluded that we learn to understand music much as we learn to understand language. The learning of both music and language involves a very complex processing system, with intimate relationships between attention, working memory, motor skills, auditory processing, visual-spatial processing, and long-term memory. Imaging also shows that both brain anatomy and brain function change as a result of the perceptual, cognitive, and motor abilities that develop over years of intense musical practice (Besson et al., 2011), and theories of embodied cognition point out that our perceptions affect our cognitive capacities and vice versa (Varela et al., 2017, Loc. 4561).

In fact, this multilayered, multifaceted system is so interrelated and circuitous that trying to isolate each, or to talk about the process in any kind of linear fashion, is almost impossible. But I will try.

One aspect that seems particularly similar when comparing language and music learning is the importance of implicit learning and its role in making predictions, and the role of anticipation/prediction based on experience and current input. I recently had a very interesting experience with this element of prediction/anticipation.

I was in Brazil on a Fulbright teaching piano pedagogy at the University of Brasilia. I had studied Portuguese a little—not enough to be able to understand it when it was spoken to me (those dialects! those accents!) when I first arrived there, but enough to read a bit and speak a bit. Many of the students in the pedagogy class did not speak any English. I had a colleague there who translated for me during the class period, but I asked the students at the first meeting to write a paragraph about why they were taking the class and what they hoped to learn. I encouraged them to go ahead and write in Portuguese, knowing I could, with my colleague's help and Google Translate, figure out the gist.

What was most interesting to me was that my limited experience with Portuguese allowed me to read their short essays sufficiently, even when written in cursive, to figure out what they wrote well enough to use Google Translate and work it out on my own.

You might be thinking, "well, duh," but try an experiment. Read the following sentence about someone getting ready to go to work: "*She wanted to know what time it was, so she looked at the dock on the wall.*" You might have read that she looked at the *clock*. Now look again.

Or consider the two series shown in Figure 1.1.

THE BEGINNING MUSICIAN

A B C   12 13 14

Figure 1.1.

And now look carefully at the B and the 13. They are actually the same image, copied and pasted. This shows the impact of context, expectations, and predictions.

Recognizing the impact of my exposure to Portuguese on my ability to read what the students had written, I wrote a short paragraph in cursive, in English, took a picture of it, and emailed it to everyone. A few days later, I rewrote the message in Portuguese, and sent it again (Figure 1.2).

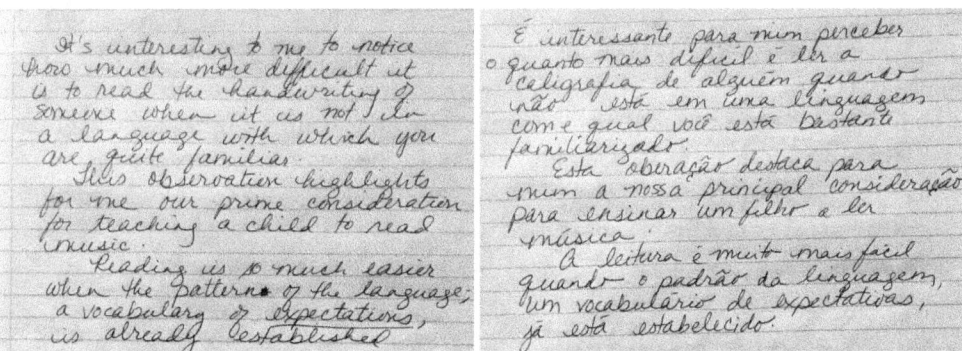

Figure 1.2. Comparing ease of reading handwriting in English and Portuguese.

At the next class meeting, I asked how many thought my handwriting improved when I was writing in Portuguese. The students laughed, and *all* raised their hands.

Prediction, anticipation: the foundation of implicit learning as related to our understanding of language, including our ability to learn to read,[3] and our ability to become efficient at learning and performing a musical instrument.

Much learning in the early years of childhood is implicit, meaning it is acquired in an incidental manner, without completely verbalizable knowledge of what is learned or how the learning happened. Implicit learning is also seen as a fundamental characteristic of the cognitive system, enabling acquisition of highly complex information that may not be acquirable in an explicit way. Despite the complexity of both language and musical systems, sensitivity to the syntax and structures in each does not require explicit learning. In fact, children exposed to multiple languages as youngsters will learn to speak each language, addressing their Spanish-speaking father in Spanish and their English-speaking mother in English, for example, and rarely if ever mixing them up (the language, not the parents, although they probably don't mix them up either). We have also learned that children can comprehend language well beyond their ability to speak it, encouraging parents to read to their children at higher and higher levels of text well after the child has learned to read.

In music, this implicit knowledge involves a sophisticated understanding of the harmonic syntax of the music of one's native culture, including recognizing functions of tones and chords in a given key, the relationships between different keys, even the change in function of events depending on the context. These internalized representations influence musical memory, musical expectancies, and the ability to mentally restore missing events, for example an omitted resting tone at a cadence (Tilman et al., 2000, pp. 885–887, 906). We could therefore make a multilingual comparison, and stress the importance that young children be exposed to as much music from as many different cultures as possible, and when they begin to learn to play an instrument, to learn pieces in a variety of modes and meters, not just major/minor and duple/triple.

The connection between language and music learning has been well established. Brain imaging shows development in *language areas*, even changes in brain anatomy, after years of *musical* study, including differences in the auditory, motor, somatosensory, visuospatial areas at the cortical level; and in the cerebellum, the corpus collosum, and in Broca's area[4] (Ettlinger et al., 2011; Milovanov & Tervaniemi, 2011). These differences in some respects are affected directly by the age at which the subjects begin to play an instrument—the younger the start, the greater the effects (Milovanov & Tervaniemi, 2011). In fact, complex internal representations of syntactic musical structures are called into play even when just tapping to a beat, something most children can do at an early age. Mere exposure to Western tonal music results in the development of the internal representations of pitch relationships by which we understand tonality. Even *infants* show the ability to track continuation probabilities in three-note patterns, and our ability to track common outcomes seems to be the basis on which our affective responses to music is formed. A marker in the brain that notes violations of syntactic language (again, in Broca's area) also appears in response to syntactic violation of musical "grammar," and violations of expectation for both language and music occur in the right temporal-limbic areas of the brain, which are associated with affect and emotive processing (Ettlinger et al., 2011).

The importance of all this brain science to us as teachers and parents of young beginning musicians is its reinforcement of the theory of many music education experts, such as Suzuki, Kodaly, Orff, and Gordon: that music is processed as a language and therefore ideally will be taught as one.

There are many stages of language development that can be paired with comparable stages of musical development. Table 1.1 summarizes and compares the foundation of implicit language and music development and the appropriate sequencing from babble to reading and beyond.

Following are some more details about aural processing and language acquisition that are relevant to our early-music-learning discussion.

Aural Cognition, Language Acquisition, and Musical Processing

Rousseau and Darwin each believed that music and language evolved together—Rousseau that first languages were sung, and Darwin that song evolved from speech

Table 1.1. Comparing Stages of Language Development (left column) to Stages of Musical Development (right column)

Infant is spoken to from birth, ideally by people who use a mature and nuanced vocabulary. All learning at this stage is "passive."	Infant is exposed to music that utilizes a broad vocabulary of meters, tonalities, and expressive characteristics. All learning at this stage is "passive."
Infant attempts speech ("babble"), any attempts met with great enthusiasm and reinforcement. There is no concern here with "right" or "wrong"; learning is without "risk."	Infant "babbles" musically, singing and humming and moving freely to music, with caregivers joining in with great enthusiasm and reinforcement. There is no concern here with "right" or "wrong"; learning is without "risk."
Infant/toddler begins to speak coherent words, then word combinations, and eventually, sentences. Caregiver responds with enthusiasm, generally makes few if any corrections.	Infant/toddler begins to sing short patterns, along with recordings; moves more rhythmically or regularly to music. Caregivers may participate by singing patterns in echo or response, dancing along with toddler, etc.
Child may begin to "read" books. S/he might be paraphrasing books s/he knows well, or "reading" what s/he thinks the picture on the page is about, etc. These attempts are met with positive reinforcement and encouragement. Parent(s) and caregiver(s) continue to read to the child, including advancing difficulty of texts as child's comprehension advances.	Children who sing in tune, move rhythmically and regularly with music, and can sing short patterns back correctly may be introduced to an instrument at this time. Focus at this stage is on a relaxed and appropriate physical technique at the instrument and the realization of patterns that the child can easily sing or chant back, moving on to playing rote songs by ear. Exposure to a broad variety of music continues, including sing-along songs of as wide and varied a nature as possible so as to develop the child's audiation skills and advance their music aptitude.[1]
After MANY years of natural and successive language development, the child is taught to read. First reading experiences focus on asking the child to read words with which s/he is already quite familiar.	When the child is able to sing in tune, move rhythmically with music spontaneously or with direction, and play a (large) number of short rote songs at the instrument, the child is taught to read music. First music-reading experiences focus on asking the child to read patterns with which s/he is generally familiar and able to play at the instrument with a relaxed and appropriate technique. Reading is a support system, a map for things that are mostly already understood, and a reminder of what comes after what.
After foundations of reading are established, expansion of reading skills through study of phonetics and exposure to more advanced texts initiated, with the child taught problem-solving strategies and verification of their comprehension of the text by teachers or caregivers at appropriate times.	After foundations of music reading established, and the child demonstrating an ability to play from music without sacrificing relaxed and appropriate technique, expansion of reading skills can commence, with the child taught problem-solving strategies and continuing audiation development as new concepts are learned.

1. *Music Play, Jump Right In: Music for Young Children*, and other such CDs available through GIA Music are a great source of child-friendly songs in many modes, meters, and rhythmic characters.

heightened by emotion. It may not be possible to figure out who was right—it's basically a what-came-first-the-chicken-or-the-egg sort of question. Unlike Rousseau and Darwin, however, we do have the benefit of advanced imaging techniques that allow us to observe which parts of the brain are most activated when perceiving and producing both music and language (Besson et al., 2011). Research and imaging studies have demonstrated many incontrovertible connections between the two. Following are just a few.

Aniruddh Patel points out that neuroimaging has revealed significant overlap for musical and linguistic processing in "normal" individuals, including similar brain operations between the processing of linguistic syntax and harmonic structures (2012, p. 205), and that musical training benefits the neural encoding of speech (2011). (To further support my argument for early music experiences and early music study being primarily positive experiences, he also notes that Chandrasekaran and Kraus found that musical training only enhances the neural encoding of speech *if the musical activities engaged strong positive emotion*, were frequently repeated, and were associated with focused attention.)[5]

Music and language share similar acoustic attributes and perception through the auditory system, and analogous generative syntactic systems. For the latter, research shows interactive effects between music-syntactic and linguistic-syntactic processing, theoretically because both are rule-governed systems, where the "rules" organize events over time and implicitly define the syntactic principles that organize them (Hoch et al., 2011).

Music (audiation) and language (comprehension) are both acquired implicitly, through what we might call "acculturation," without the aid of explicit instruction, especially in the young.[6] Implicit memory plays an important role in acquiring grammar and in the acquisition and understanding of rhythm, pitch, and melodic structures. Comprehension of both language and music involves expectation and tracking of dependencies between sequential elements, involving a three-way overlap of brain structures: those implicated in implicit memory, those involved in learning language, and those involved in learning music.

This expectation-as-a-result-of-acculturation does call into question the theory of music as a universal language. While it's true that all cultures have some form of music, what our music means to us in the West, that is, major = "happy," will not necessarily be true for someone raised in a different culture where major = "sad" (if they even have such a thing as "major," which is another question entirely).[7] Since I am writing this book in the "West," which is where my target audience lies, we will proceed with the belief and expectation that young musicians learning to audiate the difference between major and minor, or duple and triple meter, is not only relevant, but advantageous.

We can take this even further.

Many traditional methods focus almost exclusively on [C] major for a level or two, and duple meter using quarter and half notes. (They also are often written in enormous notation, which someone has decided makes it easier for youngsters to read, but which actually makes it much harder to see the *patterns* inherent in notation.

A soapbox for another time.) Minor and triple meter finally make an appearance in the second year, and gradually 8th notes might appear.

The thing is, the student will understand major better if they also know minor, Dorian, and Mixolydian; rhythms with moving notes such as quarters and eighths are more easily felt than slow pieces constructed of halves and quarters. We walk around on two feet, so duple may seem easier to feel, but triple meters are inherently paired, so they're not actually that much harder to learn, especially if the musician is exposed to them right from the start. GIA has a CD called *Music Play* that includes a song, "Scrubba Dubba," in 7/8 time, with two layers going on simultaneously. When my children were around twelve, ten, and *two*, they would sing along to this song in the car *without any "instruction" on my part*. You might imagine how much I loved this.

Language learning also shares a number of important similarities with the learning of sensory-motor sequences that have been classically associated with implicit memory and that are also implicated in acquiring a musical system (Ettlinger et al., 2011).

Neurofunctional accounts show activations in the same areas of the brain when the subject is listening to music and with the comprehension and production of language. Both language and music benefit in fluency and performance if exposure and practice is begun at a relatively young age, generally considered to be prior to the onset of puberty (Milovanov & Tervaniemi, 2011).

There even seems to be an interactive benefit—adult musicians demonstrate a better ability to detect tone and segmental variations in speech, *even in languages with which they are unfamiliar* (Besson et al., 2011), and musician children show more sensitivity to syllabic duration, to voice onset time (i.e., how we discriminate between "ba" and "pa") and are better able to detect incongruities in both music and language. In addition, adult musicians perceive pitch variations in an unknown foreign language better and are also better at reading irregular words (Milovanov & Tervaniemi, 2011).

Gordon (2001) relates language acquisition to musical vocabulary development in his discussion of the acculturation stage of auditional development. He writes:

> Young children become sequentially acculturated to music in much the same way they become sequentially acculturated to language: by listening to sounds, unconsciously formulating theories about [how] those sounds are put together, and organizing them into patterns to create meaningful communication. In language, for example, children first learn to hear and discriminate between the sudden shifts in "ba" and "da" and only then begin to speculate about the different ways [those] sounds are used. The more varied the language children hear, the better they will be able to learn to communicate when they are older, because it is our acquired listening vocabulary that serves as a basis for the development of our initial babbling vocabulary and for the later development of our speaking vocabulary. Our speaking vocabulary, in turn, serves as the basis for the development of our reading and writing vocabularies. So it is with music. (pp. 6–7)

Let us look now at aural processing from a merely musical standpoint, starting with a discussion of how we develop understanding of tonal music through exposure and implicit learning.

Continuing with Gordon for just another moment:

> In acculturation, young children are exposed to the music of their culture through live and recorded sources, and so they are able to base their music babble sounds and movements on the musical sounds they hear in their environment. *The more varied the music that children hear, that is, the richer their musical environment is in tonalities, harmonies, and meters, and the more they are encouraged to interact with what they hear through structured and unstructured informal guidance in music, the more they will profit* (emphasis mine). (Gordon, 2001, p. 7)

Experimental data shows that mere exposure to pieces that conform to the Western tonal system suffices to develop implicit but sophisticated knowledge of Western harmonic syntax.[8] This acculturation process develops without any conscious effort on the part of the listener, which puts the process as a whole squarely in the category of implicit learning. The perceived and understood hierarchy of tonal stabilities is based on the harmonic "language" of the listener's cultural background and is quickly established—presenting fairly early in a child's development. In fact, some infants can match pitch, most two- and three-year-old children are able to reproduce contours of short phrases, four-year-olds can maintain scale steps within phrases, although they may shift to different key centers at phrase boundaries to stay in their vocal range, and five-year-olds can maintain key throughout extended melodies (Krumhansl & Keil, 1982). This sequencing of development supports Gordon's theory of scaffolding through the development of tonal function audiation and indicates that what Krumhansl and Keil call "gross structural features" are acquired earlier than the more subtle aspects of structuring pitches. In fact, learning music based on its "gross structural features" is appropriate at all levels—playing the root/bass movement while singing the melody, practicing Sonatinas with blocked chords, memorizing advanced repertoire by generalizing, blocking, and performing the underlying harmonic progression or even what is on each downbeat only (I call this strategy *scaffolding*)—are just a few examples.

Tonal frameworks and prior learning also affect a listener's initial response and resistance to disturbances in the established hierarchy such as those brought about by a radical key change (perhaps from major to the parallel minor, or to a key not closely related), which is generally quickly accepted as long as the key change is reinforced by ensuing context. People who are familiar with 12-tone music also show a higher ability to wholly suspend any expectation of tonal hierarchy *when the situation warrants*. These flexibilities of expectations show that we are capable not only of establishing expectations, but of altering them, noting deviations therefrom, or even suspending them, given appropriate prior learning (Repp, 1991).

When considering and evaluating the understanding of tonal hierarchy, listeners with the least musical background will relate pitches based on pitch "height";

those with a moderate background will become more aware of octave equivalence and show a preference for tonic and diatonic tones; and "expert" listeners will show preference for tones of the tonic triad, have octave equivalence firmly established, and completely ignore pitch "height" when considering relatedness and function. By the first or second grade, children also show an increasing preference for phrases that end with a diatonic pitch, and third and fourth graders strongly prefer phrase endings on ^1 or ^5 of the tonic triad[9] (Krumhansl & Keil, 1982).

In our judgment of pitch relationships, "psychological distance" has an impact—moving from an unstable note or event (leading tone, tritone) to a stable one will be perceived as a smaller motion than when moving the same distance from stable to unstable. And while stable events are perceived as "closer," they are also more easily confused with each other. In fact, context seems to be relatively easily established, and has an impact on much of our musical perception long before we can identify how or why. Even our processing of harmonically related chords is *faster* than the processing of unrelated ones, or of chords that have not had an initial sonority to establish tonality, probably because previous musical context generates expectancies for the chords to follow (Tillman et al., 2000, p. 890). You might experience this delay of processing (understanding) if you routinely listen to a CD in order (say the Beatles' *White Album*) but have Beatles on "shuffle" on your MP3 player, resulting in unusual and jarring progressions that cause a few seconds of what we would call cognitive dissonance.

There are many other examples of how our understanding of the relationship between tonal elements is subjective, affected by context-generated expectations. For example, intervals at a higher register are perceived as larger than those at a low one. Register and timbre also affect perception of relative distance between ascending and descending intervals (Forde Thompson & Schellenberg, 2006, p. 84). Our perception of melodically presented pitches is impacted by both context and relative diatonicity, with consonant intervals being more likely to be remembered than dissonant ones. Also, the two pitches a perfect 5th apart between tonic and dominant will be judged to be more closely related than the two pitches that form the perfect 5th between the supertonic and the submediant, which will in turn sound more closely related to each other than a perfect 5th between two nondiatonic pitches. Nondiatonic tones are also more often confused with diatonic ones than vice versa (Krumhansl, 1979).

On the other hand, intervals that occur rarely in the diatonic set, such as the tritone between the 4th and 7th scale degrees, or the two minor 2nds of a major scale, are distinctive enough to imply a tonal center. The order of presentation also affects the impact of the tritone, so that going from Fa to Ti provides a stronger impetus than going from Ti to Fa (Butler, 1989), although this could just be result of our desire for the Ti to resolve up to Do, where the resolution of Fa to Mi is less compelling and/or conclusive (see above re: preference for root and 5th of the tonic triad).

Krumhansl and Keil (1982) write:

> Perhaps the single most impressive feature about the development of the hierarchy of stabilities is that it is implicit knowledge that [is merely] extracted from experience with music in the tonal tradition. All children and most adults are unable to describe this knowledge. In a manner similar to natural language syntax, it develops without conscious awareness. In music, the structure is stable and tightly organized, and even young children are able to use surprisingly abstract distinctions to guide their intuitions about what are and are not well-formed musical sequences. (p. 250)

The impact of context on aural processing emphasizes our need to *use* context when teaching young beginners, and to be aware of its effects. Asking a young beginner to identify isolated intervals ignores the effects of context; therefore the activity serves no audiational, and therefore no pedagogical, purpose. This activity also asks them to access a level of abstraction that lies beyond their abilities, which can only serve to discourage rather than encourage.

On the other hand, there are more appropriate and beneficial aural activities for a child in the first couple of years of instrument lessons. These include establishing a tonal center and singing tonic and dominant patterns in call-and-response fashion; singing rote songs and asking a child to sing "Do"; asking the child to identify whether two short patterns are the same or different, or whether a three-pitch pattern is "tonic" or "dominant." If we do need to teach them to identify intervals for some reason, say participation in an evaluative procedure, teaching them through established context first will help provide a foundation for identification of isolated intervals later.[10]

It is also of utmost importance to establish a tonal center as shown in Figure 1.3 before singing a pattern, for example, or teaching a rote song (unless, for the sake of inference learning, you want to sing the rote song and see if the child can identify the mode); or to move and tap to large and small beats before chanting rhythm patterns so as to establish metrical context. Gordon would emphasize the importance of presenting melodies and tonal patterns in the vocal range of the child (a fairly small one), and that rote songs *to be sung* always be presented at the same pitch level.

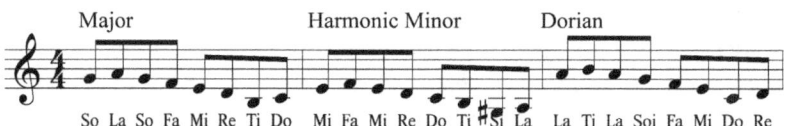

Figure 1.3. Tonality-establishing tonal patterns.

Even "perfect pitch" may not be the lodestone many think it is, but rather an indication of being made to deal with notes prior to having a syntactical understanding of musical context, so that the notes become fixed in isolation rather than understood in relationship to each other. Forde Thompson and Schellenberg (2006) write, "Absolute pitch can be a valuable skill for musicians, but it can also interfere with the ability to perceive pitch relations. Because melodies are defined by pitch and duration relations rather than with reference to any absolute pitch, relative pitch is arguably a more musical mode of pitch processing" (p. 82). As someone with perfect pitch, yet woefully inadequate relative pitch, I would testify to this assertion. I find it interesting that I was taught to read music right from the very first piano lesson, and don't remember a single instance of being asked to *listen*, to identify harmonic function, chord quality, even modality, until I was a college student. I was an excellent reader, but the notes triggered a physical/digital response, not an aural one, and despite my accomplishments as a pianist, I had to work very hard for a very long time to get to the point where I no longer need to *remind* myself to listen to what I am playing.

MUSIC PERCEPTION AND PREPARATORY AUDIATION

What does all this mean to teachers or parents of young beginners?

In the first place, it establishes the importance of building as strong a musical foundation as one would a linguistic one. This starts ideally with caregivers providing a lot of passive listening experiences for children from birth—from as many cultures and traditions as possible, in recordings, singing by parents and caregivers, moving to music, etc. Active listening experiences and developing aural and physical responses should be embarked upon from a young age, with things like Music Together classes or other early childhood music activities. Those that focus on singing (tonal) and chanting (rhythm) patterns, rote songs, moving freely and rhythmically to music or chants, exploration of simple instruments such as drums, xylophones, or boom-whackers, and those allowing for willing (never coerced) participation are the best. In fact, if a parent brings a young child to a teacher to begin instrumental lessons, asking whether they have participated in such programs is an important interview question. If the answer is "no," and your evaluation shows that the child is still in what Gordon would call "music babble," sending them off to find just such a program, or tailoring your instrumental lessons accordingly, would be an appropriate step.

Gordon calls these early stages of music language development "preparatory audiation" and stresses that children should have moved through each of these stages before instrumental lessons are begun. He divides them as shown in table 1.2.[11]

Being able to audiate, that is, to hear and understand, to *think* music, is the foundation of effective music learning throughout a person's musical development. This starts with the ability to audiate a piece's tonality and meter. With appropriate instruction, this can then inspire audiating musical elements such as harmonic function, harmonic progression, even later, style, form, and various aspects of expression. The development of audiation skill must be undertaken before, and then in parallel with, the use of verbal *identifiers* ("resting tone in major," "duple meter") before definitions of notational *symbols* or concepts of *music theory* are taught. The ability

Table 1.2. Stages of Preparatory Audiation Development

Acculturation From birth to ~age 2	Absorption: hears and aurally collects the sounds of music from the environment
	Random Response: moves and babbles in response to, but without relation to, the sounds of music in the environment
	Purposeful Response: tries to relate movement and babble to the sounds of music in the environment
Imitation ~Ages 2–4	Shedding Egocentricity: recognizes that their own movement and babble are not matching the sounds of music in the environment (accompanied by the "audiation stare")
	Breaking the Code: imitates with some precision the sounds of music in the environment, specifically tonal and rhythm patterns
Assimilation ~Ages 4–6	Introspection: recognizes any lack of coordination between singing, chanting, breathing, and movement
	Coordination: coordinates singing and chanting with breathing and movement

Source: Gordon (1997).

to audiate tonality and meter allows verbal descriptions and music theory concepts to be meaningful. Without audiation ability, notational symbols such as notes, durations, time signatures, key signatures, etc. live only as abstractions, and students will embark on what I call nonmusical solutions to musical problems. We must bring meaning to the music to perform and read it well, just as we bring meaning to text we are reading. As Sloboda (2005) points out, in order to *see* musical structures, one must first be able to *hear* them (p. 247).

Once a child has moved out of music babble and is able to sing reliably in tune and to move rhythmically and chant rhythm patterns, ideally using a context-derived solfège system such as that devised by Gordon,[12] he or she is ready to embark on instrumental lessons. Again, the focus should be on discovery and play, with lots of time spent singing, moving, chanting, and improvising. Learning note reading at this point is probably inappropriate, and certainly unnecessary.

OPTIMAL TEACHING STRATEGIES FOR THE YOUNG BEGINNER

It might be tempting, given the importance of reading music to most of you reading this book, to focus on reading from the very first lesson. But no one refrains from speaking to their children until it is time to teach them to read text, and then introduces them to their first word by showing them what it looks like on a page. In fact, that idea is so absurd I would be willing to bet some of you even snorted with derision when you read the sentence. Similarly, our earliest (very, very early) musical experiences should be just, simply, acculturation—music is playing in the background, and the child interacts with it *however he/she would like*: listening, singing (on or off pitch), bopping along to their own little beats, etc. Even toddlers and preschoolers

THE BEGINNING MUSICIAN

in early childhood music classes should never be *forced* to participate in a particular way. Encouraged, invited, welcomed, yes. Coerced, never. There are many stories about children who sit and observe and don't participate in these early childhood music classes, and then go home and sing all the songs they learned that day to their dolls. Remember, how children feel about these first experiences will dictate how they feel about the domain as well as their ability to learn in it, *for the rest of their lives*. (No pressure or anything.) Gordon points out that children's attention is not always continuous, but that children are generally aware of most of what they hear, whether they give visible evidence of their awareness or not. Just as young children require time to absorb the spoken language around them, they also require time to absorb their musical environment before being expected to sing, chant, or move in a musical manner (Gordon, 2001, p. 8).

Their first experiences at an instrument are still playful—exploring, experimenting. Young beginners at the piano almost always do better if they have had a (tuned) piano in their home from whenever they can remember and were allowed to sit on a bench and make up their own pieces, create, improvise, maybe even play some "duets" with their parents, learning simple patterns or basslines, *by rote*. (If it is not tuned, lock it up. The potential damage to development of audiation is too great to risk.)

Their first lessons continue in that vein. Yes, reading is VERY important for most of you, as it should be. But building that aural and oral vocabulary first supports that importance in irreplaceable ways.

As the lesson activities and "practice" expectations become a bit more structured, we will want to keep in mind some important principles of music learning handed down over generations of educational philosophy.[13] The general approach is still that the child is learning almost without realizing they are being "taught." Any increases in structure or rigor (in terms of "right" vs. "wrong") should be done with subtlety, care, and affection. In this way can we maximize the development of musical aptitude and set these young musicians on a road for secure development over years to come. The specific principles can be outlined in just a few points, each of which will be explained in more detail below.

1. Sound, before sight, before theory.
2. Lead the student to observe by hearing and imitating rather than explaining.
3. Context—in the audiation of rhythm and tonality.
4. Teach one (new) thing at a time before asking the child to attend to all at once.
5. Require mastery of one step before progressing to the next.[14]

Each of the above, in turn:

1. Teach sound before sight before theory. One would never ask a child to diagram the grammar of a sentence s/he couldn't read, forbid him/her from using a word that s/he doesn't know how to spell, or expect him/her to read a sentence or book full of words s/he doesn't understand or has never heard before.[15]

Likewise, when presenting a new musical *concept* (such as Dorian, unusual meter, syncopation) to a child, s/he should have aural familiarity with it first. If s/he can audiate it, can sing or chant it, s/he is ready to learn to apply this concept on his/her instrument. If you are working on music reading at this stage, s/he can be shown how notation conveys the concept,[16] and at some point in the future, when it is established and understood in an aural and a physical sense, taught how to write it or answer theory questions about it. In fact, cognitive scientists who work with music learning have pointed out the high level of abstraction and multiplicity of most theory questions, which would seem to imply that they should be (a) worded very carefully and (b) asked later rather than sooner. In fact, at the aural/oral level of learning, children should not be asked to read or notate any of these patterns (Gordon, 1997, p. 94).

This does not mean that there will not be appropriate times to ask developing musicians to solve a new problem using a bit of inference learning.[17] But these situations should be carefully designed and follow an aural—physical—visual—abstract sequence (sound before sight before theory) in some respect, not skipping more than one of the first three. We will get into this a bit more in the section on intermediate musicians and practicing.

Appendix A includes a sample lesson plan and sample practice assignment for a beginning (piano) student, in which I will demonstrate some proper sequencing as well as the elements from the list above.

2. Lead the student to observe by hearing and imitating rather than explaining. I have already mentioned the importance of approaching practice, at all levels, but especially for beginners, from the standpoint of discovery and exploration. We want to spend as much time as we can doing what it is we are trying to teach. Therefore, if we are teaching music, the majority of the input to the student should be musical.[18] So, play more, sing more, move more; talk less. In fact, this adage applies to music study throughout all levels.

That being said, there are lots of opportunities to "teach" without talking. Playing tonal patterns in call-and-response, or question-and-answer, singing tonal patterns that end with a cadential ^5 rhythm pattern and then a grand pause as you wait for the child to sing the resting tone. (This is so easily learned it will probably surprise you. You may have to pause, then sing it for/with him/her a few times, but that's generally it. See the YouTube video "Bobby McFerrin hacks your brain.")[19]

An important part of fostering an attitude of exploration and discovery is through the removal of anything that might be considered a "risk"—primarily, being "wrong," or told "no."[20] Perhaps most importantly, being given the opportunity to compare what was done with what was asked provides the opportunity to learn *both* things.

Let's say you are teaching a rote song that your student will practice over the upcoming week. First, in preparation, sing a few tonic and dominant patterns in the keyality[21] of the song for the student to sing back, and then chant some related rhythm patterns for the student to imitate. The student gets the first couple of rhythm patterns right but makes a mistake on the third one. Rather than saying "no," or "that's wrong," or "oops," saying something like, "You chanted: Du- Du-De DuTaDeTa Du; I chanted Du- Du-De DuTaDe Du; can you chant back what I chanted?"[22] gives them the opportunity to compare the two (and notice I did the one

I want them to imitate last). You will often see the audiation stare when s/he make a mistake, or when you chant the two patterns again. This is great! It means that s/he is remembering what you did, what s/he did, and comparing the two *in his/her mind*. That's audiation!

In fact, when I send beginning students home with their practice assignments, there are always two points that I stress:

1. If you can't remember for sure how it goes listen to the CD[23] extra times (I always assign tracks, including current rote songs as well as upcoming ones).
2. Try to figure it out, using the mapping (I will demonstrate this soon), the CD, and your ear. If you are still not sure, make up something that sounds good and we will work on it again next week.

The student almost always has it figured out by the next lesson. And if not, s/he has "composed" what I call a "variation," which we often add on to the rote song after s/he has finished learning it "how the composer wrote it," and which the student can insert as the B section of an ABA form.

This practice encourages the musician to listen, problem solve, and experiment while continuing to develop audiation skills and encouraging independence—a great start for their years as an advancing instrumentalist. And since they are not practicing via dozens of repetitions, the learning of a variation doesn't seem to cause interference with learning to play it "correctly." Also, at this point the motor skills required are larger, less refined, so there is less concern about learning something "wrong."

3. *Context.* A couple of really important points to remember: the audiation of rhythm is founded in movement and awareness of our body's location in space; the audiation of tonality requires establishment of tonal context.[24] Therefore, all rhythms/durations should be presented within the context of a *pattern*. Just like we want children to read text by recognizing word patterns and making predictions, so we want them to read tonal and rhythm patterns.

Consider this:

I cnduo't bvleiee taht I culod aulacity uesdtannrd waht I was rdnaieg. Unisg the icndeblire pweor of the hmuan mnid, aocdcrnig to rseecrah at Cmabrigde Uinervtisy, it dseno't mttaer in waht oderr the lterets in a wrod are; the olny irpoamtnt tihng is taht the frsit and lsat ltteer be in the rhgit pclae. The rset can be a taotl mses and you can sitll raed it whoutit a pboerlm. Tihs is bucseae the huamn mnid deos not raed ervey ltteer by istlef, but the wrod as a wlohe. Aaznmig, huh? Yaeh and I awlyas tghhuot slelinpg was ipmorantt! See if yuor fdreins can raed tihs too.

Now read it again more slowly—o n e l e t t e r a t a t i m e—and you will probably notice it is much more difficult, like you're overthinking it or something. (You are.)

Individual durations (and individual pitches) mean *nothing* without context. From a musical, cognitive, and experiential standpoint, the hierarchical relationship demonstrated in common representations such as that of Figure 1.4 is quite useless.

Figure 1.4. The rhythm "tree."

But asking a beginning musician to move side-to-side to the macrobeat (the half note in the case of Figure 1.5); tap arms on the microbeat (quarters) and chant and then observe the notation[25] of each of the patterns teaches each pattern as well as how each relates to each other.

Figure 1.5. Rhythms as patterns.

And if one of the patterns is chanted wrong—say ♫ instead of ♬, merely pointing and chanting/responding to each back and forth (maybe twice) until it is chanted correctly without being "given" will serve to correct the error. It will only take a few seconds for each of the patterns to become well established in the child's audiation vocabulary.

People familiar with the Suzuki Violin School recognize the use of mnemonics for rhythms. The first "Twinkles" feature patterns such as "huckleberry," "blue-berry," hap-py, I'm hap-py," etc. Words can certainly be used, but using a neutral syllable and/or rhythm solfège[26] actually helps develop a context-based vocabulary that is both more meaningful and more generalizable. So rather than "huckleberry," "Du-Ta-De-Ta" (pronounced Doo-Tah-Day-Tah); for "blueberry," "Du De-Ta," and finally "Du De—De Du De—De" for "Happy, I'm Happy."

Remember what we learned about tonal audiation in the section on aural and musical processing, especially how diatonicism and context affect our perception of the distance between and/or relatedness of pitches and harmonies. Therefore, if we want to learn and sing patterns in major, we first establish tonality by singing or hearing something like the first tonal pattern as shown in Figure 1.3. This puts context into recent memory, just like the first sentence of this paragraph did. Then we sing simple patterns, ideally based on implied harmonic functions such as those shown in Figure 1.6—(young children still in the preparatory audiation stage may be more successful singing stepwise patterns at first)—on neutral syllables (i.e., "Bum"), and/or on solfège.[27] If the young musician has more advanced audiation skills,[28] similar function[29] tonal patterns that present a bit more difficulty might look something like those shown in Figure 1.7.

Figure 1.6. Simple tonal patterns.

Figure 1.7. Similar function tonal patterns for musicians with higher audiation ability.

It is also of utmost importance that there is a short gap—around two seconds—between a given tonal pattern and the sung response. Gordon calls this the "audiation pause." The theory is that it is within this gap that the child actually learns the pattern. If a pattern is sung back without the pause, it might be sung correctly, but it was most likely a result of "imitating" rather than "audiating," which means it probably has not been learned and therefore won't be available to be built on later. We learn in the gap, like taking an aural picture. This allows the brain to *store* the information rather than merely *echo* it. I have found this listening—audiating—response to be particularly effective for both my students and me, improving more accurate singing and responding to sung tonal patterns.

Interestingly, we don't pause between presentation and echoing of rhythm patterns. In this case, the meter, pulse, and rhythm are being audiated as the pattern is presented (we do establish pulse and meter before presenting), and maintenance of the tempo and meter is more helpful through continuity.

We should also take care to establish tonality and/or meter before singing, playing, or teaching a rote song.

4. *Teach one (new) thing at a time before asking the musician to attend to all at once.* As musicians develop and/or are working on inference learning, elements can be paired or grouped and still managed and beneficial. But especially in earlier stages, it is generally better to divide and conquer. Besides the benefit when teaching new concepts, this can be especially helpful when determining the cause of an error.

Let's work our way from effect to cause for a moment—for example, a student is playing a piece in the lesson, and makes what seems to be a rhythm mistake. But are you *sure* it was a rhythm mistake? Maybe the rhythm was wrong because s/he was not feeling the pulse—which makes it a tempo and/or pulse error. Maybe s/he didn't look at the measure signature and was thinking of an incorrect number of beats and divisions? Maybe the pickup was played with too much emphasis, which threw off the conceptual downbeat. Or was it maybe because s/he was not reading far enough ahead and just wasn't ready for the next note? Is there a facility problem that prevented him/her from getting to it in tempo? Maybe s/he used a poor fingering and just didn't have anywhere to go. Taking a step back and breaking the problem down into its components can help us diagnose the source of the problem, making it much more likely that we will fix it quickly and effectively.

Learning one thing at a time, especially when that "thing" is a new concept, ensures understanding of each component. And *that* goes a long way to ensure a better chance of having correct, effective reinforcement in their practice at home. (And we all know what happens when something is practiced wrong!)

So let's say it is mid-November, and little Johnny, who has been reading music for about six months, wants to learn to play "Silent Night." An arrangement you have found for him, of appropriate difficulty, has a key *signature* of B-flat major (a key he has played rote songs and patterns in, but has not yet encountered in notation),[30] and is written in 6/8 time. Johnny has a deep familiarity with triple meter but has not yet *seen* 6/8 notation that uses dotted 8th and 16th notes.

Rather than sitting Johnny down in front of the score and asking him to read through the piece, a couple of preparatory activities would be well suited to this situation and can present some of these new ideas individually and in careful sequence.

1. Johnny reviews previously-learned-by-rote five-finger patterns, arpeggios, and cadence patterns in B-flat major, perhaps even with instructions to improvise incorporating some of these patterns over the coming week. Graphic notation, as shown in Figure 1.8, with which Johnny is already well familiar, is used.

Using this type of graphic notation has the young learner comparing what they see in a picture to what they are using in the real world—an important step toward instrument- and hand-awareness as well as an early "reading" experience, comparing symbols to the actions they "command." Removing things like letter names and finger numbers from the discussion means that everything the student is dealing with is concrete, laying a much stronger foundation for abstractions down the road.

At the next lesson, after performing his prepared improvisation and playing some motivic patterns related to the piece in call-and-response with the teacher, the teacher shows Johnny how each pattern played looks in notation, perhaps first with accidentals, and then with the key signature. Similar patterns are then found and identified in the score.

THE BEGINNING MUSICIAN

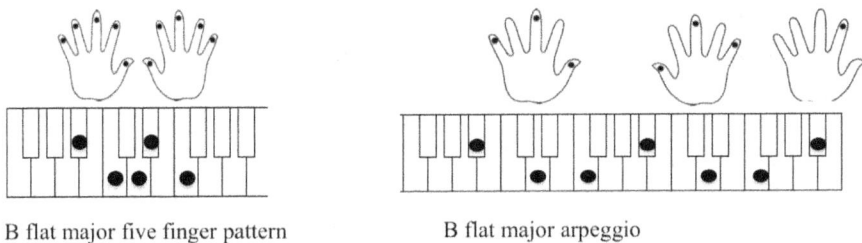

B flat major five finger pattern   B flat major arpeggio

B flat major chord sequence

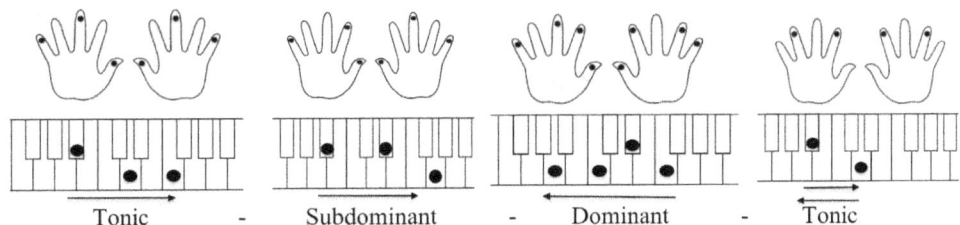

Tonic - Subdominant - Dominant - Tonic

Figure 1.8. B-flat major patterns in graphic notation.

2. Teacher and Johnny stand up and move in triple meter, chanting two-measure (four-macrobeat) rhythm patterns shown in Figure 1.9 in echo/response in the demonstrated approximate sequence.

Figure 1.9. Rhythm patterns in 6/8 time.

There are many important things to notice about this activity:

a. Each pattern ends on a long duration. This is how most music phrases work, and until the child has sufficiently advanced audiation skills, ending on the last 8th of a measure or on a syncopation may interfere with their metric audiation rather than help it.

b. The patterns move from simple to complex, beginning with patterns already known, moving incrementally toward the new division to be taught, and presenting the new, dotted pattern last.
c. The first several patterns include a literal repetition, resulting in implicit reinforcement of fundamental concepts.
d. The fundamental rhythm patterns of the piece are included, but not in a way that is trying to teach the entire rhythm of the entire piece from start to finish. If the individual patterns are understood, they will also be understood within a larger and more varied context. There is actually no benefit to repeating the Du—Ta-Di Du—pattern over and over and over again. In fact, the result of that will be repetition for repetition's sake (tedious, a deterrent to practice), rather than to learn and understand (fun!). Not only can excessive repetition lead to disorders such as focal dystonia;[31] it is boring and unmotivating in a lesson or in practice. My motto is always, if you can do it well, mindfully, comfortably, and with confidence several times, maybe five at the most (usually), in a row, you know it well enough for that practice session.

After having moved and chanted each rhythm, come again to the notation, and look at each of the patterns. At this point, a teacher or practice assistant might point and chant each pattern before the student chants back.

NB: *There has been no counting.* If you take away anything from this book, let it be this:

Rhythms are not counted—
Rhythms are felt

At a certain point, recognizing which beat a note coincides with, and maybe even resorting to mathematical solutions to very complex rhythmic configurations, is appropriate if not necessary. But if something is to be played *musically*, with appropriate metric emphasis, a steady pulse, and nuanced rhythmic divisions, the rhythm must be felt in the body.

This begins with moving, tapping, and chanting. Then patterns are played after they have been chanted. New rhythm durations are taught through physical experience before they are explained or identified. If an error is made that seems to be a rhythm error, the pulse is tapped and the rhythm is chanted. If the chanted rhythm is wrong, you know where to start. If the chanted rhythm is correct, it is a matter of rhythm + execution, and you have some ideas of where to look for a different solution. If it's a pulse/rhythm problem, we want to solve it using large motor groups (moving, tapping, and chanting), before we ask for its representation with the note patterns of a melody or piece requiring small motor control and that many more parts of the body the mind needs to keep track of.

Once these patterns have been experienced, finding one or two of the rhythm patterns in the piece itself brings their physical, aural, and notational experiences to the music rather than trying to decode something in a purely digital or pointillistic way.

If you are dealing with a new tonal configuration, such as a disjunct melody, a large leap, bow crossings, a new harmonic, etc. a similar, carefully structured approach can be very beneficial. Figure 1.10 shows a sequence for teaching and practicing "May Song," a popular folk song found in the Suzuki violin method. You will notice this sequence presents one new thing at a time, teaching pitch and rhythm

mm. 1-4

mm. 1-4 tonal patterns

Each one-measure pattern sung by teacher or parent, sung back (in proper voice range); then played and played back. If parent can't play or sing, teacher can record the patterns, with pauses included for the student to use for playback. There should be two half-note pulses before the student plays. These can be tapped or clicked by the presenter on the recording.

If string changes and/or intonation presenting a problem, short "tricky" patterns can be practiced (each repeated 3-5 times, no more):

mm. 1-4 rhythm patterns

As above

mm. 1-4, measure to the next downbeat ("Measure + 1")

As above

If measure 2 to measure 3 presents a difficulty, practice the "seam" between the two:

Figure 1.10. "May Song" sequence.

independently, incorporates a bit of listening-audiating-playing, focuses on preparing for potentially challenging physical movements, and incorporates practicing of shorter sections that will hopefully generate a bit of meaningful-unit anticipation as the student learns the whole piece.

5. *Require mastery of one step before progressing to the next.* You may recognize a connection between this and the previous principle. Look again at the 6/8 rhythms from our moving and chanting exercise from Figure 1.9.

If the third pattern is incorrect, it is pretty likely the fourth one will be wrong too. Or, if you still get the fourth one right, it may not be built on a foundational understanding of the meter, pulse, and divisions. In either case, your understanding is going to be less secure, and going off to practice a piece in 6/8 using these rhythms when you have not yet demonstrated your ability to move and chant those rhythms will be much more likely to lead to erroneous practice and more problems later.

There are times when there may be benefit to pushing through or even jumping ahead and circling back—perhaps not routinely, especially at the beginning levels—and if chosen, *don't forget to circle back!* The foundation must be broad, deep, and secure. If this is the case, everything built upon it will be that much stronger.

Whole-Part-Whole

McGilchrist's (2009) fascinating book on the workings of the two hemispheres of the brain sent me down a rabbit hole of sorts. Most of the book didn't pertain directly to the music cognition discussion here. But he shines a light on some conceptions and misconceptions about how the brain works and which side of the brain is responsible for what. To state some concepts somewhat simplistically, the left hemisphere of the brain is primarily concerned with readily identifiable *parts* that can be assembled into *facts*, and dealing with concepts once they are familiar; the right side of the brain is looking at the whole, the big picture, the *Gestalt*, concerned with the relationships between things, and dealing with concepts that are new, no matter which side of the body is sensing or manipulating them. He also writes about how one side of the brain might make a rather quick decision about it being the correct hemisphere to deal with the job at hand, and we will often persist favoring that hemisphere, even after further evidence perhaps indicates that it was not the best choice.

These elements make strong arguments, at least in my mind, for the importance of being as ambidextrous as possible in our learning to play an instrument, and to strive to attend to both the whole and its parts. In this way perhaps we can avoid a predominance of one hemisphere or the other, to the expense of the subjugated one, resulting in both a better understanding of larger structures *and* the details of which they are made, and in better development of facility in our nondominant hand.

Gordon highly recommends a whole-part-whole approach for structured learning experiences of young musicians. Listening to the entire song a couple of times while attending to some foundational detail such as tapping the pulse or macrobeat, or singing "Do" at the end of every phrase, lays an important acculturative foundation. Chanting some of the fundamental rhythm patterns in call-and-response, practicing the cadence pattern in the key of the song, and singing a few of the tonal patterns divides the elements into individual units. The song can then be learned by rote, phrase by phrase, perhaps beginning with the final phrase (teacher or parent plays the first three phrases, or student listens to a recording; student plays the last), and gradually expanding. Teacher or student then plays the whole song again; perhaps this time the student plays and the teacher taps the pulse or macrobeat, or sings "Do" at the end of each phrase. This moving back and forth between whole and its parts seems to provide young beginners with the opportunity to listen, compare, and contextualize, all of which benefit their learning both now and later.

APTITUDE

I can't really move on from this section to the discussion of the intermediate musician without addressing the idea of "talent" or "natural ability."

There are a number of biological contributors to "talent"—which I am defining for the purposes of this book as purely innate, domain-specific ability. *Aptitude* is considered a product of innate ability plus environmental factors—bolstered if the environment is beneficial, and allowed to degrade if it is not.[32]

It is also important for us to use any considerations or opinions of aptitude very carefully. All children, of all levels of ability, deserve music and instrumental lessons, and should be taught the same concepts in approximately the same sequence. The difference is the pace at which we expect them to progress and the difficulty of the tasks themselves that we ask them to perform. Especially in the earliest years of instrumental study, really any time before the age of eleven,[33] we can look at appropriately designed lessons and practice assignments as an opportunity to develop and advance the child's aptitude. One can hopefully see how important it is, then, that these early experiences focus on developing the child's audiation, along with comfort and ease at the instrument, *before* any emphasis is put on music reading or things like scale technique or theory.

For example, for most young children, playing individual fingers in succession is quite challenging. The fine motor skills for most will have not yet developed, and often tension will ensue. Start with simple soft-fist songs, then rote songs that move by step but are played with the third finger[34] only, focusing on relaxed motions of the arm from the elbow. Finally, when the student is ready, using fingers 2-3 and then 2-3-4. This is a more appropriate approach for most young beginners. Most five- or six-year-olds will lack the small motor skills to play a pentascale, for example, with ease and appropriate hand position at their first piano lesson. This is an area where aptitude might make a difference, and evaluation of this ability and encouragement of relaxed shoulders and free arm motions first, proper hand position second, support of the "stronger"[35] and more independent fingers third, before finally using fingers in scale-wise motion, is crucial.

While focusing on innate abilities may contribute to teaching and learning, especially in terms of pacing, motivation, and favored styles of communication, *learning style* theories have been mostly debunked, with research showing that it is actually more important to align the type of learning with the type of activity being pursued (Brown et al., 2014, p. 133). In fact, learners who can utilize a variety of learning styles, adapting their approach to the task demands at hand, are shown to be more creative than subjects with fixed style preferences (Lubart & Mouchiroud, 2003, p. 130). This means, for example, that aural skills should be taught aurally, even for strongly visual learners; reading should focus on observing the patterns of notation and linking them to an extensive, established vocabulary of tonal and rhythm patterns. This ensures an appropriate connection between the task and the associated cognitive processes.

A friend, fellow teacher, and former co-student from my undergraduate days was kind enough to be a reader for me as I worked on this book. Her biggest question regarding this section on the young beginner was whether there was a way to adopt these strategies without reinventing the wheel, or whether perhaps a reinvention was necessary. My answer to both questions was a resounding "yes."

That being said, the overhaul doesn't need to happen all at once. It is quite possible to adopt one new teaching strategy at a time. You might start by teaching new rhythm patterns through movement and chanting before looking at them in notation. Or maybe you use movement and chanting to isolate and fix rhythm errors in a piece. New pieces might be taught through exploration of related tonal patterns first, then some improvisation in the keyality and/or with fundamental rhythm patterns related to the piece before the piece is taught from the score. Each lesson can include a brief improvisation or composition assignment, and varieties of interpretation can be explored with repertoire currently known. Transposition is encouraged, and opportunities for students to accompany each other on the piano or on rhythm instruments carefully designed. I've had siblings play together on recitals, one playing a "Jingle Bells" arrangement written for both hands, his younger brother playing a bass line accompaniment, and his even younger sister shaking hand bells on the quarter note beats. They are each participating at their own level, but they are working together in an ensemble. The next year the younger brother maybe plays the tune, with the sister playing the bass line, etc. These experiences are priceless, and not just in charm.

When I first learned about Music Learning Theory, as a doctoral candidate at Michigan State University and taking a psychology of music course with Gordon himself, I was actually quite dubious. I had always believed, given the importance of reading music to being able to learn independently and quickly, that the focus of learning and progress at all levels should be reading based. But I had a couple of students with some profound learning disabilities, and on a whim tried out some of Gordon's pattern-singing and movement-with-tapping-and-chanting activities for passages that were persistently incorrect in lessons. When I found that these strategies not only helped correct the errors, but that the corrections stuck from week to week, I started to wonder. Over the next few months, as I used more and more of these strategies in my teaching, I realized not only the benefit, but that they could be incorporated much earlier in the process. It is not an exaggeration to say that I completely changed the way I teach young beginners.

One switch in focus was to small group lessons given with only one piano. This provides multiple opportunities for the young student to audiate by the need to take turns (which provides extra opportunities for listening, and teaches them to audiate rhythm, pulse, tempo, and meter so as to come in in tempo and on the appropriate upbeat or downbeat), and to play various types of duets with each other, which allows for flexibility based on aptitudes. Young children will also generally be much more participatory when in groups with other children close to their age. I find that in a solo lesson, I might sing a pattern and the student will just stare at me blankly when it is his/her turn to sing. In a group, the student is not only more likely to sing alone, but always has the group interactions to build familiarity and confidence. A group of three or four students works perfectly well, even with varying ages and levels of ability.[36] Students who are catching on to a new concept more quickly can be taught a new rote song perhaps in one lesson, while other students are moving to the downbeats, chanting recurrent rhythm patterns, or playing a simple tonic whole-note bassline or a rhythm instrument in accompaniment. These partnered experiences provide the opportunity to learn the song by ear for another week or two before they begin to play it themselves. There is lots of singing, chanting, and rote songs, with learning in the form of "play." I've also found that students in these group lessons become quite adept at listening and preserving ensemble in their duets in a way that some more advanced students, those who have not learned to audiate, that is, are quite incapable of.

I also changed from teaching students to read music in the first month or two to teaching music reading a couple of years down the road, at which point the musician can do things like transpose rote songs to any number of keys, improvise, play in small ensembles, sing in four-part harmony (even one to a part) while following simple hand signals, and audiate in major, minor, various modes, as well as in duple, triple, and unusual meters.

The transition to reading takes care but places them quickly in learning intermediate repertoire with superior audiation skills.

NOTES

1. Don't worry—I will get to very detailed, disciplined, specific practice strategies very soon!

2. I had a student once who loved G minor. Every piece he learned he also transposed to G minor. It brought him joy, so we went with it.

3. Children learn language aurally (by ear) first, orally (speaking) second, and visually (reading) last. Adults often approach learning a new language from the opposite direction, probably because the innate language-acquisition ability actually fades quite early—some predict by the age of three.

4. A region in the frontal lobe of the left hemisphere of the brain, with functions linked to speech production.

5. Something that is really interesting to me but perhaps too tangential to include in the main portion of the book is that Patel reports a surprising link between dyslexia and deficits in *auditory* processing, directly related to the aural segmentation of words, and the need for this segmentation so as to map sounds onto symbols. There seems to be a relationship between what is called the "amplitude envelope" both for the perception of the rhythms and boundaries that segment speech, and similar problems dyslexics have with musical rhythm tasks. For more detail, see Patel (2011), Thompson and Goswami (2008), and Huss et al. (2011).

6. Gordon actually claims that musical exposure and audiation development can improve a child's musical *aptitude*, up to around the age of eleven, at which point it becomes "fixed."

7. There are other cultural challenges, such as the positive impact singing patterns using movable Do with La-based minor has on developing audiation ability, competing with cultural tradition such as those of Brazil or France, where Do is fixed. The fact remains that different systems of solfège are better for different things—a topic for another book perhaps.

8. Related to the tangential discussion of whether music is, or is not, a "universal language," given our audiation's dependence on just this exposure.

9. In this book, as is now the custom in writing about music, the carat symbol, ^ = "scale degree."

10. In fact, Gordon would claim that the only appropriate evaluation of one's listening ability is same-or-different questions. Anything else requires theoretical knowledge, reading ability, etc., which muddies both the question and the result.

11. Gordon (2001) ages are estimates and might vary by as many as several years. The important thing is the quality of the preparatory audiation activities, not necessarily the age at which the child moves to the next stage, although younger is always better.

12. There are many excellent sources to familiarize yourself with Music Learning Theory and Gordon's tonal and rhythm solfège systems. I recommend Eric Bluestine's *The Ways Children Learn Music* as a very reader-friendly place to start. *Rhythm: Contrasting the Implications of Audiation and Notation* (Gordon, 2001) is a bit drier, but includes an extensive explanation and demonstration of Gordon's function-based rhythm solfège system.

13. From Pestalozzi to Mason to Gordon.

14. This does not include acculturation-type learning, which will be generally more holistic, or the inference-based learning we might ask of musicians as they progress. It does encourage care in mastery of specific skills in careful sequence, such as not asking a young beginner to play with all five consecutive fingers in stepwise motion before they have developed a relaxed arm approach to the instrument, an appropriate hand position, and the ability to play with two and then three consecutive fingers in stepwise motion while preserving the relaxed arm and appropriate hand position.

15. However, reading experts encourage caregivers to continue to read to their children through middle school—trying to select books that are slightly above the child's current reading level to build vocabulary and comprehension in an implicit, unpressured, and ongoing way. Therefore, children can and should still be *listening* to "real" music; we're just not asking them to play it yet.

16. This is exactly how I teach students to read music. I will walk through this in much more detail in the section on intermediate students.

17. The application of former learning in a new context.

18. More on this in the section on "More Relevant Than Learning Styles: Personality, Character, and Motivation " in chapter 2.

19. See https://www.youtube.com/watch?v=E2yAddhsLlg&t=3s

20. Besides the emotional impact of being told we are "wrong," there is evidence that we learn messages with "yes" answers better than those with "no" ones (Baddeley, 1990).

21. A Gordon/Music Learning Theory term referring to resting tone + mode, so C major, D Dorian, etc.

22. If they can't a second time, maybe it is time to back up a bit and chant some simpler patterns and work up to that pattern again. For beginners it is usually best to assume that if the student is unable to do correctly whatever you are asking after a few tries, you are either teaching something that is too difficult, or you are teaching it incorrectly or too soon. If the student is really stuck, I might even say something like, "Let me think about whether there's a different way I can explain this," and then try again the next week so the student feels that it's "on" me, not him/her if s/he doesn't understand.

23. I use *Music Moves for Piano* by Marilyn Lowe for beginners, which comes with either a CD or online access to all the songs as well as some other tonal and rhythm patterns for the upper levels. If you are interested in and/or new to rote methods for beginners, each book of this method has a teacher's guide, which may be useful.

24. At first we do this through singing the little melodic pattern shown to establish tonality in Figure 1.3. Eventually, the child learns to establish tonality him/herself as s/he listens to or performs music.

25. If the musician is learning to read notation.

26. Kodaly's system reflects durations only; Gordon's system creates a hierarchy, so that "Du" is always the downbeat, "De" the pulse in duple, "Da Di" the pulse in triple, "Ta" the divisions; and "Be" and "Ba Bi" are used to teach duple or triple divisions in unusual meters. While at first glance it may seem tricky to start learning this as an adult, I started using it in my forties, and the learning curve was pretty quick. I find it extremely helpful for teaching, as well as teaching myself complex rhythms such as those seen in Kennan's "Sonata for trumpet and piano,"discussed below and shown in Figure 6.26. Once meters and rhythm patterns are heard and audiated, traditional counting systems can be useful and occasionally appropriate, say, for identifying starting places for practice or ensemble work.

27. Gordon's research shows that movable-Do with La-based minor, Re-based Dorian, etc. is the best system to use for melodic patterns and to help children audiate tonality. It can create some difficulties with harmonic function, but by the time we are teaching this in any great detail or level of difficulty, the solfège system has established the foundation, and more flexibility of approach might be suitable. There are additional difficulties with cultures that focus on fixed Do (French, Brazilian), etc. Any system has its challenges and shortcomings. For example, La-based minor makes the most sense melodically, Do-based resting tone makes the most sense harmonically, and fixed-Do makes the most sense for nontonal music. Our job is always to try to find the one that makes the most sense to our students and is as consistent as possible. For young children, if possible, moveable Do with La-based minor is the best.

28. This is where learnedness and aptitude start to come into consideration.

29. Function in terms of tonic, subdominant, dominant, etc.

30. If he has never encountered B-flat major at *all*, back up a few steps and make sure that he has before embarking on this sequence of activities.

31. A neurological condition that affects a muscle or group of muscles in a specific part of the body, causing involuntary muscular contractions and/or abnormal postures.

32. The relationship between music aptitude and intellectual ability or academic achievement is still being evaluated, with some studies showing some slight improvements in IQ scores as a result of years of music study. There have been clear demonstrations of benefit to factors such as discipline, creativity, divergent thinking, working memory capacity, problem solving, and auditory processing.

33. Gordon would say that aptitude "freezes" at age nine, but I have had students score quite differently on his aptitude tests up to the age of eleven or twelve, so I tend to believe in a bit more malleability for longer than that.

34. This centers the hand and encourages the free arm movement from the elbow and support of the proper hand position.

35. Fingers aren't actually "strong," but stabilized through support of the tendons, for many requiring attention and rehearsal. By "stronger" here I mean in terms of integrity of position.

36. To a point. I found that personality combinations became the most important consideration. Two very active boys in a group lesson with one shy, retiring girl might help draw the girl out of her shell, or it might intimidate her to the point of nonparticipation. These factors must be carefully observed and adjusted for.

PART 2

2

THE INTERMEDIATE MUSICIAN

Fluent Music Reading and Early Problem Solving

All effective use of declarative and procedural learning presupposes pattern recognition. (Kellman & Massey, 2013, p. 148)

FROM "BEGINNER" TO "INTERMEDIATE"

For my teaching practice and the purposes of this book, I will label a musician as an intermediate when s/he is ready to learn longer pieces, to read music with ease and appropriate audiation,[1] and to begin to adopt more systematic and disciplined practice habits. This is another level that is beneficial to spend a fair bit of time in. According to perceptual learning theory, our ability to discover which features are crucial and to build a broad and deep structure of understanding comes from encountering a variety of instances of any single concept (Kellman & Massey, 2013, p. 146). Taking the time and opportunity to learn a lot of different music from different eras, in myriad styles and textures, helps develop reading and problem-solving skills, and build the technical facility and comfort with the instrument necessary for expressive playing. A thorough, comprehensive, and multiple-intelligences problem-solving approach should also help avoid the plateaus and discouragement that often accompany moving into more advanced repertoire. This approach assumes beginning lessons that focus on developing audiation and how to play with comfort and ease, pattern-based music reading built on a foundation of musical understanding, and the focus of practice on the pursuit of proper problem-solving skills and self-observation. (If this was not the case, some remedial work may be necessary.) Guiding intermediate musicians' attention and effort toward learning how to observe relevant structures and relationships aids learning, maximizes agency and motivation, and encourages them to categorize and predict, contributing to durability of learning and more transfer between tasks (Kellman & Massey, 2013, pp. 153–154).

Discouragement is often a result of being given challenges far beyond one's capabilities—something most individuals are aware of if/when it occurs. Feeling that what you are trying to do is beyond you can lead to crippling performance anxiety. If a learner can't see a way to a solution, especially if this individual has gotten a great deal of self-esteem from his/her ability to *play* rather than an increasing ability to *learn, problem solve, strategize,* and to observe *progress,* s/he will quickly lose interest and want to discontinue lessons. Conversely, if we carefully select music of appropriate difficulty[2] and in an appropriate sequence, and if we are equipped with a toolbox of effective, efficient, and enjoyable practice strategies, practice will be more enjoyable, and more will be achieved in less time. In fact, how a learner approaches the first pieces that are going to be learned from notation can lay the groundwork for his/her approach to notated music for the duration of music studies. Since one of the important developments for musicians at the intermediate level is comfort with reading music notation, cognition as it relates to visual processing seems an appropriate next topic.

VISUAL PROCESSING

There are two temporal stages in eye movements: *fixations* and *saccades*. Saccadic movements are very fast, and input during them is essentially shut down (it would make us dizzy if this were not so). Useful pattern information is acquired during *fixations*.[3] As our familiarity with the patterns increases, the duration of fixations shortens, and fewer are needed before recognition occurs. Rehearsal increases the number of elements in a pattern that can be perceived within one fixation, reflecting an expanded area of perception rather than any strategic change in gaze (Burman & Booth, 2009, p. 315).[4] We then organize small units of visual[5] input into groups, which construct our perception and recognition of larger forms (or patterns), where each form/pattern is perceived as a meaningful unit (Henderson, 2013). Various psychologists identify slightly different laws of organization,[6] but the basic principles are:

1. We look for the *simple*st structures (Figure 2.1).

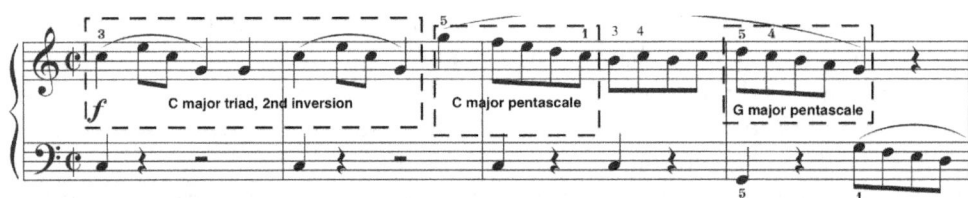

Figure 2.1. Clementi, "Sonatina in C major," Op. 36 No. 1, mm. 1–4, showing simplicity.

2. We group according to things that seem *similar*[7] (Figure 2.2).

Figure 2.2. Bach, "Musette in D major," mm. 1–8, showing similarity.

3. We look for *continuation* (Figure 2.3), grouping straight or conjunct lines that follow the smoothest path.

Figure 2.3. Bach, "Prelude in C major," *WTC I*, mm. 1–2, showing continuation.

4. We group according to *proximity* (Figure 2.4)—things near each other, in musical time/physical space. This seems to be the most powerful grouping cue, although often not the most useful one from a musical standpoint. Note the disadvantage, in Figure 2.4, of focusing on each successive 16th note in the right hand as a series of intervals: 4th, 3rd, 6th, 4th, 6th, rather than grouping by continuation (same excerpt, 2.3) or similarity.

Figure 2.4. Bach, "Prelude in C major," *WTC I*, mm. 1–2, showing proximity.

Different grouping principles function independently of each other, but their combined grouping is additive. And while proximity seems to be the most powerful cue, a variety of subjective factors affect grouping and segregation, including past experience, the location of fixations, and *attention*—something we can learn to control intentionally according to the structures of the piece. This also means that, if musicians are taught to read too early, before those subjective factors and organization are established, the tendency may be to attend to individual notes (proximity), rather than patterns, which is detrimental to good reading (Peterson & Kimchi, 2013) and confounds the way music is actually understood.

A challenge arises when we are receiving information simultaneously that involves both hearing and vision; we tend to attend instinctively more to one stimulus and ignore the other. There is an innate preference in general for visual stimulus. If you really want to rock your world, put this book down right now and watch this video: https://www.youtube.com/watch?v=G-lN8vWm3m0. This is an excellent demonstration of how the eye "hijacks" the ear.

Often, beginning musicians who have been approaching their instrument for months in a relaxed and efficient manner and are capable of playing dozens of rote songs will seem to become rigid, tone-deaf zombies when music is first put in front of them to read. If this happens, it is a good cue that maybe they are not ready to read yet. It is also a good reminder that, if reading is being pursued, these other elements must be carefully and conscientiously preserved.

While we want to tailor our teaching and learning to the specifics of the domain itself, our innate learning style may impact our approach. If we tend to be a visual learner, we might fail *entirely* to listen; if we learn well by ear, our eyes may be directed at the score, but they are effectively blurred and not contributing to the input. As musicians, *it is of utmost importance that we learn to attend to both*. Therefore, our goal should be to develop reading skills that focus on identifying and audiating patterns, recognizing which features at any given moment in the score are most relevant to the grouping of information to construct these patterns, making predictions according to those patterns, and trusting the physical self to execute the visual cues without needing to look at the hands. Learning to simultaneously read the score, send motor signals to the body, feel the execution of hands/fingers/embouchure, and listen, in a constant feedback loop, is the key to success at this stage of learning.

BEGINNING MUSIC READING: BRINGING MEANING TO THE SCORE

> *I wish to argue . . . that reading facility is not simply a useful additional skill for a musician to have. It is, in a sense, necessary for full membership [in] the musical community.*[8] (John Sloboda, 2005, p. 5)

> *PL [perceptual learning] is the type of learning that leads to mind as pattern recognizer.* (Kellman & Massey, 2013, p. 145)

I hope that previous sections have succeeded in explaining why, despite the importance of music reading ability, it is best if not embarked on too early in the process. When done so, the goal is to recognize patterns that represent symbolically that which we have already "represented" (in terms of knowledge representation) cognitively. Possessing a vocabulary of tonal and rhythm patterns and rote songs, and linking known patterns to patterns in notation, will lead to relatively quick adaptation of music reading as an appropriate perceptual input without sacrificing audiation or technical integrity.

Kellman and Massey (2013) point out that systems that involve symbolic content use representations that pose important information-extraction requirements and challenges. To interpret these symbols, we use spatial, configural, and/or temporal structures that connect the representational symbols to our experience with and perception of those structures in the real world (p. 129). In many ways music notation looks like it feels, and like it sounds. Having an established sense of how it feels, and how it sounds, can only help.

To take this further, we ideally understand music as being made up of patterns. Therefore, we read best when we read in patterns, and have enough of a musical vocabulary that we can bring meaning to the page. An established audiation ability and a relaxed, effective physical approach to the instrument allows the learner to add visual input to the complicated loop of things s/he must do and think about in relatively quick and, ideally, fluid succession. If the individual reading music already knows what the music means and can *hear* what makes musical sense, s/he will be much more effective not only in how they learn the piece, but in making that meaning explicit to the listener.

> This vital information is plain for any reader to see, without his having to execute a single note. When he does come to perform the notes, therefore, he already *knows* what the music means and can perform it in such a way as to make that meaning explicit. *The poor reader can't do this* [emphasis mine]. . . . The meaning is not apparent to him on inspection so he has to listen to what he plays or sings and try to make sense of that. Whether he succeeds will, in part, depend on his musicality, that is, his ability to hear what makes musical sense. (Sloboda, 2005, p. 6)

An important element in successful music reading is the ability to preview—to take in visual information well ahead of execution—which gives the performer time to "decode" the information in the score and provide a steady flow of output in the form of signals to the motor control network (Sloboda, 2005, p. 16). A lack of refinement in this ability can also be seen in poor readers, who might remember there is a difficulty ahead, but, in their efforts to plan for it, mentally skip over where they are currently playing, leading to a different error entirely. Good readers are looking "through" as they look "ahead."

Visually, the taking in of information happens during fixations; mentally, the process can be understood as "buffering." Buffering is a concept familiar to any child who watches YouTube, streams movies, or plays online video games—information has to "load" before it is accessible. During musical performance, the buffering must occur in such a way that execution is steady and rhythmic, even when the visual and working memory processes encounter temporary snags posed by unusual patterns or passages that are more challenging to execute (Sloboda, 2005). The visual/memory/playing span is therefore impacted by the relative conventionality of the passage being read and performed. Nonmusicians who are good typists are probably aware of this perceptual/processing span. Even the best typists will have to slow down when typing unfamiliar words, or when they are prevented from preview. Musically, this means that, when dealing with familiar vocabularies (patterns, expectations) one will be able to organize more information into fewer groups, which will allow one to read further ahead. When dealing with unfamiliar vocabularies, one would expect the opposite.

Buffering is discussed at length in the article on threaded cognition by Salvucci and Taatgen (2008). While in some respects this may be more appropriate to discuss in the section on advanced musicianship, because I've mentioned buffering here I'll elaborate slightly.

According to their theory, which supports at some level my belief that musicians can and do "multitask," there are several "task threads" in operation simultaneously, coordinated by a serial cognitive processor and distributed across multiple resources, which include cognitive, perceptual, and motor systems. Each of these contains a module that performs the actual processing and one or more buffers, which serve as communication channels between the module and the resource. Rather than central cognition translating perceptual stimulus into a motor response, Salvucci and Taatgen theorize that there are two distinct resources: a declarative one that facilitates storage and memory for factual knowledge and a procedural one that integrates information and effects new behaviors. This separating of the memory and procedural processes helps us avoid the cognitive interference that can occur with multitasking (pp. 102–104).

While "central processing" is only able to process one "thread" at a time, some cognitive systems allow for multiple rules to "fire" simultaneously when the multiple rules align with the buffer state. In addition, one thread's resource processing can proceed in parallel with another *as long as they do not require simultaneous procedural processing* (Salvucci & Taatgen, 2008, p. 110). Therefore, while "multitasking" is in evidence in terms of thought being ahead of execution, the processing itself is still working in a rapid sequence of input, rule firings leading to motor execution, making room for more input. I see it somewhat as the much-simplified representation shown in Figure 2.5.

Visual and auditory processes deal with "what" and "where" information, and a procedural resource maps that information into a request to perform a motor command. A production "rule" defines a set of conditions and/or actions, which utilize buffers for the transfer of information. If the set of conditions and actions align with the "rule," the rule fires, the cue for the motor command is sent, and the buffer empties, making room for more information. At this point the action places a new request for more resource processing (Salvucci & Taatgen, 2008, p. 105). Imagine

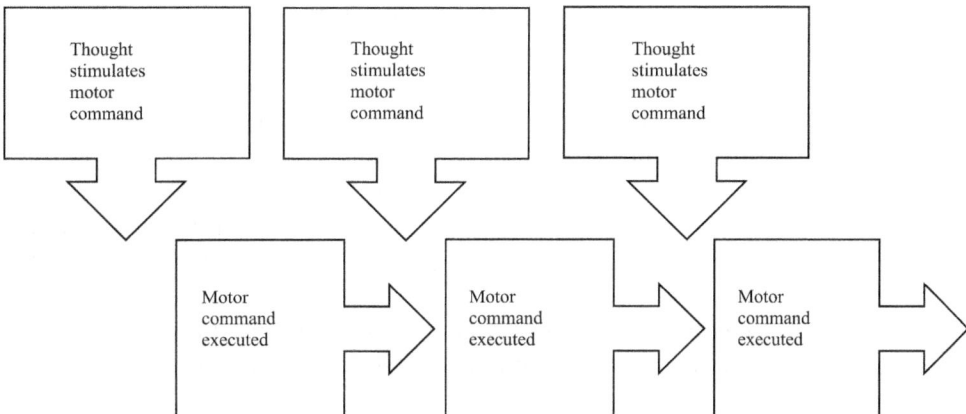

Figure 2.5. Thought-to-motor command.

a series of containers, with liquid flowing in from one to the next, but only as liquid also is able to flow out, making room for more. You may also have had this experience: playing, and thinking about something that has just occurred, leading to a new and unexpected error. One can see this as a result of holding something in the buffer (container) rather than allowing new information to enter.

An important element in this "dual cognitive resource" is in the transformation of "declarative task representations" into "procedural" ones through practice. Salvucci and Taatgen (2008) write:

> Once instructions are stored as declarative knowledge, a general set of interpreter production rules[9] retrieves each instruction and executes its desired actions. As these interpreter rules execute the declarative instructions, the production compilation mechanism begins to combine the general interpreter rules and the instructions into task-specific production rules. Production compilation is a slow process in the sense that a new rule must typically be relearned multiple times before it is able to compete successfully with existing rules. (p. 107)

The need for retrievals from what they call "declarative" memory is frequent in early stages of learning but becomes less frequent as the learner becomes more familiar and intuitively adopts more (and perhaps more generalizable) procedural rules, which further contributes to decreasing interference between these two parallel threads. In addition, the learning thread requires fewer production rules overall, requiring even less processing from the procedural resource (Salvucci & Taatgen, 2008, p. 110). So, a win-win-win for the learner.

Whether this convinces you that we can actually multitask, or you hold to the more common belief that we are switching rapidly between quickly-in-succession tasks, what it means for us as musicians is that, as we progress, we want to continue to develop the ability to hear, read, and think ahead of where we are playing (at just the right increment, carefully calibrated according to the piece demands), so that we are able to play in this moment while planning for the next.

We just begin to see the importance of buffering at this level, and it will become more and more important as the musician progresses. We can aid this buffering process consciously through mindful observation of visual patterns, aligning them in our memories to audiated and played patterns, and focusing on thinking/processing ahead rather than behind. If the situation warrants that we do stop and think about what has happened previously, that is certainly appropriate, especially in our efforts to avoid making the same mistake in the same way numerous times. But the focus is always on *visual* chunks, representing *audiated* chunks, being processed in *mental* chunks.

Prereading, there is an interaction of three processes, shown in Figure 2.6: audiation, motor coordination, and evaluation (also sometimes called *monitoring*).

- Audiation—we hear and understand the patterns that make up the music.
- Motor coordination—we have learned how what we hear and understand works on our particular instrument, and our brain sends the appropriate signals to the appropriate muscles to bring those patterns "to life."
- Evaluation—we listen and evaluate whether we performed what we audiated.

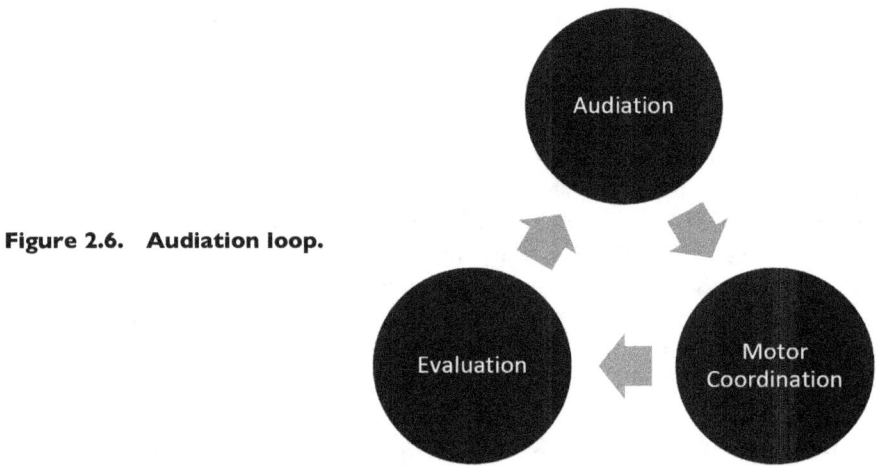

Figure 2.6. Audiation loop.

With the additional task of reading music, a fourth process is added to this loop—visual processing; *and* a fifth—working memory, which holds the notes we have observed but not yet performed in our minds until the time at which we perform them (Figure 2.7). By that point, we have taken in another group of notes and they are being held in working memory, having discarded the previously observed patterns, etc. Of course during all of that, we are still, we hope, audiating the patterns, the brain is still sending signals to the muscles, and we are still listening and evaluating whether what we saw is what we played and heard.

Phew! It's a wonder anyone can do any of this at all!

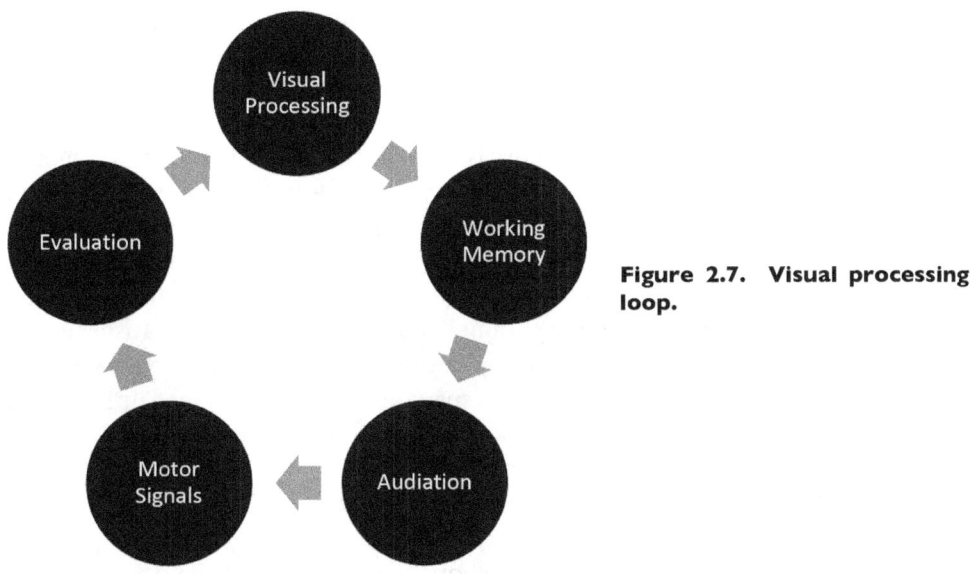

Figure 2.7. Visual processing loop.

It helps, a LOT, if what we are reading is organizable into groups of notes with higher-order interrelationships. The more notes per group, the better. This seems like a good place for a brief tangent, after which I will return to a bit of practical application toward effective music reading.

[Long-Term] Working Memory, Chunking, and Template Theories

Deciding where to put this section presented a bit of a challenge. In most cases, the scientists and topics to be discussed next address how someone becomes an "expert," which would implicate its placement in chapter 5. It also seems a bit tangential, but since I'm writing about reading in "chunks" (forming and processing meaningful units) and the demands reading places on working memory, I've decided to place it here.

The chapter on beginning musicianship focused on developing audiation skill based on pattern learning, but intermediate musicians are facing more complex problems. I argue that if they learn the important skills of reading and thinking in chunks and building a wide, deep repertoire of patterns, pieces, and solutions, their transition into the advanced levels of playing will be eased. Therefore, understanding and contemplating the implications of each of these theories is important for the teacher of musicians of these levels. If we wait to learn "well" when we are "advanced," we might not ever get there, or may find we have that much more remedial work to do.

Working memory is an important element in visual processing, and therefore to music reading. Working memory is actually critical to *many* cognitive functions, and the fundamental determinant of proficiency in a wide range of tasks (Hambrick & Engle, 2003, p. 180). Some researchers even consider working memory capacity to be the most important factor in general fluid intelligence (Conway et al., 2001). Working memory is also important in the suppression of undesired retrievals, which helps us avoid intrusions of deceptive information when encountering misleadingly similar problems.

While the capacity of working memory is somewhat fixed and limited by genetics, a person's memory capacity *for a particular type of information*, or within a certain task, can be expanded through the acquisition of appropriate skills (Ericsson, 2003, p. 47). This seems to be directly related to the ability to chunk information into meaningful units, an important feature in the development of expertise in any domain, and a feature of many of my recommended practice strategies. Musicians also demonstrate a general increase in focused attention and working memory capacities, advantages in reading and operation span, and an improvement in long-term verbal memory (Besson et al., 2011). These correlations also support the music and language connection previously addressed.

In the article "Long-Term Working Memory," Ericsson and Kintsch (1995) discuss two different working memory systems: one with which most are probably already familiar, "short-term working memory," (ST-WM), and a system that links short-term working memory to long-term memory (LTM), which they refer to as "long-term working memory" (LT-WM).

Tasks with a large cognitive load require access to a large amount of information contained within a meaningful context. Like knowledge retained in LTM, information in LT-WM is stable, but reliable access to it is temporary, triggered by a series of retrieval cues in ST-WM (Ericsson & Kintsch, 1995, p. 211). Ericsson and Kintsch believe ST-WM to have a maximal capacity of around seven "chunks," or meaningful units, *if* they correspond to a familiar pattern already in LTM; in most cases it is more likely to be around four. If/when attention is diverted to another demanding task, the information in ST-WM becomes unavailable, sometimes in a matter of seconds. On the other hand, LTM is primarily associative, relating different items to one another and to attributes of the current situation or context. But while there may be a great deal of information in LTM, there is often a bottleneck during retrieval since retrieval cues are triggered in ST-WM, and, as already mentioned, we can only manage a few at a time.

This is where LT-WM comes in. Ericsson and Kintsch believe that LT-WM serves as an organizer of ST-WM cues—which, in addition to our limited capacity, tend to be very brief—and a link from these cues to information encoded in LTM.

According to Ericsson and Kintsch, good "readers" perform better than poor ones because they have *superior comprehension strategies*,[10] which lead to the construction of *better retrieval schemata*, and more extensive retrieval structures result in an effectively larger working memory. Conversely, a *lack* of prerequisite knowledge impairs both encoding and storage in LTM, as well as the ability to generate inferences needed to create an integrated representation. Forming integrated representations in LTM requires prerequisite knowledge as well as encoding skills. Encoding and retrieval are at least somewhat dependent on the individual learner's ability to successfully anticipate future retrieval demands. Perhaps the most important feature these authors have found in terms of integrated encoding and retrieval is the ability to "chunk," which, not at all coincidentally, is one of the most important practice strategies we can develop (Ericsson & Kintsch, 1995, pp. 230–233).

> To meet the particular demands for working memory in a given skilled activity, subjects must acquire encoding methods and retrieval structures that allow efficient storage and retrieval from LTM. In the same manner that skilled subjects must acquire relevant knowledge of the demands of an activity and develop efficient procedures for completing a task, they also refine methods for encoding information in LTM. The structures that are generated to represent information guarantee accessibility with respect to specific future retrieval demands. Retrieval demands differ greatly among different activities. . . . LT-WM is therefore closely tailored to the demands of a specific activity and is an integrated, inseparable part of the skill in performing the activity. (Ericsson & Kintsch, 1995, p. 239)

In other words, if we understand it better, and can imagine what we will need to do to retrieve it *while* we are encoding it, we will encode it better. Better encoding means we will not only be more likely to remember it, but will be able to remember it more quickly, more reliably, and when we need it. It will also be more likely to help us when we meet future, related, and/or more challenging problems.

Kellman and Massey (2013) propose a theory of perceptual learning, where experience in a domain induces changes in how we extract information from our sensory perceptions. These mechanisms are complex, abstract, selective, and often not limited to modality-specific sensory features. "With practice in [a] domain, [we] become attuned to [both] the relevant features and the structural relations that define classifications [of information] over time, [and] come to extract [information from our perceptions] with increasing selectivity and fluency." These mechanisms provide complex descriptions of reality that overlap and interact deeply with what is considered to be "higher" cognitive functions, and the information delivered becomes increasingly adaptive. Over time and with practice, our "learning system becomes selectively attuned" to what information should be extracted, and we are able to do so faster, more automatically, and in larger chunks. Automatization of this pickup of basic information "paves the way for discovery of even more complex relationships [as well as finer detail, all of] which . . . becomes progressively easier to process." This creates a positive feedback loop in cyclic form, where "improvements in information extraction leads [sic] to even more improvements in information extraction." As a result, we can "see at a glance what is relevant, . . . [and] discern complex patterns as well as finer details, . . . with minimal cognitive load" (pp. 118–120).

Procedural learning has positive effects in both "discovery"—finding what information is relevant, and filtering out that which is not, constructing larger chunks of information with higher-order relationships; and in "fluency"—extracting information with greater ease, speed, and reduced cognitive load and using parallel processing rather than serial (Kellman & Massey, 2013, p. 123).

While increasing selectivity increases efficiency and therefore improves speed of processing, there will be plateaus. Working through these plateaus paves the way for new gains, generating a cycle of discovery leading to improved performance, leading to increased fluency, leading to higher levels of discovery, etc. (Kellman & Massey, 2013, p. 124). Pattern recognition and fluent processing of structure contributes to attaining expertise and can and should be encouraged at this stage of study, not just so that good habits are formed, but so that the foundation of pattern recognition so important to efficient and effective music reading and performance is well and securely established.

In his survey on four theories of "expert memory," Gobet (1998) takes a bit of issue with Ericsson and Kitsch's long-term working memory theory and acknowledges that each domain imposes constraints[11] that will "critically shape behavior" (p. 43). He claims there is much more support in the experimental evidence for template theory, which has evolved from chunking theory.

Chunking theory, posed by Chase and Simon decades ago, proposes that expertise in a domain comes from having learned and encoded a large database of "chunks," which are indexed by what they call a "discrimination net" and which are compared with new problem situations. Two forms of chunking are identified in their model: deliberate, which is goal-oriented and under our conscious, strategic control and automatic, which is continuous, and linked to perceptual processes. A chunk "collects a number of pieces of information from the environment [and assembles them] into a single unit. . . . [This theory] explains how greater knowledge can lead to an increased ability to extract information from the environment, in spite of constant cognitive limitations [such as the capacity limits of short-term memory]. . . . Chunking underlies many aspects of human learning," and the construction and retrieval of chunks "affects the types of generalizations made, and . . . predicts typical errors or successes" (Gobet et al., 2001, p. 236).

Chunking theory allows for seven (±) chunks available at any given moment in short-term memory. Familiar chunks in LTM are recognized when stimulated by new perceptions with similar characteristics, and an action is evoked—in experts to the point where the response seems automatic. Chunks also provide access to semantic memory, including productions and schemas, and Gobet uses the presence of chunks to explain why experts can recall larger amounts of information than novices, even when the short-term memory capacity is basically the same. This superiority is due to each chunk containing more information, and being stored in LTM (Gobet, 1998, pp. 5–6).

"This model proposed that [experts'] skill is based on their stock of configurations in LTM [long-term memory], which allows them . . . to recognize known patterns." These chunks in long-term memory are represented with an "internal name" that is "associated with a set of instructions that permit the patterns to be reconstituted as an internal image" in what Gobet refers to as the "mind's eye." The "mind's eye consists of a system that stores perceptual structures, both from external inputs and from memory stores, and that can be subjected to visuo-spatial mental operations. . . . It also contains relational structures, [allowing] new information to be abstracted from it" (Gobet, 1998, p. 11). According to chunking theory, expertise is a result of the learner having (a) a large database of chunks in long-term memory, all of which are indexed by a "discrimination net," and (b) a large knowledge base, whose encoding includes production values, plus (c) a schema, which couples the chunks from (a) to the index in (b). Some "nodes" will evolve into more complex data structures, with several paths to them, creating redundant networks (Gobet, 1998, p. 16).

Gobet and Simon's template theory expands on chunking theory, combining the concept of chunking with a retrieval structure that connects low-level to high-level knowledge (Gobet, 1998, p. 15). There is a perceptual element, with chunks accessed from LTM through filters, pointers to the chunks placed in short-term memory, and visuo-spatial structures (based on these same chunks) built up in "the mind's eye." If the material is behaving as expected, a discriminated node will provide access to the learner's semantic memory, which leads to deeper understanding. Chunks, after having been experienced (processed) many times, develop into higher-level templates, with slots that are created to receive new data when new information is perceived (Gobet & Clarkson, 2004). These templates include a large chunk at their core, with the addition of slots that are created after multiple experiences with some element or variable that differs from the core template chunk. These chunks and templates are organized schematically, "accessed by visual information, contextual cues, strategic or tactical features, [and] labeling," with multiple routes that allow for "highly redundant," and therefore, probably more secure, "memory management." While this redundancy is evident in chunking theory, template theory explains how chunks evolve into these more complex structures (pp. 15–16, 33). Templates also allow specific details of a stimulus to be "plugged into appropriate slots," which facilitates rapid recall and may "account for much of experts' superior memory skills" (Gobet et al., 2001, p. 240).

Template theory claims fewer chunks are available at any given time, probably around three, and holds that the limits on short-term memory capacity are the same for experts and novices, but that experts hold (much) more information in each chunk.

I hope you have persisted through this somewhat dry explanation, and recognize the myriad overlaps among the above theories. To summarize: with time and practice, we develop an internal encyclopedia of knowledge based on perceptual cues leading to motor commands. This basis of knowledge and experience leads to an informed set of expectations that eases our recognition and execution of familiar patterns, and helps us identify potential problems. Experiences that vary slightly expand the depth of the chunks in long-term memory; experiences that differ greatly instigate the creation of new chunks.

In a practical sense, our intentional practice can help this process through:

- the contribution of chunking both mentally and physically to both long-term storage and to ready access to information in long-term memory by short-term and working memory;
- the importance of coherent and relevant retrieval cues;
- the important role of perception in cognition; and
- the impact of higher-level organization.

But what does this mean for the intermediate music reader?

If each note constitutes one "thing," we can only think one note at a time. But if we group—visually, aurally, mentally—one "thing," one chunk, one meaningful unit may contain an entire beat, an entire measure, a chord pattern, etc. Compare the ease of reading and performing the first rhythm pattern in Figure 2.8 with that of the second, where the beaming makes the meter and pulse much clearer. And notice how individual notes in the excerpt in Figure 2.9 belong to groups such as "G major triad," "D dominant 7th," "G major scale from D to D," etc. Or, even better, "tonic triad in G major," "dominant 7th in G major," and "scale on ^5."

Figure 2.8. Unbeamed vs. beamed rhythms.

Figure 2.9. Mozart, "Sonata in G major," K. 283, I., meaningful units.

Young musicians can learn how to do this (or not) from their first experiences reading music.

For example, "Broken Record Boogie" by David Kraehenbuehl[12] is often one of the first pieces I use to link a student's playing to learning a piece from a score. In my teaching, this is usually after a couple of years of lessons where we have been singing, tapping pulses and chanting rhythms, playing rote songs that are often transposed, improvising, playing basslines while singing melodies, playing melodies while singing basslines, and playing lots of theory games that incorporate elements of music reading and notation, etc. "Broken Record Boogie" is an excellent place to begin reading notation because there are only a few patterns to learn and the bass-boogie pattern is familiar because the beginning musician has been playing rote pieces that use the 12-bar blues progression throughout their previous year(s) of study. But this piece is a bit longer and has a few "curveballs" in it, which make the notation helpful for the intermediate musician to keep track of what happens next.[13]

For the first week of practice in preparation for this piece, one can practice the blues-boogie bass pattern on I, IV, and V in C and the main melodic motive by rote, and improvise using those. The "notation" would look like Figure 2.10.[14]

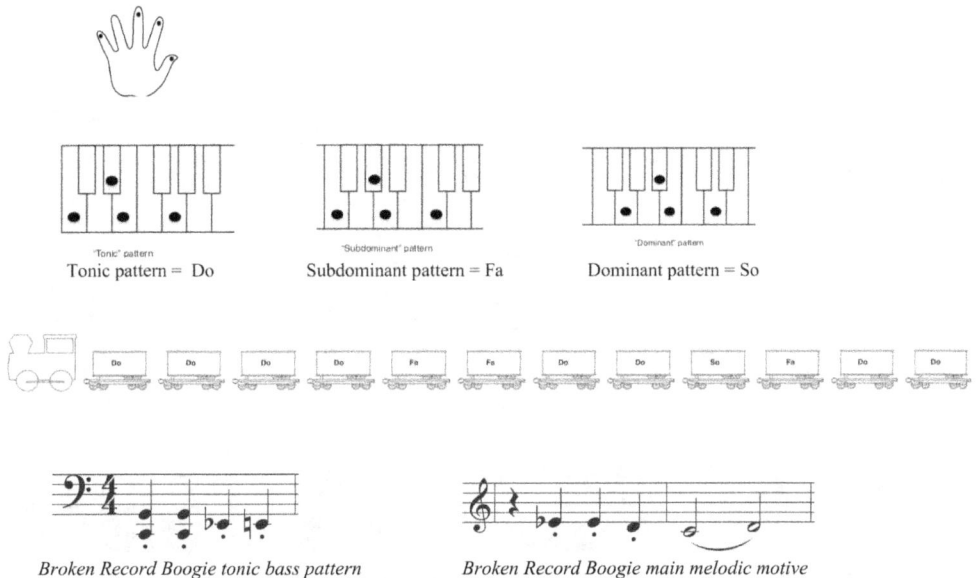

Figure 2.10. "Broken Record Boogie" first "notation."

The next week, after the learner has demonstrated that each of the above patterns is understood and can be played successfully on demand, the landmarks Low C, Low F, and Middle C[15] are introduced using a grand staff and flash cards. Each note is shown, and then the flash card placed behind the appropriate key, as shown in Figure 2.11.

Identifying each landmark within the score, and perhaps even circling each occurrence in the notation with its own color, links the landmark on the keyboard to the landmark in the music; playing the tonic bass pattern as it appears on low C, the subdominant pattern on low F, etc. links the rote patterns to the notation. For the first week, the piece can even be practiced with the landmark cards placed as above. You might even draw the little keyboard pictures, as in the "first notation" in Figure 2.10, in appropriate places in the score.

Also learning to play and then identify the basic melodic pattern, circling each occurrence and then finding any that differ makes similar connections for the right hand. This would also be an appropriate time to talk about the two different names—D♯ and E♭—for the key at the top of the pair of black keys, and then maybe

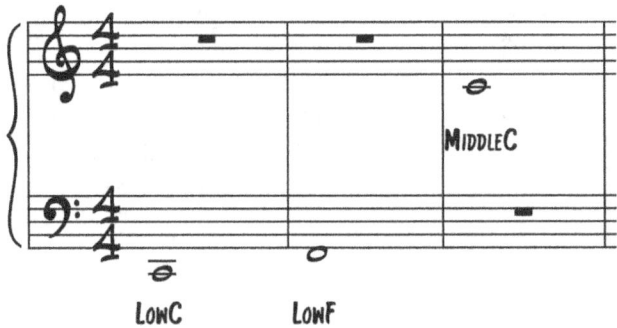

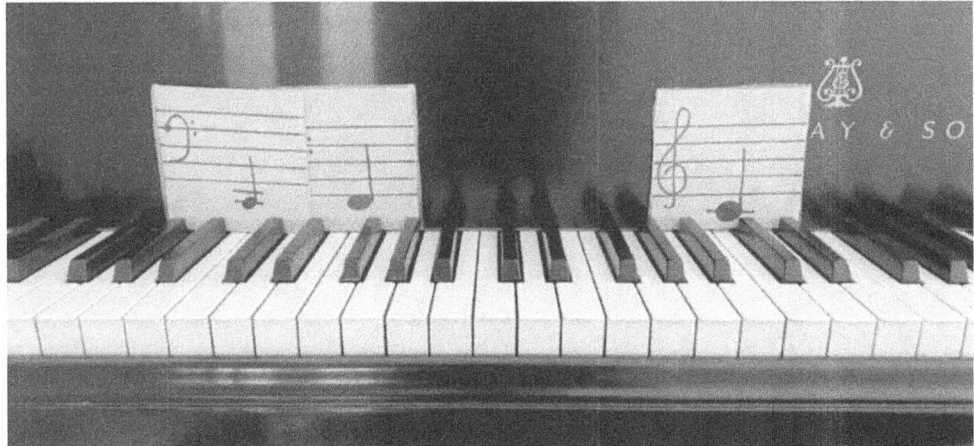

Figure 2.11. "Broken Record Boogie" landmarks and keys.

a brief exploration of other sharps and flats for the rest of the piece, deeper learning, and future reference.[16]

The music is now serving as a map, and the musician is bringing a lot of meaning to the score along with a basic physical understanding of how each pattern works. This helps the visual processing loop, shown in Figure 2.7, work well and comfortably, and introduces music reading as a process by which we read and recognize *patterns* rather than focusing on individual entities.

Part of this cycle of pattern reading and prediction includes the honing of what may be our most important skill—knowing what to think about, when—while building a reliable motor-signal network so that we can trust our physical selves (our procedural resources, to use cognitive science terminology) to execute that which we have just thought. What struck me most about Salvucci and Taatgen's (2008) theory of threaded cognition is the emphasis it puts on the evolution of reliance on declarative knowledge in the early stages of learning to reliance on procedural skill, and that practice hones representation of what might be called compound tasks, which are easily integrated or separated as needed, allowing for flexible combinations according to the situation demands (p. 127).

From a practical what-are-we-actually-thinking-about-when standpoint, this will work best if we are thinking about meaningful units as substantial as possible so that we are not overwhelmed by declarative types of information, and therefore mentally frantic. Good readers have been shown to hold larger chunks of musical material in their memory because they are able to organize the notes into groups with higher-order relationships. A more advanced understanding of music and the expected functions therein leads to more proficient reading and reading-and-performing.

In his book *Exploring The Musical Mind*, Sloboda (2005) recommends exactly this approach to music reading:

- Learning music that is "understood before it is played."
- Development of audiation, and then development of audiation while looking at the score without actually playing.[17]
- Development of musical knowledge as it relates to form, style, and harmonic language.[18]
- Practice of chunking skills.

He also stresses the importance of beaming according to beat structure (as shown in Figure 2.8) and using appropriate accidentals according to key structure (such as an F♯ in G minor rather than a G♭); both principles with which I strongly agree; these reinforce context and preserves the *meaningful* in the expression "meaningful units."[19]

Taking this approach to a handful of pieces lays a very important foundation—one that focuses on reading music that is already understood, audiated, and, at least in some respects, performed. Early reading pieces should be chosen carefully so that they consist *mostly* of rote-learnable patterns (both tonally and rhythmically) and explore a wide range of the keyboard (or whatever instrument) as soon as physically possible for the musician[20] so that all appropriate landmarks can be taught and reinforced through experience. But the pieces should also be of sufficient length or difficulty that the notation is helpful to the learning process.[21] These practices introduce the concepts of music reading in a way that encourages pattern recognition and links to already established audiation skill.

Then, just as would happen with language learning and reading of text, as the musician becomes more and more experienced with music reading, a musical equivalent of phonetics can be applied, based on problem solving and applying former knowledge through recognition of contextual cues.

EXECUTION, AND BENEFITS, OF MENTAL PRACTICE

Coffman (1990), Davidson-Kelly et al. (2015), Gentili et al. (2010), Schuster et al. (2011), and Yágüez et al. (1998) all testify to the benefits of mental imagery practice. The benefits seem to be particularly relevant to improving cognitive components of perceptual and motor tasks. Yágüez et al. postulate that imagining the target movement assembles the appropriate motor programs, and that the central processes during mental imagery practice are largely identical to those required for performance of the same material. The areas that fire the motor command are much less active during mental imagery, but are evoked, and there is significant overlap in the supplementary motor areas, premotor cortex, and parietal areas (Yágüez et al., 1998, p. 104). Gentili et al.'s findings (2010) indicate that the brain uses what they call "state estimation, provided by internal forward model predictions to improve motor performance," that "mentally stimulated and physically executed movements trigger similar motor representations," that "motor-imagery training has been repeatedly shown to improve motor performance," that it "reduces movement variability," and "is also associated with changes in brain activation" (p. 774). Gentili et al.'s findings also indicate that motor performance can be even more improved when physical practice and mental imagery practice are combined (p. 781).

A simple form of mental practice can be seen in the early experiences of a well-taught beginning musician, with the young learner audiating and able to sing in response or to improvise tonal and rhythm patterns. It can be nurtured through the intermediate stage through developing reading skill as it relates to audiation and pattern reading. The benefits of mental imagery are well documented for experts, but I would argue that the ability should be learned and rehearsed at an earlier stage so as to be mastered and useful before the challenges of the repertoire become too great.

Musicians who read music well can hear it in their minds while looking at the score. This ability is established if taught to read with a pattern-reading approach, and should be reinforced at every stage. A musician reading with audiation ability will be able to recognize recurrent motives or melodies and rhythm patterns, and will make connections with technical patterns they know and practice as well as to other pieces that presented similar material or challenges.

"THEORY"—WHEN, HOW, AND WHY

> *Abstract knowledge . . . is created through the interaction of the world and the mind.* (Perlovsky, 2015)

It may have occurred to some that I have not started talking about the teaching of music theory topics yet. This is intentional; we want to learn according to the Pestalozzian principles previously mentioned of sound, before sight, before theory.

Our first forays into "theory" are really just labeling, which can happen fairly soon at the beginning levels. *After a number of patterns have been learned*, they are named:[22] "major," "minor," "Dorian," "duple meter pattern," "tonic triad pattern"; and the naming can eventually become more detailed and specific: "two-macrobeat duple meter pattern"; "tonic triad pattern when Do is G," "subtonic pattern in Dorian." Eventually, the identifications of the keys on the keyboard or notes on a string instrument (etc.) evolve from being, "Can you find another note that looks like this?" with the teacher indicating a particular key on the piano or position on a string, to being called[23] "the white key below the group of three black keys" or "2nd finger in first position on the A string," to "F" or "C♯." You might also label triads, such as calling the three notes C-E-G played in succession, first, a "major triad," then maybe "tonic triad when Do is C," or "C major triad," which might also, when appropriate, be identified as the subtonic triad in D Dorian, or the dominant triad in F major. (It is not necessary to spend a lot of time on this, but these connections will begin to be made if the patterns are labeled often enough, within context.) Likewise, this rhythm pattern: ♬♪♬ which can already be chanted using neutral syllables or rhythm solfège, can eventually be described as being made up of "two-16ths 8th note, 8th two-16ths," although this is certainly not necessary in order for it to be chanted or performed correctly. At this stage of learning, labeling for any new concept should only be after the concept has been heard, sang, chanted, and/or played.

After a musician has begun to read music, identifying note names, individual rhythm durations, etc. will become more and more a part of the discussion, and useful especially for selecting a starting place, or in passing as early introductions to what will become more focused study. But the focus should, and for a great while, be from within an established context. Therefore, note names are first closely linked to their relative position around recognizable structures at the instrument (CDE around the two black-key group on the piano keyboard, or the treble clef G-D-A-E to coincide with open strings for young violinists), and notational landmarks on the score as they relate to the clefs used (the five Cs and the two clef notes for treble [G] and bass [F] clef, for example; middle C for alto or tenor clef, etc.). Individual durations are identified from their occurrences within a complete macrobeat/microbeat rhythm pattern. Triads are identified first by mode, then function within a keyality, and then later by the note names by which they are formed. In every instance, individual entities are taught, practiced, labeled, and understood as part of a larger meaningful unit. This supports audiation, and how we want music to be read: as patterns, functioning within a larger whole. More involved theory work comes later, gradually, with great care, and at least at first, at the instrument.

Music cognition experts actually talk about how any one theory question is actually many, and the *process* by which we work to answer each underlying question *in proper succession* is of utmost importance, like learning the proper solution order for complicated math problems.

An intermediate student was struggling to work through this process correctly, so he and I listed the number of theory "questions" behind being asked to play a randomly chosen melodic minor scale from a large number of learned ones:

1. Identification of the relative major
2. Identification of the key signature of the relative major (which involves its own series of multiple steps)
3. Identification of which scale degree(s) is/are altered in a melodic minor scale

4. Identification of the specific note(s) that/those alterations affect in this particular scale
5. Knowing to what fingering group the scale belongs
6. Knowing how that fingering rule applies to this specific scale,
7. ... in each hand
8. And whether there is a difference between the ascending and descending versions

And these are "only" to play the scale. To write the scale one also has to have knowledge of clefs, placement of notes on particular lines and spaces, how to shape the notes, etc.

Theory questions are generally abstract, and often will not lead to the right conclusion unless they are asked and answered in a particular order. We want to understand not only the process, but why step 2 must follow step 1, etc. In any case, it is almost always better to learn how to "find" a solution rather than to try to "memorize" one, especially when the problems are presented with as much variability as they are in music.[24] There will be more about rule learning in the section on the advanced musician.

Identification is always easier than writing, so it is also best if that comes first. And there are added difficulties with notation, such as needing to know how to read the chosen clef, whether the 7th scale degree of the *a* harmonic minor scale is a G♯ or an A♭, and why that matters.

MORE RELEVANT THAN LEARNING STYLES: PERSONALITY, CHARACTER, AND MOTIVATION

> *Solving a complex problem requires more than mere knowledge; it requires the motivation and personal resourcefulness to undertake the challenge and persist until a solution is reached.* (Zimmerman & Campillo, 2003, p. 233)

I don't think that anyone would disagree with the proposition that most people have innate preferences for how they approach new material, receiving and processing new information accordingly. This might be attributed to learning style, personality, etc. But research shows it is *most important to align the style of approach to the parameters of the task*[25] itself, and that learners who are most adept at choosing the appropriate learning *mode* are more creative and successful at problem solving than those with fixed style preferences. Subscribing to a particular belief as regarding your own learning style can also have a negative impact on your perceptions of your learning abilities, while it has been demonstrated that using multiple intelligences elevates the number and variety of tools that can and will be used. Adaptability ensures appropriate connections between the task demands and associated cognitive processes. It is also possible that, if you overembrace an innate learning preference, other crucial elements may be permanently hobbled. For example, if you learn well by ear and are never taught, or expected, to learn music from notation, reading skills will fail to develop.

That being said, personality, character, and motivation play an important role in learning success. While personality is pretty much innate, character and motivation are things that can be developed, taught, and encouraged, so those are elements I want to write about next.

An effective, disciplined work ethic can certainly be learned and cultivated, along with the motivation to persist through increasingly complex problem-solving tasks necessary to excel at an instrument. In this respect, character traits as they relate to motivation can play a role, but when learners have confidence in their ability to solve a problem, they will be that much more motivated to try. This is where a strong foundation in our early music learning really pays off. At the beginning levels, the focus is on the development of audiation skill, a relaxed and playful approach to the instrument, and listening to/monitoring the results. As learning progresses, and more strategic problem solving begins to be required, focusing positive feedback on curiosity, creativity, and diligent investigations of alternative problem-solving strategies builds belief in self-efficacy, and the more self-efficacious people believe themselves to be, the more effort and persistence they will display (Zimmerman & Campillo, 2003, pp. 240–241). Learning the tools by which they can solve their own problems will not only make them more successful, but they will work harder for longer in more difficult situations and believe in themselves more while doing so.

As a teacher, then, we want to praise *disciplined investigations and applications of various/appropriate problem-solving strategies* above achievement so as to encourage self-motivation.

Research has shown that intrinsic motivation is more likely when self-evaluation is learning-goal- and problem-solving-based rather than performance-based, and that attributing errors to having chosen the wrong solution strategies, or having implemented them incorrectly, rather than to one's innate ability, is more effective for sustaining motivation. Strategy attributions will actually sustain perceptions of efficacy until *all possible strategies* have been tested. Thus, highly self-regulated problem solvers attribute errors to controllable variables and are therefore more confident and willing to persist. These self-motivational beliefs form the basis for the learner's sense of personal agency and encourages the learner to continue his/her cyclical self-regulatory efforts until s/he eventually reaches a solution (Zimmerman & Campillo, 2003, pp. 244–246).

Recognizing problems, defining them, identifying and exploring potential solutions, and evaluating the relative success of those solutions are important stages in the representation of the problem and in finding solutions. Consciously enacting this process is key to productive practicing. Certain personality traits will make a person more (or less) likely to engage in seeking out and identifying the problems, even ill-defined ones, and more (or less) likely to experiment with various ways to solve them. Identifying these qualities and cultivating this mindful curiosity in young learners is an important task for parents, teachers, and caregivers. The first steps in this direction may be in encouraging problem *solvers* to be problem *finders*, to think flexibly, and to suspend judgment while engaging in a playful search of a variety of solutions. It is important that the learner be engaged in all stages of this process, learning to listen for and identify problems and to be an active participant in investigating, experimenting with, and identifying the success or failure of various solutions.

Many of us have experienced a lesson where we play something over and over as our teacher gives feedback—"too loud," "too soft," "not staccato enough," "the top wasn't voiced properly," etc. until finally s/he says "That's it!" And we have no idea what we did, or what s/he heard.

How could we possibly do it again?

Rather, the musician must learn to be both producer and evaluator.

The teacher can certainly help this by asking more questions than s/he answers. I don't know who said it, but *teaching isn't telling*. Often, it's asking . . . and waiting . . . and asking again, or asking something else.

An element that has come up frequently in my research is something that we don't always think about when we are thinking or talking about practicing—*creativity*.[26] We have already discussed the importance of an adaptable learning style so as to best meet task demands. In fact, creativity in problem solving is an important aspect of maintaining motivation. One of the points I am planning to make by the end of the book is that there are really only a handful of *types*[26] of practice, and having the ability to identify which will be most effective for the given situation is one of the keys to efficiency, like a carpenter picking just the right tool. But creativity of approach plays a role in most of them. Asking questions like, "What would it sound like if I did x instead of y?" and listening carefully to the result while observing the physical sensations provides a learning opportunity of exponential benefit. Creativity is a learnable trait, and can be maximized by parents and teachers, as well as through the experience with diverse cultural and social environments, which have been demonstrated to promote creative thinking. On the other hand, time constraints, competition, and external evaluation *during problem solving* tend to have negative effects (Lubart & Mouchiroud, 2003, p. 134).

For the intermediate musician, all the above indicate the importance of choosing repertoire judiciously, continuously developing and refining technical facility, and using problem-solving strategies that involve exploration, self-observation, and creativity so as to develop a focused work ethic and maximize motivation as well as results. We also want to be sure to encourage and reward mindfulness at the instrument, analysis, mapping, scaffolding, and practicing in layers so as to encourage establishment of useful retrieval cues and higher-order organization. Listening, observing, and planning in cohesive patterns and a constant looping cycle establish a framework of performance that is reliable and secure, and therefore provides sufficient mental space to play with stylistic and personal expression. Specific practice strategies can support these elements, and most facilitate chunking on many levels, both physically and mentally.

NOTES

1. I realize many teachers teach "beginners" to read music; I hope that at the very least this book encourages a delay of some months if not years until appropriate audiation ability has been developed first. Whether you do or not, the practice strategies in this section would be generally appropriate for students in their third or fourth years of lessons, with exceptions depending on aptitude.

2. Usually, just a little bit more challenging than what has just been mastered, or similarly challenging but with a variation in surface structures or one or two new concepts or additional technical demands.

3. Fixations are also strongly linked to memory, so that, when remembering something, a person will replicate the eye movements from when they were looking at what they are remembering, or when imagining the stimulus. And similarity in eye movement patterns from encoding to imagery predicts memory accuracy.

4. As the selection or passage becomes more familiar, the musician eventually remembers the *sequence* of notes, at which point the musical notation becomes a cue for evoking a *motor* command (Burman & Booth, 2009, p. 317). (More on that later.)

5. Aural, also, but we've talked about that already.

6. Goldstein (1984); Peterson & Kimchi (2013).

7. Similarity and continuation affect our aural processing as well, and explains the ability to hear a compound melodic line such as one might find in a Bach violin or cello suite, and which Gestalt psychologists refer to as "auditory stream segregation."

8. In light of current understanding on diversity and inclusion, and in terms of how music is performed and understood in many cultures, this statement is perhaps both controversial and overstated, and clearly directed to those involved in music study as it is approached in "Western" and academic cultures. Music is pursued to a great degree, complexity, and satisfaction in many cultures and by many musical artists—jazz, rap, the Beatles—that doesn't involve or even require notation. For the arguments of this book, music reading is one of many important pursuits, and one that we want to approach in a cognitively sound way and at an appropriate stage in development. In that respect, it is "necessary" for "full membership" in the musical community of which I write.

9. Put simply, a *rule* is an if/then statement, and can be thought of in terms of this (input) leads to that (output).

10. An important thing, and one that can be actively cultivated in how we approach our practice.

11. Referring specifically to Vicente and Wang's proposal of a "constraint attunement hypothesis" to explain domain expertise in memory recall (Vicente & Wang, 1998; Simon & Gobet, 2000).

12. Found in "Supplementary Solos Book 1," Summy Burchard, a division of Alfred Publishing. I regret I was unable to obtain reprint permission to include the score.

13. Using notation to tell us something we already know is actually how and why notation was designed in the first place. Tradition was that pieces were learned by rote/ear. Notation became necessary when the pieces became long enough or complex enough that rote learning was inefficient or cumbersome, or when people wanted to transmit their music to a new location without having a few weeks to spare so as to teach it to the ensemble by ear. Anyone reading early notation already had a pretty good idea how the music went. The score was used to help fill in the details or remind the performer of what was next.

14. The type of "notation" used in *Music Moves for Piano* by Marilyn Lowe, and which I would draw into the practice assignment book for other pieces.

15. In my teaching practice I teach Frances Clark's landmarks: the five clef Cs, the treble clef G and its octave-higher "high G," and the bass clef F and its octave-lower "low F." These are introduced gradually, as needed for the first several pieces, and then expanded and eventually "memorized." We start with identifying which is which, then extracting them from a collection of flash cards that include some red herrings (like the middle E in the bass clef due to its resemblance to the high C, etc.), which they place or play in the appropriate place. It is MUCH later that they are asked to write them. Other instrumentalists may learn different landmarks, based on the register and appropriate "landmark" notes on their instrument.

16. Especially G♯/A♭ and A♯/B♭, since the sharp versions also appear in the boogie pattern.

17. An important "mental practice" approach that I will talk about more specifically later in the book.

18. In fact, a developed understanding of expected functions within context of a given style—that is, recognizing the 12-bar blues pattern in the piece above, or the likely chord progression in a Mozart Sonata—leads to greater proficiency in reading that particular style. Of course, proficiency at reading Mozart will not predict proficiency in reading Schoenberg except where there is overlap—perhaps in this case more likely in a rhythmic scenario than in a harmonic one.

19. Full disclosure: I don't agree with every one of Sloboda's proposed solutions. He also recommends changing the key signature even if key changes are just a few measures long, which seems unnecessarily fussy, and adding rampant courtesy accidentals, which confounds the ability to think in a key and actually often results in the performer mentally removing that accidental from the key signature.

20. I actually teach young beginners with them standing at the keyboard so that they can walk up or down to an appropriate register as needed. Their stance must be at an appropriate distance and the focus is always on relaxed shoulders and appropriate arm movements. When tall enough to sit at a proper height at the piano on an adjustable bench, they must then sit exactly in the middle of the keyboard unless they are playing duets, so as to build theme physical sense of where those notes are in relation to their position, which gives them physical security throughout their development.

21. Only if the musician has spent a length of time developing audiation ability and using it at their instrument through rote songs and patterns. If you are teaching a child to read at the first lesson, which I strongly discourage, start simple, and teach the pattern.

22. Since part of learning what something is, is learning what it is not.

23. Which comes only after the musician is able to match it easily with graphic notation, as discussed in the section on the beginning musician.

24. Obviously, some things need to be "memorized," such as landmark notes, order of sharps and flats for the key signatures of the circle of 5ths, etc. That being said, the order of sharps and flats subscribe to a rule, based on the evolution of the tetrachords of the scale, sharps ascending in 5ths, flats descending in 5ths, etc.

25. Brown et al. (2014).

26. See Table 9.1 in Appendix D.

3

PRACTICE STRATEGIES FOR MUSICIANS OF BURGEONING INDEPENDENCE

Practicing is problem-solving, and being a good problem-solver is exhilarating in itself. (Westney, 2003, p. 47)

In a previous version of this book, the first section covered music cognition topics and the second presented practice strategies that parallel cognition. At a certain point in the research and early in the stage of writing, I (briefly, facetiously) considered writing "Chunk It!" for the second section and having that be that. While that wouldn't make for much of a book, it does sum up several of the most important practicing strategies we can develop that closely align with how our brain wants to learn music, so we will be talking about several chunking strategies in greater detail. As mentioned earlier, encoding and retrieval is at least somewhat dependent on the individual learner's ability to successfully anticipate future retrieval demands. Integrated coding and retrieval occur when we observe and store chunks of notes in relevant and meaningful units, allowing for effective prediction and/or anticipation while in the act of retrieving (performing). In fact, many cognitive theorists consider chunking strategies to be one of the most important practice strategies we can develop.

But a few other, more general, things, first.

Much writing on effective practice makes some important points that I will not be addressing here: have goals, set up a pleasant and amenable-to-focus practicing space, concentrate, warm up first, be careful to avoid injury, fix mistakes. These are all good points, and I imagine most agree, as do I, but they are not very specific, are they?

Even those writing on deliberate practice and its effects such as K. Anders Ericsson don't go into a whole lot of *practical* detail about what "deliberate practice" might look like. It may be defined as effortful, disciplined, designed so as to meet particular goals, teacher directed. The first three are certainly true, but still not specific. As for the last, some of my best practice has occurred since I stopped working with teachers; some teachers don't actually know how to practice effectively; some common recommendations can actually be detrimental, such as learning one or two measures at a time, or weeks and weeks of hands alone or slow practice. Some practicing philosophies focus on avoiding mistakes at all costs—which, in practice, often leads to different mistakes such as stopping, stuttering, or an inability to continue through errors in performance.[1]

The strategies I want to talk about are much more specific, but with governing strategies that can function as general precepts, and that will link common problems to how we process music so as to find the most effective solution. They also adhere to some really important considerations for performance, especially that:

- Some mistakes in performance are probably going to happen,
  - unless they are rampant and/or disruptive they really don't matter that much,
    - and they are only going to be disruptive if we don't learn how to play through them.

And to some important cognitive considerations:

- Our eyes, ears, and brain will seek out patterns, whether we direct them to or not.
- We read and process these patterns (chunks) as much as we process language.
- We learn and understand new concepts best during pauses, and should approach new concepts aurally/orally first, then physically, and only then theoretically.
- Our short-term/working memory can only deal with so many things at a time, so we must learn to organize and generate a succession of meaningful units that include as much information as is possible within the parameters of logic and reason, linking our current actions to encoded information in long-term memory.
- We stay most motivated if the evaluation of our efforts is problem-solving-strategy based rather than performance based.

We also want to keep in mind that how we approach something will reinforce how we understand it. This might involve practicing our scales in the order of the circle of 5ths as a way to reinforce our understanding of the circle of 5ths, or practicing our scales by fingering rule so as to reinforce our understanding of the fingering concepts, etc. For example, when students are telling me a key signature for a piece or scale, I insist they name the sharps or flats in key-signature order rather than the order in which they appear in the scale so as to reinforce their memory of this important foundational concept and encourage them to think in a "chunk" (a key) rather than a series of individual events (each note of the scale).

Conversely, after we have learned and firmly established the foundational concepts, mixing things up creates *effortful* learning, requiring us to make multiple, perhaps contradictory decisions in short succession, and is an excellent way to test whether we really do understand the concepts being studied or their application. Therefore, every once in a while it is useful to practice our scales in a random order, perhaps through selecting from a pile of flash cards; or practice our memorized pieces working backward by section, or starting in the middle of the most difficult passage. This also supports the benefits of a desirable level of difficulty, which encourages the continuation of effort and helps avoid mindless repetition.

You may have noticed intermediate musicians making errors in the "easier" sections of a piece they are learning, or moving too quickly through suddenly longer note values. This may reflect that they are not paying as much attention at that point, or that they are striving to maintain a certain level of mental tension in their making of predictions, or physical tension in their execution. (I think the latter is also often why musicians will begin to rush while playing fast pieces as their facility improves. They are used to a certain amount of mental/emotional stress, and as they become more masterful, subconsciously strive to preserve it.) It is important to determine which of the above might be causing the difficulty. If it is a result of an excess of automaticity,[2] consciously preserving a level of attention and deliberateness while playing and discouraging mindless repetition should help solve the problem.

This point bears repeating: foundational understanding should be fairly well established before effortful retrievals are asked for. Discrimination learning, what something is versus what it is not, supports our initial understanding of new concepts; inference learning, or a focus on the abstract, encourages transfer of learning to new, relevant concepts (Department of Education, 2007).

For example, I first teach minor scales as relatives to the major, natural form only, so as to encourage the student to think "in" the key, then harmonic (one alteration), then melodic (two up, natural minor down). They are also grouped by fingering rule. After the student has worked on these for a while I will mix them up in different ways.

In all cases, our best learning will happen if we approach the piece with an open yet analytical mind, clear intentions for what we want to accomplish, coherent and exploratory strategies for trying to attain those accomplishments, and an honest, nonjudgmental evaluation of our relative success or failure.

As already mentioned, beginning musicians are ideally approaching "practice" in a playful manner—improvising, creating, transposing, learning songs by rote that they can also sing, moving and chanting rhythmically—and making "corrections" based on comparisons to aurally presented patterns or pieces.

Musicians at the intermediate levels are usually older, are reading text and notation, have established audiation skills as well as more refined small motor control, and have more experience with increasingly disciplined and focused work efforts through educational expectations. For many learners, this will be the first stage of learning their instrument where they notice they can't make significant progress with just a few corrections or repetitions. If equipped with appropriate audiation and the "power tools" of effective practicing strategies, though, they will still observe progress at a pace that helps maintain motivation. Preserving that playful approach and remembering that the path to learning is through being willing to stretch, expand, challenge yourself, and observe mistakes as "fascinating bits of evidence" (à la Westney, 2003), rather than something to take personally or as an indicator of abject failure (meaning you should therefore stop playing altogether) is perhaps the most important thing at this stage. I'm sure there's fodder for another whole book on middle schoolers and the paradoxical pressures of finding/becoming yourself while also somehow managing to conform perfectly. But know that preserving their sense of agency as well as their feelings of dignity and joy are as important to the process (if not more so) as teaching them how to play their melodic minor scales hands together.

Well-known practice strategies include hands alone (for pianists), slow practice, and working in sections, often from the beginning and moving forward painstakingly. Many intermediate musicians believe that mistakes are "bad," and that a "perfect" performance is the goal. Many also recognize the value of repetition in reinforcing good habits and strongly desire to make improvements before they come to their next lesson or performance. As teachers or parents, our goals might also include that they progress, that they are able to perform securely, and that their playing is musical/expressive.

So how do we link these myriad goals?

- Preserving a sense of joyful self-discovery and embracing of new challenges without imposing crippling personal self-judgment
- Practice that maximizes the way our mind works, making our practice sessions as efficient and effective as possible (getting more done in less time)
- Self-evaluation that focuses on problem-solving strategies and progress toward a goal so as to maintain motivation and creativity
- Performance that is expressive and allows for continuation through mistakes

I have a few practicing precepts of my own that apply well to the intermediate musician. These include:

- If you're not thinking, you're not practicing.
- Don't do it again until you know why.
- The audiation pause equals the learning pause.
- Hands together as early and as much as possible.
- Always try to find, and attend to, the patterns.

My case for each follows.

IF YOU'RE NOT THINKING, YOU'RE NOT PRACTICING

> *Elite performers must frequently engage in problem solving and challenging learning to make the necessary modifications to reach their new and higher levels of performance. Consistent with the characteristics of problem solving, elite performers report a very high level of focus and concentration during deliberate practice. In fact, master teachers and expert performers claim that full concentration is a necessary prerequisite for deliberate practice. . . .* When concentration wavers, practice must stop. (Ericsson, 2003, p. 67, emphasis mine)

Almost every musician has had this experience: you are playing along in a performance and everything is just ducky, and then your brain chimes in with some super-detailed and not-very-helpful question: What finger am I putting on that B? Am I sure I know the next chord in the left hand? Wasn't that tuna melt I had for lunch delicious? Am I in the Exposition or the Recap? Why does that person keep coughing?

And that's it. You knew where you were, and now you don't.

There are lots of books out there about maintaining focus, dealing with performance anxiety, and various philosophical attitudes.

But what a lot of people don't talk about is what causes those mental glitches in the first place. And I would pose the theory that, a lot of the time, it is because you are not paying enough attention when you're practicing. Or in practice, you are thinking one way, and when performing, you are thinking completely differently. Practicing with a different series of thought processes than will be used in performance is like training someone to do a job, and then sending someone else to do it. In effect you are rehearsing *not* paying attention, and failing to develop awareness of what it is you should be paying attention to.

I have heard stories about people practicing their scales or warmups while reading or watching television. I have personally experienced practicing and realizing that my mind has gone to about one hundred places, very few of which had anything to do with what I was playing.

Perhaps part of the difficulty is that the word "practicing" is thrown around so much that we stop thinking about what it really means. In the broadest sense, it is rehearsing, one could even call it choreographing, what we want to *think about* and what we hope to *do* when it comes time to actually do it. In another sense, it's problem solving, and, of course, developing the physical awareness and facility to play with ease. If we are not paying attention, not only are we likely to miss problems that need solving; we are also not noticing what we are doing when we do something correctly, which makes it a lot less likely that we will be able reliably, at will, to do it again.

This means that a crucial element of effective practicing is self-observation. When it went well, I was doing this and thinking that; when it went poorly, I . . . didn't plan, forgot what note I was supposed to be leaping to, missed the fingering, got hung up in the passagework, wasn't reading far enough ahead, etc. And while self-recording can be a very helpful tool in evaluating a performance, the monitoring of one's efforts and results during the act itself is of utmost importance, especially because this is the only option during an actual performance. One of my favorite recommendations of William Westney is that upon making a mistake, the first thing to do is to play the passage again *without trying to fix it* (just once!) to see if you can find where the mistake actually begins. *It is often not where you think it is.* This gives us a much better picture of what needs to be done.

In this approach, a mistake, *made once (or maybe twice, if your goal is to observe and determine the what/where/how/why elements of that mistake)*, is a learning opportunity,[3] and errors can be as informative as accuracies.

DON'T DO IT AGAIN UNTIL YOU KNOW WHY

Often in practice a mistake is made, and the practicer either stops and, without thinking or strategizing, goes back and immediately plays the passage again. Or perhaps s/he keeps going, reassuring him/herself that s/he will "fix it next time."

It's never next time

There are problems with both approaches. In the first, the mistake caused a complete derailment and interruption, which will not lead to the habits we want to develop for convincing performance. Also, and perhaps even more dangerous, the practicer has tried to fix something but has not taken the time to figure out what exactly needs to be fixed, why the error might have happened, or what they want to do differently. So they play it again, and sometimes again, and again, often exactly as they played it just before, and now the mistake is reinforced.

Rather, for the sake of reinforcing continuity, I recommend playing just a few beats past the mistake,[4] just until composure and accuracy have been regained. Then and only then go back to where the mistake occurred, try to think and play in exactly the same way (once) and see if it is possible to identify (a) the nature of it *exactly*, (b) possible reasons that it happened, and (c) what you want to do/think differently so as to correct it. Play in your head once,[5] with those intentions firmly in mind, first starting on or near the spot. Then play in actuality and evaluate the result. If effective, work backward to begin from a beat or measure before, then maybe a couple, gradually expanding the excerpt by a few beats or measures in either direction,[6] aiming to *think* and execute correctly each time. For each repetition and/or expanded increment, until you're putting it all back together again, "play" it in your head before playing it on the instrument.

The practice of starting in various places is actually much more important than people realize. If the musician can only begin at the beginning of a phrase or section, his/her ability to recover seamlessly in performance is grossly impeded. Rather, it is extremely beneficial to be able to start just about anywhere, with the music and from memory. Granted, sometimes midgesture, or being in the midst of a tangle of tied notes, might present problems that prevent this, but other than that, I strongly encourage this approach.

The alternative scenario is where something happens that the practicer notices is wrong (or not), but does nothing about it, and is surprised by the same glitch, over, and over, and over again. I refer to this as being a "passenger" on the bus rather than the driver. Observation so as to diagnose is perfectly appropriate. Observation in the hopes that maybe it won't happen this time—oops, there I did it again!—not so much.

Never be surprised by the same thing twice

AUDIATION PAUSE = LEARNING PAUSE

We learned about the audiation pause in the section on beginning musicians. This refers to the time between when a pattern is heard and when it is performed in response, and is foundational to establishing a vocabulary of tonal patterns. Zimmerman and Campillo (2003) point out the need for individual learners to observe, encode, and recall prior solution strategies effectively, not just for current learning but to develop the ability to adjust strategies optimally to meet new situations. And this encoding seems to happen best *in the pause*. This also helps our practice be much more intentional, and therefore effective, and helps avoid the buildup of physical tension, which can lead to injury and/or frustration, which helps no one ever.

In practicing, what I call the "thinking" pause begins the work toward a solution *mentally* before it is tested *physically* and paves the way for more substantial mental practice, which will just increase in importance. These thinking pauses help us avoid habitual repetition of a previously made mistake and provide important *planning* information for when the piece or section is being played from start to finish. After the fact, think of it as a learning pause: if it went well, we "take a picture"; if it went poorly, we make the correction mentally before we attempt it physically.

Plan » execute » observe/plan » execute » observe/plan » execute, etc.

This approach has the added benefit of building in breaks, allowing the muscles to relax and helping the practicer avoid a buildup of frustration and/or tension. It might seem odd to talk about focal dystonia here, since many equate it with more advanced practitioners, but it seems that the potential to develop this problem may begin earlier than people realize. While the disorder itself is physical in presentation, it is neurological in nature, beginning perhaps with too much repetition and the difficulty this poses for the brain to keep track of what goes with what. An analogy I like to use is that you have five cooked spaghetti noodles in your hand, and you plop them down in a loose pile on the counter. You can probably, without touching any noodles, track each individual noodle from start to finish. This seems to be, in an exceedingly simplistic form, a lot like what your brain has to do to keep track of the individual pathways formed by the learning and reinforcing of a specific task. Now hold one hundred cooked spaghetti noodles and try the same thing. Aha!

And yes, a certain amount of repetition is crucial so that the thought can lead to a reliable action, and stamina in terms of physicality and concentration does need to be developed to a certain extent. But fewer intentional, mindful, observant repetitions of individual tasks do the job quite well, encouraging focused concentration, and may help the musician avoid potential problems related to tension or overuse. A certain freedom of approach and interpretation also seems to help protect against dystonia, as it is seen in many fewer instances in musicians who tend to improvise a lot or who approach music without exerting unnecessary pressures on their expectations of success. Altenmüller (2003) writes: "In summary, the development of hand dystonia in musicians is related to the *intense and prolonged* [emphasis mine] practice of fast and highly precise externally predefined actions. Movement patterns, which are worked on extensively and which require force and skills in one hand at the same time, seem to be affected predominantly" (p. 531). So if we can avoid excessive intensity, distribute the practice of any one thing[7] with practice of other things (discussed at length in the section on distributed and interleaved practice later in the book), and characterize our practice with a spirit of exploration, creativity, and observation, perhaps that can serve as a sort of vaccine against this dreadful disability.

While it is believed that there may be a genetic factor contributing to a predisposition to dystonia, it does seem to be something that even then might be avoidable with care. Altenmüller (2003) reports a study in which monkeys who demonstrated chronic overuse and repetitive strain injury through *highly stereotyped movements* had degraded cortical representation of somatosensory information guiding their fine motor movements. *A similar degradation of sensory feedback information and concurrent fusion of the digital representations* in the somatosensory cortex was confirmed in musicians with focal dystonia through a magnetoencephalography study, although the musicians had no history of chronic pain. There also seems to be an emotional factor, with strong linkage between musicians wanting to express emotion but also fearing mistakes, resulting in a strong internal reward-punishment system. These fears—of false notes/movements—may paradoxically enhance the memory for unsuccessful movements (Altenmüller, 2003, pp. 532–533). This makes a strong argument both for cultivating "yes" messages: "do this" rather than "don't do that," but also of avoiding excessive repetition, and for approaching practice and performance with a spirit of mindful observation and acceptance.

HANDS TOGETHER!

Brain imaging shows us which areas of the brain are most active when particular tasks are being performed. Imaging of the brains of pianists shows that the areas of activity for playing individual hands are *not* the same as areas of activity when both hands are playing at the same time, even when the imaging for each hand is overlaid.

This shows us that, while there are some advantages to hands alone practice for certain tasks such as refining gesture, working out fingerings, checking accuracy of particularly thorny chord constructions, etc. it is very important that, if the piece requires both hands play at the same time, as much time as possible be spent working hands together.[8]

While this part of the discussion is most important for pianists/keyboard musicians, there are times when other musicians may practice the equivalent of hands alone (e.g., a string player working on their fingerings/position changes without bowing, or brass players practicing with just the mouthpiece or just working through the valve plan). These approaches are all useful and certainly have their place.

I do recommend that for however much time is spent working hands alone (or its instrumental equivalent) an equivalent amount of time is spent working hands together, although there are some concessions that will be discussed in the next section on chunking.

PATTERNS AND MENTAL "CHUNKING"

Much of intermediate musicians' success will depend on their established audiation and technical ability, how "prepared" they are to meet the challenges of the piece (which also affects their motivation, which impacts their likelihood of trying and persisting through challenges), and how they are instructed to sequence and structure their practice.

In the discussion on teaching music reading, I have already demonstrated a pattern approach to learning new pieces and to learning to read. I am going to assume that, for this section, the musicians I am addressing have been reading music for several months or even years now and are beginning to work on pieces that require a bit more independence through application of a disciplined, step-by-step practice approach in order to master all of the difficulties of a piece of music.

There are several ways to encourage "chunking" habits in musicians at this level.

For example, rhythms ideally are taught and understood as made up of durations grouped into patterns. The understanding of these patterns is connected to our physical bodies through moving, tapping, and chanting, and connected to function through the use of rhythm solfège whenever possible.

Recognition of recurrent patterns is encouraged. For example, tap and chant a prevailing rhythm pattern throughout the piece while listening to a recording or as a teacher or parent performs it; then listen again while watching the score and locate each occurrence of the pattern.

Chord, sequences, or other technical structures can be identified. At first perhaps this is done with a teacher playing the piece or from a recording, with the intermediate musician listening for x or y. As reading improves, the musician can seek and find x or y in the score. For a piece that uses recognizable chord and scale structures, these can be practiced and identified before work begins on playing the piece from the score. Preparing to learn Burgmüller's "Arabesque" by first reviewing the A minor five finger pattern, the A minor scale, and the i-iv-V-i cadence in A minor—perhaps even improvising using these structures for a week before beginning to learn the piece—will imprint those patterns in recent memory, where they will be more readily accessed by short-term working memory. This will make it more likely that they will be recognized within the piece, as well as when they are slightly altered, often without external direction to do so. One doesn't need to pre-learn *every* pattern in an upcoming piece ahead of time. But a few of the essential ones will encourage pattern reading and demystify the piece as a whole.

Incorporating preparatory mini-etudes that utilize these technical patterns in musical ways; a continuous development of component skills such as scales, arpeggios, chording, harmonization, transposition; the performance of rhythm patterns through movement, tapping, and chanting; and utilization of appropriate practice strategies—each reinforces the connection we want to make between mind and body for secure performance and effective practice. Scaffolding, chunking harmonic patterns into chord structures, and think-it-then-play-it practice strategies link these conceptual elements to rehearsed, fluent motor commands. So on to that, then.

NOTES

1. Being able to recover from an error is an important skill; consistency of tempo and a certain amount of "faking" can often convey a successful performance to many but the most discriminating listener.

2. Practicing at half tempo is an excellent test of this.

3. A second time, a choice; a third time, a habit, and a bad one!

4. This would be appropriate after the first few sessions with the piece; at first there is little risk of continuity errors because it is just being learned.

5. I call this "think it then play it." Research shows that imagining oneself doing something generates brain activity in many of the same areas that fire during actual performance (Meister et al., 2004), which indicates mental practice can be an important tool in problem solving. If you think about it, your body only does what your mind tells it to. If you think your way into the correct execution, often the body will follow. If you make the mistake *only* mentally, you also don't risk reinforcing inaccurate physical habits. This is much more thoroughly addressed a bit later in the book.

6. I call this "zooming in and out."

7. If a single challenging moment takes several seconds to perform, it's probably reasonable not to spend more than a few minutes on it *at the most*, before moving on to something else.

8. I would also recommend that, once a musician is playing hands together on the piano beyond simple accompaniment lines or parallel motion, the time to introduce playing-while-reading music has arrived, as the thinking/acting/observing loop becomes so much more complicated both with reading and playing and with playing differing parts in the two hands.

4

SPECIFIC PRACTICE STRATEGIES FOR THE INTERMEDIATE MUSICIAN

Finally, the moment you may have thought would never come, where I outline specific, physical practice strategies! You will notice that the following approaches attempt to link audiation ability, pattern reading, and the formation and processing of meaningful units to efficient ways to solve problems and reinforce facility and ease.

PREPARATORY PRACTICE STRATEGIES

I will use Burgmüller's well-known "Arabesque" from *25 Easy and Progressive Etudes* to demonstrate some preparatory and early practice activities.

To facilitate pattern reading and to promote physical comfort and accuracy in the myriad shifts of this piece so that it eventually can be played at a suitable tempo, there are a few things the intermediate learner can do early in the practicing process. These are shown in the same numbered sequence in Figure 4.1.

1. Before beginning work on the piece, review all white-key minor five-finger patterns, and then incorporate the turn-around gesture as well as the ascending pentascale gesture, using a loose, rotating, or scooping wrist from 16ths to the quarter, and light but legato fingers. Practice by rote, descending by step, in each hand and hands together because why not?[1]
2. Practice playing five-finger patterns ascending in and diatonic to A natural minor. Move up by step, first watching hands (for accuracy) and then with eyes closed. Focus on developing familiarity with the feeling of each five-finger group, as well as the physical sense of the shift. Continue to use scooping wrist gesture practiced in step 1. With each iteration, we ask ourselves: What did I do? How did it feel? How did it sound?

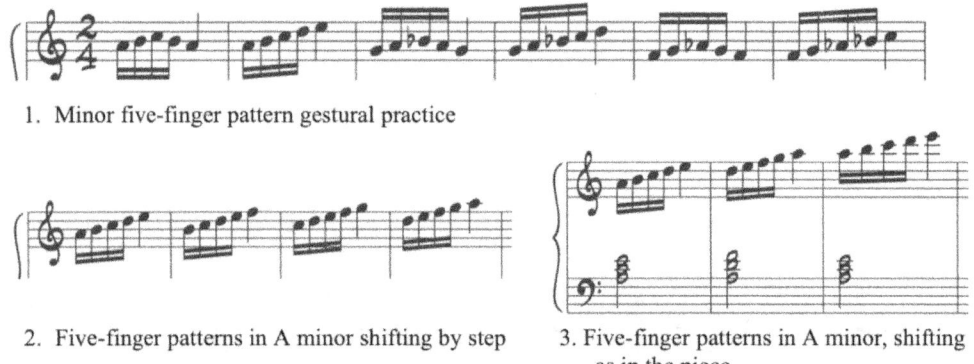

1. Minor five-finger pattern gestural practice

2. Five-finger patterns in A minor shifting by step

3. Five-finger patterns in A minor, shifting as in the piece

4. Three-beat chunks

mm. 17-18, practice pattern 1   *mm. 18-19, practice pattern 2*   *mm. 19-20, practice pattern 3*

Figure 4.1. Burgmüller, "Arabesque," sequence of preparatory and practice strategies.

3. Practice the ascending/gestural pattern on i and iv of A minor and a few other keys.[2]
4. Measures 18–19 often seem the most problematic, so why not learn those first, maybe starting at measure 17, in shifting chunks of 3 beats, thinking it before playing it (mental chunking/thinking pause) each time?

The approach in step 4 allows the practicer to solve the coordination challenges one measure at a time, *hands together*. And notice the overlap, with the second practice pattern starting on the beat that the first practice pattern ended on. This is *very important* so as to avoid inadvertently reinforcing gaps/pauses that can develop when practicing in small bits but without practicing the seams that connect them, which can leave a persistent gap, and we all know that continuity is key.

When each measure-to-the-next-downbeat is mastered (I call this "Measure + 1") and executed with facility and ease, one can expand the group to two measures (which again goes to the downbeat of the third measure), as shown in Figure 4.2. Next, one should probably take the opportunity to compare the expected chord structures in A minor to the ones that Burgmüller actually uses, shown in Figure 4.3.

Figure 4.2. Burgmüller, "Arabesque," two-measures-to-the-next-downbeat groups.

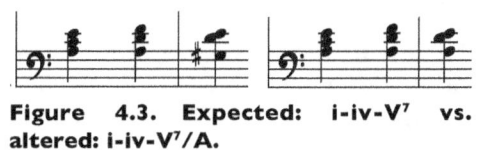

Figure 4.3. Expected: i-iv-V^7 vs. altered: i-iv-V^7/A.

Comparing expectations to actualities is not only important to ensure that the musician plays the chord correctly, but an opportunity to discuss alternatives to traditional dominant (V) chords as well as the concept of "pedal point."[3] Bassok (2003) calls this "abstraction-by-intersection training"—where two or more analogous problems are presented for the learner to evaluate, compare, and identify their structural similarities—which can significantly increase logical transfer of the solution. Multiple analogs provide an opportunity for a successful problem comparison that can lead to structural abstraction, making the information a contributor to successful understanding of future problems (pp. 352–353).

Effective practice strategies actually help us learn more than "just" the piece or passage we are practicing, contributing in myriad ways to the encoding and storage of patterns, which helps us anticipate and predict what might come next. This will serve us well when playing the piece from start to finish, *and when it comes time to learn the next one*, as a more comprehensive understanding of music and expected functions within the context of a given style leads to more proficient reading and reading-and-performing skills. These approaches also actively connect information we are holding in short-term memory to patterns we are encoding in long-term memory and help us practice the mental buffering necessary for the passage as a whole while building short- and long-term working memory capacities.

Ritter et al. (2013) write: "One of the most important issues in learning is *transfer* of learning. After a skill has been learned, the goal is often to reuse the knowledge or apply it to a new situation. If no transfer occurred, every situation would be a new situation" (p. 132). Imagine if, for every new book you wanted to read, you had to learn how to read all over again.

There is a strong argument for learning a wide variety of pieces with similar structures or demands, especially at the intermediate stage. This is how learners come to compare input, and to compare, recognize, and understand appropriate solutions—including why, when, and how they worked—and to what similar situations they might be applied. Therefore, several pieces written in Sonata-Allegro form, or that utilize transitioning from 8th notes to triplets and back, will encourage deeper understanding, which facilitates transfer. I also realize that without care this approach could become rather tedious and burdensome, placing an enormous burden on the teacher to construct scenarios that overlap enough to provide this depth of learning yet varied enough to maintain that perfect level of desirable difficulty.

CHUNKING STRATEGIES

Moving from preparatory activities to chunking strategies helps link technical patterns and facility to the repertoire. Since we read best if we read in chunks and learn best if we think in chunks (meaningful units), practicing in chunks forces the issue, in a beneficial way. These strategies are most obvious for pieces that use accompaniment patterning such as broken chords or Alberti basses. In these cases, the piece can be practiced hands together pretty early in the process, but with the chords played as blocks at first. This will more closely manifest the desired brain activity than learning hands-alone will, and encourages reading and thinking in chunks. Once learned in this way, the physical execution of the bass patterning can be refined through a relatively simple technical/gestural exercise. Again, practicing tonic-dominant-tonic or other simple cadences in a similar pattern and relevant keys will help prepare you to meet these challenges.

These strategies can be quite intuitive for much of the piano repertoire, but can also be deliberately investigated in less obvious scenarios, as well as in repertoire for single-line instruments, which I will discuss shortly. Clementi's Sonatina Op 36 No 1 provides many opportunities to explore some of the more obvious contexts for chunking practice strategies, so let's start there.

In order to put relevant patterns into more recently encoded long-term memory, the week before beginning the piece, practice:

- C and G major scales, hands alone
- C, G and D major triads and inversions (broken and solid) and arpeggios, hands alone
- Tonic-Dominant-Tonic Cadence in C and G major, blocked and in Alberti patterning
- Dominant 7th in C and G major in root position, broken and solid
- Major—Dorian—and Phrygian[4] scales in keys of C and G, hands alone, using typical C-fingering rules (RH 4th finger on the 7th scale degree, LH 4 on the 2nd), shown in Figure 4.4.

Figure 4.4. Major, Dorian, and Phrygian scales in C and G major key signatures.

At the lesson, and for first week of practice with the piece, you:

- indentify and block each recognizable chord pattern (Figure 4.5);
- find and practice each full and partial scale passage (Figure 4.6);
- practice the piece hands together, but with all chord structures practiced blocked as well as "as written." Identify any other chord structures that are discovered in practice, such as the C minor 2nd inversion chord in the 2nd measure of the Development, the dominant 7ths previously unidentified, etc. and note occurrences of the major and modal scales that were practiced at the preparation stage.

Figure 4.5. Clementi, "Sonatina," Op. 36 No. 1, mm. 1–19, showing chord blocks.

Figure 4.6. Clementi, "Sonatina," Op. 36 No. 1, mm. 1–19, scales and scale fragments.

If these investigations are done well, the thought process while reading and playing the piece will look a lot like table 4.1.

So far, our practice strategies have been mostly proactive in nature—preparing for and approaching a new piece in such a way as to maximize the linking of new

Table 4.1. Clementi, "Sonatina," Op. 36 No. 1, mm. 1–15, showing conceptual process.

measure	1	2	3	4	5
RH	Tonic triad in 2nd inversion, broken, beginning on ^1	same as measure 1	Descending scale from ^5 to ^7171 "noodle"	G major 5fp	same as measure 1
LH	I	I	I	V 5fp	I
	6	7	8	9	10
RH	Tonic triad in root position	G major scale in 3rds starting on ^5	GM scale	A 8ve/repeated	B Phrygian scale
LH	I F# (new LT)	1---4---5---5---	G (new I)	V6 Alberti	G (I)
	11	12	13	14	15
RH	C 8ve/repeated	G major 2nd inversion arpeggio, descending 5fp	Noodles, 4-note scale from ^2	4-note scales from ^6 and ^5	G
LH	V4/3	B (^3)	^4	V	GM arpeggio

information to established auditional and technical skill. This is very important for early intermediate levels and will become much more learner-directed as the musician progresses.

But consider the probably-not-that-remote possibility that despite all of this careful preparatory work and investigation of patterns, the first week of practice still produces a few learned errors. Some likely difficulties for this selection might include unsteadiness of tempo, lack of observation of fingerings, a bit of facility trouble with the alternating thirds patterns, and some inaccuracies with lengths of notes in the accompaniment line. What is the best way to practice these difficulties so as to maximize cognitive inclinations and to build good mental and physical habits?

TEMPO AND RHYTHM

Tempo and rhythm problems are usually best solved first with movement, tapping, and chanting. A sequential approach would be:

1. Moving side to side/foot to foot on the big beats, tapping the small beats, and chanting patterns previously performed in error. This could be done in call-and-response form with the teacher at the lesson, or from reading the notation in practice. I would argue that if you can't tap the pulse and chant the rhythm, you probably can't play it correctly, and even if you can, it is through luck and therefore not reliable.
2. Then observing the notation and playing—perhaps still chanting "Du" on the strong beats, or tapping the pulse with the other hand.[5]

One can make this progressively a more musical construct by gradually expanding the length of the pulse. So perhaps at first you are tapping the quarter notes with one hand (or chanting "Du" or "Bah" thereon) as the other hand plays its part, then you are tapping or chanting the half notes, then the whole notes.[6] "Tempo" and "pulse" are abstractions, and only exist in the physical world when we "put" notes on them. Tapping while playing or chanting provides a physical manifestation of these abstract elements, providing a helpful structure on which rhythm patterns are built.

Playing one hand and tapping the rhythm of the other requires observation of both lines of music, but only execution of ~50 percent of one of those lines, which is an excellent intermediary between hands alone and hands together.

Tapping and chanting (rather than clapping the rhythm) also facilitates attention to durations—if chanting a half note, for example, sustain the sound, "Baaaaaaah" or "Duuuuuuuuuuu" with the cutoff carefully placed. Clapping a rhythm pattern offers no way to sustain *sound* for a duration. But one could, as shown in Figure 4.7, play the melody part and chant the rhythm of the accompaniment part on "Bah,"

mm. 1-4, showing chanting of quarter-note accompaniment rhythm

mm. 13-19, showing chanting of whole and half notes in accompaniment

Figure 4.7. Clementi, "Sonatina," Op. 36 No. 1, mm. 1–4, 13–19, rhythm chanting.

paying careful attention to the placement of the rests and the sustenance of the whole notes.

Many of the above activities can be done using side-to-side movement, and/or with a metronome. Learning to keep tempo with a metronome while moving, tapping, and/or chanting is an excellent introduction to metronome work, and should be accomplished before trying to play with a metronome. Using a metronome on the "big" beat (let's say a half note in duple meter), tapping the smaller beat (in this case, then, the quarter note), and chanting rhythm patterns in call-and-response is an excellent early metronome activity. Gradually adding activities such as playing five-finger patterns or quarter note scales with the metronome ticking the quarter, then the half, etc. develops this important skill incrementally. What is important is to get familiar and comfortable with the metronome early, and find ways to interact with it successfully before trying to play a piece with it.

FACILITY

When working on passages requiring facility, reinforcing mental chunking while working on physical execution can be done in partnership.

Learners of the Clementi Sonatina above frequently have facility/execution difficulties with the patterns in measure 7 and measures 13–14, so we will use these passages as our next examples. In our earlier investigation of the piece, we have already discovered that m. 7 is "just" a descending G major scale in alternating thirds. Practicing the top "voice," then adding the thirds in blocks, and then the left hand, reveals what we might call the structural line, and provides a useful scaffold for the alternating pattern in the right hand and the disjunct contour of the left, informing both the mental and physical approach (Figure 4.8).

STRATEGIES FOR THE INTERMEDIATE MUSICIAN

Figure 4.8. Clementi, "Sonatina," Op. 36 No. 1, mm. 7–8, evolution of structural

Of course, in addition to these types of structural approaches, the intermediate musician should always be practicing scales, arpeggios, chords and inversions, cadence patterns, etc. striving for a relaxed and efficient approach, appropriate position, and beautiful, even tone, while incrementally increasing tempo so as to develop facility in preparation for more challenging demands. Facility in these component skills presolves a lot of problems we will encounter in our repertoire, provides important perceptual information for both the storage and retrieval of chunks, and becomes a foundation of the trust we will rely on for flexible and expressive performance.

THINK IT THEN PLAY IT

Continuing with the Clementi Sonatina, then. To practice the tricky contours of measures 12–14, as shown in Figure 4.9, we can play in short groups, from beat 1 to beat 3, beat 3 to beat 1 (next measure), etc. Before each group is played, it is "thought" (encourages thinking in chunks and thinking ahead). It is practiced

Clementi Sonatina Op 36 No 1, 3-beat patterns,   then measure + 1

Figure 4.9. Clementi, "Sonatina," Op. 36 No. 1, mm. 12–15, three-beat groups, then measure + 1.

in tempo to rehearse chunking and thinking ahead at a proper pace. And the only fingerings included are those that indicate a shift of position or something unexpected—best if students learn to recognize patterns and predictable "closed" hand positions whenever possible. Having to look back and silently strategize on which finger each individual pattern starts also encourages audiation while reading from a score. Each pattern could then be paired, so that the practice is from beat 1 to beat 1 in each subsequent measure, preserving the think-it-then-play-it approach.

A similar approach can help the musician have a well-developed physical sense of two patterns that begin the same, but that require a different fingering and trajectory at the end. In the excerpt from Gossec's "Tambourin" shown in Figure 4.10, you might practice the first gesture (in the box) five times (with that thinking pause in-between each), then the second gesture (in the oval) five times (likewise), then go back and forth between them (three times each, then two times each, then back and forth) before playing the whole passage (arrow) so as to rehearse identifying and executing these competing patterns.

Figure 4.10. Gossec, "Tambourin," mm. 21–24, comparing similarities

STRUCTURAL LINES

It is also helpful to practice structural elements, such as notes on downbeats only, notes on half notes (in 4/4 time) only, or looking for and realizing stepwise motions that span figuration, in a Schenkerian-like *Urlinie*.

I might show the latter with a student by playing the structural notes—shown in Figure 4.11 with stems up in the treble clef—as he/she plays the piece as written; making the stems of these structural notes longer as shown, or circling the structural

Figure 4.11. Clementi, "Sonatina," Op. 36 No. 1, mm. 7–12, structural line.

notes; or maybe even inviting the student to find the hidden structural line on his/her own. This is particularly helpful for patterns with lots of disjunct motion, so that rather than focusing on the zigzag and getting lost in the details, building the pattern on a simple ascending line, and keeping mind and fingers in control of a much simpler pattern. The execution is shown in Figure 4.12.

Figure 4.12. Clementi, "Sonatina," Op. 36 No. 1, mm. 7–12, execution of *Urlinie*.

CONTRAPUNTAL MUSIC

Contrapuntal pieces pose particular challenges for intermediate pianists and may require a bit of strategic planning on the part of the teacher to generate appropriate chunking strategies. I will use the well-known "Minuet in G" (excerpted in Figure 4.14) as an example for this discussion.

First, take a close look and try to identify a few essential rhythm patterns, and any patterns that might link to an intermediate musician's current technical practice. You probably noticed the first two rhythm patterns shown in Figure 4.13 are pervasive, and the triplet pattern potentially tricky.

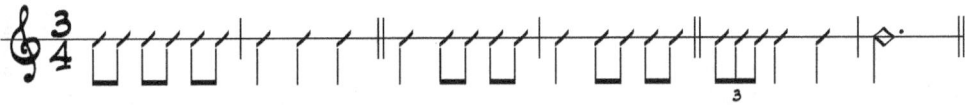

Figure 4.13. Attributed to J. S. Bach, "Minuet in G," BWV Anh. 116, essential rhythms.

Before playing, move, tap, and chant the patterns. Next show them in rhythmic notation, and then find their occurrences in the score. This encourages pattern learning, turns individual durations into two-measure meaningful units, and solves some of the rhythm "problems" before the work of playing the piece has begun (learning one thing at a time before mastering them in combination).

You have probably also noted the G major arpeggiated 4-note triad (oval, see Figure 4.14 for this and following markups), the i and V arpeggiations in E minor (rectangle), and a few interrupted and completed five-finger patterns (arrows). There are also C major triads, a D major arpeggiated chord, and a return of the A section.

Figure 4.14. "Minuet in G," BWV Anh. 116, showing analysis markup.

Reviewing those technical patterns in daily practice for the week before beginning to learn the piece, and then every day before practicing the piece, can be extremely helpful. Finding some of the more prevalent patterns before beginning to play puts them back into recent long-term memory, and will help make that link between technique and repertoire even clearer,[7] providing an advantage in the early reading of the pieces and a sense of mastery before some of the work has even begun.

STRATEGIES FOR THE INTERMEDIATE MUSICIAN

This piece is a good example of something that would benefit from *some* hands-alone practice. But it must be done carefully. There are several "risks" of practicing hands alone; one of the most significant is the amount of time it gives the musician to look down at the keyboard, a practice that will not be viable, but rather quite detrimental, to learning and playing hands together. Better perhaps to work on a few of the trickier passages in isolation, practicing one hand while tapping the rhythm of the other, and then play with hands together several times at a slow tempo; or cover the keyboard with a file folder strategically tucked into the key lid or a towel laid over the top of the hand to discourage peeking. In fact, it might be most appropriate that the first week with the piece consist of reviewing the technical patterns; listening to a recording while watching the score and tapping the quarter note and then maybe, on a subsequent listen, the dotted half note; and isolating and practicing any sections that involve "blockable" chord structures, as those shown in Figure 4.15. Finally, in places with large leaps, practicing the "seam," as shown in the same figure, should help prepare for future continuity.

Opening measures

mm. 13-20, blocks

mm. 18-20, practicing the "seam"

Figure 4.15. "Minuet in G," BWV Anh 116, blocks and practicing the seam.

This piece and others like it are also fodder for many early instrumentalists. And while those musicians learning to play flute, or violin, or trumpet, may neither need to nor be able to physically chunk things like accompaniment figures, they can certainly identify essential tonal and rhythm patterns and patterns that link to their technical practice and use mental chunking practicing strategies.

For example, the Musette from the English Suite in G minor by J. S. Bach is often played on cello. Many of the above strategies can be applied here as well.

Specifically, review of the G and D major scales and arpeggios would place those patterns in more recent long-term memory, causing them to be more readily accessible. Identifying these structures as they appear in the piece (upper portion of Figure 4.16) at the introduction stage would help link those technical patterns to the score. The instrumentalist can also look for and practice recurring motives or melodic lines, such as seen in the second portion of Figure 4.16.

Musette, from English Suite in G Minor, J. S. Bach; related technical patterns

Musette, from English Suite in G Minor, J. S. Bach; recurring motives and melodies

Figure 4.16. Bach, J. S., "Musette," from *English Suite in G minor*, arrg. for cello, technical patterns and recurring melodic material.

Noting long-term structures is also helpful, especially since they seem to govern the nonrecurring passages in this piece. This can be done by listening and observing, looking for *Urlinie*-type lines as shown in Figure 4.17. Or perhaps a teacher plays the structural notes on his/her own instrument as the student listens, or simultaneously plays the piece as written.

Figure 4.17. Bach, "Musette," from *English Suite in G minor*, arrg. for cello; *Urlinie*.

Moving, tapping, and chanting continues to be the best way to attend to rhythm and tempo, and thinking and playing small sections; perhaps 3-beat (shown in Figure 4.18), or 5-beat (Measure +1) practice is applicable to this piece as well.

Figure 4.18. Bach, "Musette," from *English Suite in G minor*, arrg. for cello; 3-beat patterns.

I recognize that many might read the words "Schenker" or "*Urlinie*" and shudder a bit. How can this possibly be an appropriate approach for intermediate musicians? While I would certainly not recommend musicians at this stage study Schenkerian analysis or try to do Schenkerian sketches of their pieces, finding long-term structural lines should be accessible. These observations feed into the Gestalt organizational principles discussed above in the section on visual processing—simplicity, similarity, proximity, continuity—and help the musician attend to the long-term melodic lines and phrase structures, which can provide scaffolding for secure learning and memory.

A good approach is to make a copy of the piece, mark it up somewhat like I have done for the Invention shown in Figure 4.19, and practice from that just for a week or two. Returning after these first weeks to an unmarked score will require tracking on your own, but the experience with the markings and/or perhaps a teacher playing

Figure 4.19. Bach, "Invention No. 1," showing long-term melodic structures.

the structural line an octave higher along with your playing of the piece in the lesson will have established the continuation in your mind.

(A bit of an aside: I encourage much marking up of music to be either lightly in pencil or colored pencil, or, if more extensive, to be done in a separate copy from the one you will want to play from. If the goal is to encourage and develop observational skills and independence, reserving markings such as dynamics, phrasing, and necessary bowings and/or fingerings for the score one is playing from, and writing all over a study-score copy seems to allow us to have our cake and eat it too. Last-minute additions can be made right before performance as necessary, at which point they are reminders rather than interfering with good learning and playing habits.)

A helpful way to encourage chunking according to the Gestalt principle of continuation in pieces with compound lines is to rewrite such passages in vertical chord structures. This approach works well for pieces such as the first Prelude from *Well-Tempered Clavier*, Book 1, where the entire movement is rewritten—by the musician, with just the first few measures done by a teacher or practice assistant for modeling purposes—in stacked whole notes (first four measures shown in Figure 4.20). At this point the musician is that much more likely to notice not only the vertical stacking of each chord structure, which can serve as the basis for analysis and mapping, but, perhaps more importantly, the horizontal motion of each individual voice (shown with connecting lines).

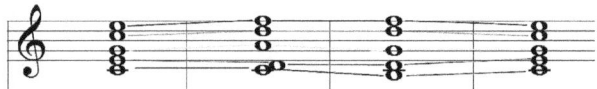

Figure 4.20. Bach, "Prelude No. 1," *Well-Tempered Clavier*, Book I, opening measures, reduction with horizontal voicing indicated.

The musician can then practice the figuration (piece as written) while reading from the reduction. After working on it from the simplified version for a few weeks, or even earlier in the process if the musician is older and/or more comfortable with abstract theory topics, it can be turned into a theory assignment, marking chords with Roman numerals, circling nonharmonic tones and finding the long dominant pedal on the second page. When the musician returns to playing it from the regular notation, alternating with playing from and studying the reduction encourages maintaining those connections and thinking in larger meaningful units. The reduction can also form the foundation for a musical map, as shown in Figure 6.35, an important learning and memorization strategy discussed at length in the next section of the book.

BENEFITS AND CHALLENGES OF THESE TYPES OF PRACTICE STRATEGIES FOR THE INTERMEDIATE MUSICIAN

Many of these approaches may sound like they would take a lot of time or make cognitive demands on a young musician beyond their capabilities. I would argue that doing things like standing, tapping, and chanting a few rhythms "fixes" tempo and rhythm patterns—in both senses of the word—making it more likely that they will be learned and performed correctly, and provides insight on how to correct them if they are not. Playing a structural line along with a student in the lesson takes little extra time, and often helps with implicit learning—the student will hear and recognize the long-term pattern underlying the line without necessarily needing to be told or to have it marked in the score. That being said, taking a few seconds to point out or to discover these long-term motions lends an organizational layer to the learning, and will provide a scaffold on which the details are built. Not only does this calibrate musical understanding to the direction and shaping of the musical line, but the scaffold itself can become a structure for memorization, leading to more secure performance down the road. Taking the time to identify chord and scale patterns or to point out harmonic progressions may add a few minutes to the first presentation of a piece to the student in a lesson, or even in early practice sessions. But when the time is taken, the ensuing practice will be more informed, and more likely correct, making ultimate learning quicker and more secure while establishing a foundation for learning not only this piece, but the next and the one after that.

Most deeply effective learning, especially beyond the implicit stages, is frontloaded. More work at the beginning means less, and more effective, work later.[8] This applies both in the long term—making sure beginning musicians are able to audiate, for example, before beginning to play the instrument or to read music, and in the short term—by approaching a new piece with foundational skills and understanding. If done properly, by the time a musician is learning advanced repertoire, there is a foundation of fundamental skills, a toolbox of effective practice strategies, and the knowledge and self-awareness to apply the correct ones to the correct circumstances. So, rather than learning being linear, it might start off seeming slower,

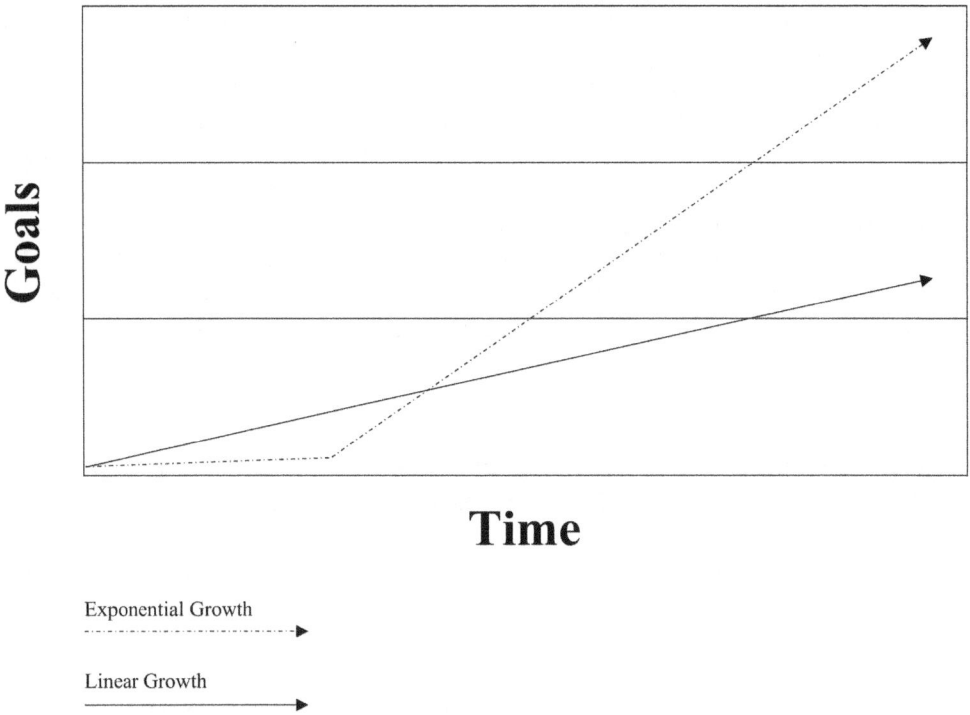

Figure 4.21. Exponential vs. linear learning.

but then rise exponentially and be both more foundational to future learning, and more secure (see Figure 4.21).

I realize as I outline practice strategy after practice strategy that it might begin to sound a little dreary. Preserving an experimental mindset and a sense of exploration and discovery can help avoid the feeling of drudgery, as can being sure not to spend too long on any one section or task. Practicing in different registers helps explore tone colors and the subtle differences in physical distance between similar constructions,[9] at different tempos highlights the physical elements and how they contribute (or not) to the musical expression. A favorite exploration of mine is half tempo, with heightened awareness of gesture and efforts to preserve *every single musical element*, followed immediately by *a tempo*, where I strive to preserve all those elements. Occasional performance run-throughs allow us the opportunities to see how all this work contributes to freer performance, and to test our ability to monitor our playing while leaving certain elements to spontaneous decisions. Westney (2003) even recommends using things like role-playing, trying *anything* no matter how wacky it might seem (pp. 168–169), and observing the result while refraining from judgment. (This practice was introduced in chapter 1 with what I call "feeling chips." See above.) If part of that self-observation includes focusing on how the moment feels as well as the outcome, so much the better (Westney, 2003, p. 113).

Before I move into more advanced cognition topics and practice strategies for more advanced musicians and repertoire, I would like to take a moment to summarize the practice strategies described above and how they link effectively to relevant aspects of music cognition.

We have learned to develop the ear first, then the body; then once a sufficient musical vocabulary has been developed, to incorporate and develop reading skills; and eventually, after the concepts are understood in each of the above capacities, to study the theory behind them. Ideally, theory is first approached at the instrument so as to establish a physical connection to an overwhelmingly abstract topic.

We have approached reading music as we read text, according to the limitations of visual processing as it is linked to working memory capacity, and to the Gestalt principles of grouping things into patterns based on simplicity, similarity, proximity, and good continuation. We understand, read, and notate rhythm in patterns according to contextual meter and organize tonal patterns guided by context and recognizable short- and long-term structures.

For practice itself, we have focused on linking various components—audiation, thinking and playing in patterns or "chunks" while observing long-term structures, and continuing to hone and refine technical skills—to the reading and learning of repertoire. These practice strategies work in parallel with the way our musical mind works, linking the processing of sensory stimuli with motor commands. This mindful alignment between input and output makes our practice sessions as efficient and effective as possible, getting more done in less time and building a foundation for more challenging repertoire to come.

We have encouraged focus, striving to observe both execution and results, to begin in different locations within any piece or section, and to practice playing through mistakes (to prepare for performance) as well as to go back and thoughtfully, mindfully, fix them.

We have stressed providing help when needed, such as writing in fingerings at position changes or when something unexpected is happening and removing help when not needed[10] so as to encourage pattern reading, focus, awareness, thinking in a key, and the application of musical solutions to musical problems.

We have made the experience enjoyable, creative, and expressive, and have rewarded creativity and application of strategic problem solving so as to bolster independence and discipline and to maintain motivation.

Our "intermediate musician" is ready for the next stage.

NOTES

1. It's actually really important that we develop the facility of the left hand along with the right. Much of the beginning and intermediate repertoire makes quite different demands on each hand, and then advanced repertoire suddenly requires more equality. Finding opportunities to develop that facility along the way is extremely helpful to preventing plateaus and discouragement at more advanced levels. At beginning levels this means that every hands-

alone piece can be learned in each hand; perhaps even played hands together in parallel if the child's coordination allows it.

2. Transposing teaches function. Students of rote methods are extremely comfortable with transposition, so this practice should continue through intermediate levels and be applied to their technical practice in books such as *Dozen a Day* or *Czerny-Schaum*, etc.

3. And this may be a good opportunity for the teacher *not* to tell the student what's different, but rather to ask leading questions and/or encourage him/her to find it for themselves.

4. Major and Phrygian appear in the piece; Dorian helps us get from major to Phrygian logically and provides a foundation for future experiences. No sense trying to do everything all the time, but also helpful to find opportunities to add just a little bit more to the learning experience. More curious students might enjoy practicing all the modal scales in each key.

5. Being your own metronome, so to speak.

6. You can use the metronome in this way as well.

7. Which can also go a long way toward *keeping* them motivated to practice their technique!

8. I outlined a very specific approach to a new piece or passage for a student once. He nodded, seemed very receptive, took notes, and then commented, very respectfully, that he would certainly do everything I recommended, but wondered if there was a "shortcut" he might learn later. He looked more than a little aghast when I told him that what I had just described *was* the "shortcut."

9. Playing the same thing in different registers will not feel the same—the breath or the angle is different, so the perceptual size/shape is different too. This is clearly visible in the "shrinking" of the octave as a string player moves "up" the instrument, but this is just as true for the pianist when they are playing at the outer reaches of the keyboard.

10. The writing in of note names, excessive fingerings, courtesy accidentals, etc.

PART 3

5

THE ADVANCED MUSICIAN

The Cognition of Expertise

To attain the highest level of performance, all individuals, even the most "talented," devote years, typically over a decade, to engaging in thousands of hours of practice.... During this extended period of deliberate practice, complex adaptations and acquired mechanisms gradually emerge, and their development is the primary cause of improved performance. (Ericsson, 2003, p. 62)

[C]urrent evidence suggests that access, ability, and willingness to engage in deliberate practice activities are the primary determinants of exceptional performance. (Boot & Ericsson, 2013, p. 154)

Many years ago a student asked me to explain the difference between "intermediate" and "advanced." I pondered the question for a moment and replied that the real difference lay not where many probably believed it did—in the difficulty of the piece—but rather in the degree of independence and problem-solving ability/discipline the musician displayed. Said more simply, "advanced" musicians need less instruction and are able to get much further, more reliably, on their own.

Given that definition, it would be entirely possible to find an "advanced" musician playing intermediate-level repertoire, or vice versa.

"Experts must at some point become their own teachers in order to succeed" (Zimmerman & Campillo, 2003, pp. 237–238). These self-teaching components include the abilities to keep oneself on task; to guide one's own thinking through complex sequences of input and procedure that are being continuously combined and coordinated with prior knowledge and to make self-regulatory adjustments when some aspect of the current situation does not align with prior experience. The latter scenario produces new knowledge, which then must be encoded so as to be available for future purposes. In addition, as already discussed in the previous section on personality, learning styles, and motivation, the learner's perceptions of his/

her own personal agency are important to self-regulative formulations as they motivate and sustain problem solving (Zimmerman & Campillo, 2003, pp. 237–238).[1]

For the sake of this book, any student who has a significant musical vocabulary, plays with sufficient facility and ease to master complex repertoire, and is able to accomplish each of those above components will be considered, and hereafter referred to, as advanced.

TOWARD "EXPERTISE"

Individual differences in performance in many domains of expertise are shown to be mediated by complex mechanisms that have been acquired for a dual purpose: to allow the performer to master tasks challenging for less skilled individuals, and to allow the performer to monitor, evaluate, and analyze their own performance. These mechanisms must be in place for a performer to continue to improve beyond the level of "everyday skill." (Ericsson, 2003, p. 73)

Experts not only know more than novices, but their knowledge is also much better organized and more readily available. (Ritter et al., 2013, p. 130)

Ericsson (2003) believes that deliberate practice activities result in evermore-complex mental representations while also facilitating development of the physical mechanisms that are required for expert performance. Therefore, it is safe to assume that at least a fair amount of achievement is related to learning and to deliberate efforts to increase in skill rather than merely to "talent." In most cases, acquiring this expertise is a complex and relatively long process, where the learner encounters increasingly challenging problems and incrementally develops the ability to meet them.

In addition to the explanation of various cognitive models found in chapter 3, it might help to consider Fitts and Posner's three discrete stages for the acquisition of skills (Ericsson & Towne, 2013): the cognitive stage, the associative stage, and the autonomous stage.

The cognitive stage, which one would see with early music learning at an instrument, is also sometimes called the verbal-motor stage. This stage features instruction, guidance, slow-motion or segmented drills (therefore, for beginning musicians, short, rote pieces focusing on developing audiation and large-motor skills), and a lot of appropriately expressed feedback from caregivers, teachers, and coaches. At this stage, fundamentals of movement are established and a constructivist[2] approach to learning and/or correcting errors is most useful. The generation of new behaviors is typically slow and characterized by frequent errors. Observation and correction of these errors, best done through comparison of result and desired result, leads to gradual improvement through repeated practice. With sufficient experience and mental concentration *on producing the correct actions*, individuals improve, especially in the performance of frequently encountered patterns. The learner may make surprisingly large gains in performance at this stage, but it will probably be a little inconsistent.[3]

At the associative stage, individuals learn and execute more sequences of associated actions, with the learner becoming better able to string together smaller motor skills, and to access and execute complex actions rapidly and with more consistently successful and intentional outcomes. Ericsson and Towne claim that this stage is usually reached after approximately fifty hours of experience with "*everyday* activities,"[4] by which time the learner can successfully adapt to the typical situational demands of the domain. I would argue that in learning to play a musical instrument many more hours of experience are needed to attain this stage and link this stage to the abilities of what might be referred to as an "intermediate" musician. At this point execution tends toward increasing automatization, a certain amount of which allows performers to monitor more discrete aspects of the skill, resulting in faster learning and execution with less effort (in some respects). However, *without adjustments in the type of practice*, this stage will often plateau, showing less improvement and smaller gains in performance. Highly skilled learners, or those with appropriate instruction, will continue to seek out ways to improve, revisiting both the cognitive and associative stages throughout their development to continually refine their technique.

At the autonomous stage, movement is largely controlled seemingly automatically, requiring minimal cognitive demands, which allows the performer to attend to and process a lot of information beyond the intended actions, which might include monitoring the position of his/her teammates on the soccer field, or keeping in sync with the collaborators in his/her string quartet. At the same time, this relative lack of cognitive demand can cause problems in that it leaves room for irrelevant, distracting thoughts to creep into working memory, something even more likely as an autonomous performer nears the end of the activity.[5]

It's not over 'til it's over

Over-automatization can also result in incorrect movements gaining hold until they become habit, causing increasing difficulties as time goes on and these incorrect actions are not reformed. Learners must take great care at this stage to continue to revisit cognitive and associative stages and to learn to control thoughts in working memory (Ericsson & Towne, 2013, p. 891; Huber, 2013).

Boot and Ericsson (2013) write that expert performance is characterized by more and better planning and more consistent and controlled actions while also demonstrating greater adaptability to changing demands (p. 154). They also claim that the expert performer maintains better incidental memory for the details of the performance, and that a critical component of expert performance in many domains is a greater ability to anticipate future events. More elaborate advance preparation of appropriate actions has been documented for expert performers in many domains, including music. This ability of an expert to anticipate future demands leads to a more rapid execution of actions without the need for faster neural processing, and also seems to reflect a larger amount of information accessible in working memory (Ericsson & Towne, 2013, p. 891).[6]

Anticipation is manifest in apparent preparative activities, such as skilled typists looking further ahead in the text, moving their fingers to the next intended key well in advance. In fact, when expert typists were constrained from previewing the text, their performance was dramatically reduced almost to the level of novice typists (Boot & Ericsson, 2013, pp. 145–154). I can often see when a student is about to make a mistake, based on where his/her hand is, or where it's not. I have also felt myself about to make an error in performance and either adjusted or dropped the (erroneous) note altogether. Appropriate preparations can and should be deliberate and rehearsed as part of the learning process. These come into play in many of the specific practice strategies discussed below.

Experts in many domains show superiority in perceiving the structure[7] beneath the surface of a problem and are better and faster at evaluating potential solutions and consequences. This then is motivation for us to identify and/or construct meaningful structures deliberately as we are learning challenging repertoire.

Experts also code brief perceptions more rapidly into long-term memory, with minimal distortions between presentation and recall (Ericsson, 2003, p. 57). As skill increases, the ability to encode and manipulate internal representations improves. Superiority in these areas, though, especially when faced with time limitations, tends to be limited to the types of patterns one would expect to see, which explains why even the best sight-readers will still probably have a harder time reading Schoenberg than Schubert. It also makes clear that recognition and understanding of the myriad patterns that form these expectations can and should be a crucial part of learning, which can certainly be approached in a deliberate fashion. The broader the experience, the broader that foundation.

> Experts' ability to generate products of consistently superior quality . . . requires the mediation of complex cognitive mechanisms. These mechanisms allow experts to perceive the structure of representative situations and assess relevant relations underlying actions. The same mechanisms allow experts to plan and evaluate various options in order to assure the generation of high-quality responses. The difference in performance between experts and less skilled individuals is not a simple difference in accumulated knowledge about past experience. Expert-novice differences appear to reflect differential ability to react to representative tasks and situations that have never been previously encountered. Less skilled performers may not even be able to generate the appropriate action when confronted with a difficult task, at least not in the time that is usually available. Highly skilled performers are likely to perceive a solution to the same task as one of several possible actions, then identify the best choice after rapid evaluation and planning. (Ericsson, 2003, p. 57)

Experts also rely on several different representations simultaneously. For expert musicians these include the knowledge representations of the music itself as well as of their performance goals—which include the capacity to modify as needed for the acoustics of the hall, a response to an unfamiliar instrument (pianists), and/or input from collaborators or conductor. This means that they are monitoring their own thoughts, actions, *and* the performance itself.

Our next question might be: How does one gain expertise?

Many merely attribute the type of superior performance that warrants this designation to talent—you are either born with it or you are not, and the only way you are going to get good enough to be called an expert is if you were born with sufficient natural ability in the first place.

On the other hand, there is the theory that the difference between an expert and a novice is simply a matter of practice. If you have put the time and work in—the famous "10,000 hour" rule,[8] for example—expertise is yours to be had.

In reality, it is the result of a complicated mix of genetics, opportunity, personality, and effort, presenting yet another loop of interactive causes and effects. As Boot and Ericsson (2013) point out:

> [T]here is no evidence that rules out the effects of genetic components on the development of exceptional performance. . . . This could include genetic determinants of individual differences in motivation and ability to engage in deliberate practice. Regardless of whether some individuals benefit from innate talent provided by an exceptional genome, we still need to understand the detailed mechanisms of how deliberate practice activities cause both innately talented and other individuals to improve their initial levels of performance. (p. 154)

Someone born with what we refer to as "talent" will be more likely to engage in the activity at a younger age; rapid early progress will make him/her more willing to work at it. Reaping rewards in terms of both positive societal reinforcement (external motivation) and self-observed progress (internal motivation) provides impetus for increased enjoyment and motivates persistence, even through ever-increasing challenges. If someone has opportunity—exposure to the domain, access to good instruction, support of knowledgeable and conscientious caregivers—whatever natural talent s/he may possess will be nurtured, cultivated, developed. And finally, if the learner has the personality and character to work in a disciplined way to develop appropriate skills and problem-solving strategies, progress will be maximized.

Of course these things are cyclical—talent affects motivation, development is at the mercy of access and opportunity and influenced by good (or bad) teaching, societal values, and parental encouragement (good) or pressure (not necessarily good, although it depends). Consider if Mozart had been born in a different city; he would have had neither the exposure to a rich musical culture nor felt the societal reward of being a prodigy. If he had had a different father he may not have been pushed to excel, and maybe would have been much less prolific. (Or, maybe, more.) Some have even speculated that if he had had access to Prozac, he might have just spent his days teaching the area merchants' daughters their little piano lessons and discussing politics at the local coffeeshop.

Edwin Gordon, Boot and Ericsson, Terman, and Sir Frances Galton are among the many who consider innate ability to be the limiting factor to an individual's achievement in any domain. They don't ignore the role of practice and training but theorize that practice and training are the factors that allow the individual to attain his/her highest potential (Boot & Ericsson, 2013, p. 145).

Since there is nothing we can do about anyone's genetics, the focus of this book has been, and will be, on that which we can control: environment, opportunity, motivation, and practice. Elements already discussed include:

- the importance of forming a strong musical foundation through acculturation and audiational development for young musicians;
- the best approach for learning to read music for intermediate instrumentalists; and
- developing practice strategies that support innate cognitive processes.

I have also addressed the importance of providing tools and problem-solving strategies for the learner, and of focusing evaluation of "success" on the ability to select and apply them appropriately. These approaches build self-efficacy and help maintain motivation, setting intermediate musicians on the right path while giving them the proper tools for meeting increasing demands both cognitively and physically. As the repertoire becomes more demanding and the learner becomes more adept, *mindful* practice and a reliance on readily accessible connections between thought and execution while avoiding excessive automatization rise in import.

I would actually argue that if we can make practice more productive, for students of *any* level of natural ability, we can help maintain their interest and willingness to persist.

MINDFUL PRACTICE AND AVOIDANCE OF EXCESSIVE AUTOMATIZATION

Research shows that expert performers intentionally avoid what may be an almost natural tendency toward automatization, as it comes with an associated loss of control of relevant aspects of performance (Ericsson, 2003, p. 75). This is probably especially important for pianists, since we rarely perform on the instrument we practice on. Striving for an intended, carefully rehearsed *result* probably means we are going to have to *do* many things differently. But the importance of avoiding automatization applies to any instrumentalist, as variants occur in acoustics, distractions from the audience, collaboration with others in ensemble, etc. There is also the risk of an automaton-like result if performance is too highly programmed, especially the risk of going off the rails completely if things don't go exactly as planned (we are human, after all).

Rather, our goal in practice should be to develop facility, rehearse expected execution patterns, observe the results, and maintain the ability to make adjustments as needed and/or recover from mistakes. Of course certain things will be "automatic" in that once we think it,[9] our bodies do it; but mindful awareness of where we are and what is next never fades in import.

Boot and Ericsson (2013) again:

> [S]uperior performers don't seem to automate relevant aspects of their performance, and strive to increase their control of their performance. . . . This control, or ability to monitor and adapt performance, derives directly from deliberate practice activities that focus on improvement rather than automated and stable performance and that continuously push learners outside their comfort zone. These true expert performers are found to be able to respond flexibly when encountering new and challenging situations. . . . To less skilled individuals in a domain, the performance of experts often seems to share characteristics of automatic performance (fast, error-free, and seemingly effortless) . . . [but] there is good reason to believe that the extrapolation of expert performance from models of skill acquisition is inappropriate. . . . Rather than performance that is rigid, expert performance is often fluid and adaptable, which is not consistent with the idea of expert performance as automated. (pp. 151–152)

In other words, don't practice like it's a closed system, because it's not!

One method that helps ensure against inadvertent automaticity is what Ericsson refers to as "variable priority training." Most simply, the participant practices a complex task, alternately focusing his/her attention on improving specific subcomponents individually—perhaps attending first to dynamics, then to voicing, then to phrasing, etc. You might recognize this principle from earlier in the book in the section on mastering one thing at a time. Variable priority training has been demonstrated to accelerate learning, maximize the mastery of skill, and encourage broad transfer of training to new or novel tasks or problems (Boot & Ericsson, 2013, p. 154). It also forms a component of distributed/interleaved practice, discussed at much more length below.

I find it particularly beneficial to move between focused attention on one or two musical parameters and striving to attend to all of them. If we are overwhelmed with input and/or technical demands, we may overlook many of the musical markings. As we become more familiar with the passage at hand, and more comfortable with our physical execution of it, we should find that we are able to observe more and more of the other indications in the score as well as our own musical intentions. Pursuing this deliberately helps us get there sooner.

Before I get into more practicing details for more challenging repertoire, I would like to expand a little bit on some higher-order cognitive topics.

KNOWLEDGE REPRESENTATION, WORKING MEMORY, AND SKILLED VISUAL PROCESSING

Future expert performers . . . start the development of basic representations as soon as they start regular practice. They learn to internalize some of the monitoring functions of their teachers, become able to evaluate their own performance, diagnose weaknesses, and identify appropriate adjustments.[10] These representations then allow them to identify desired goals, construct plans for how they will achieve them, and develop methods for monitoring their progress and performance. These representations are tightly integrated with their acquired skills. Refinements in representations usually precede improvements in performance. Deliberate practice is that which pushes the limits of the current representations, and leads to refinements and modifications through problem-solving efforts. (Ericsson, 2003, p. 75)

The construction of an integrated representation . . . in LTM [Long-Term Memory] is a skilled activity that requires prerequisite knowledge as well as encoding skills if an individual is to be able to successfully anticipate future retrieval demands. . . . Lack of prerequisite knowledge impairs both encoding and storage in LTM and the ability to generate inferences needed to create an integrated representation. (Ericsson & Kintsch, 1995, p. 232)

Many of us observe an apparent plateau at the late-intermediate stage, and attribute it to "teenagedom"—rebellion, succumbing to societal pressures, shift of focus, etc. In fact, much of the plateau and then falling off of interest may come because these musicians have not been properly prepared for the higher-level challenges of advanced learning. If learners don't have, or don't believe they have, the knowledge, experience, and/or problem-solving tools necessary to meet challenging problems, they are much more likely to give up. Conversely, if equipped with a strong foundation (audiation ability, technical proficiency, experience reading and thinking in chunks) and the tools with which to approach new problems—as well as the confidence and discipline to work hard toward solving them—the transition into more advanced problems and performance will be eased, and the learner will be better equipped and motivated to meet them. At the same time, the methods and discipline of the approach will have to evolve along with the difficulty of the repertoire.

At this stage, learning benefits from and utilizes two different systems, identified by Daniel Kahneman (2011) in *Thinking, Fast and Slow*: automatic and controlled.

Automatic systems, as you might imagine, are unconscious, intuitive, and immediate, and use sensory input and memory to make quick decisions about a situation. Malcolm Gladwell (2007) calls this "thin slicing." This type of learning is dependent on a fair bit of transfer, is deeply influential, draws on accumulated experiences and deep emotions, and is susceptible to illusion.

On the other hand, controlled learning processes are conscious, where choices are considered, decisions are made, and self-control reigns. This process is slower, and a result of analysis and reasoning. Impulses are checked, plans are made, and options are identified and evaluated for possible implications.

Perhaps one of the biggest challenges at the advanced stage is learning when to trust your intuition and when to question it. This in and of itself will also become more and more intuitive (pun unintended, but certainly relevant), and effective, with lots of practice. At the same time, learning is guided by our judgments of what worked and what did not, as well as why or why not, which can be helpful, but we can easily be misled. Learning how to apply models through different contexts and paradigms[11] gives the learner the opportunity to truly evaluate whether mastery has been attained, or merely a superficial memory of surface elements (Brown et al., 2014, pp. 106–125).[12]

As you've already learned, experts categorize problems differently from novices, with experts focusing on deeper structures and categorizing things into a *schema* that includes potential solution methods (Chi et al., 1981, p. 140). For effective transfer of problem-solving strategies, the structure of the problem must be included in the knowledge representation. In fact, transfer is magnified by a level of abstraction that can usually only be achieved through a rich and varied wealth of experience. Good problem solvers will be more likely to check the appropriateness of considered problem-solving strategies (Bassok, 2003, pp. 353–355), and choose better ones more often and earlier in the problem-solving process.

As William Westney (2003) points out, everything depends on how you represent the problem space. He writes about a dog who can see a bone on the other side of a fence. Some dogs will bark and bark and bark (and bark) at the bone;[13] others will run along the fence until they find an open gate and go through it (pp. 155–156). This is an excellent analogy for how we want to practice. Much as the dog, in moving down the fence line, actually *moving physically away from the bone* so as to find an opening and get closer to the bone, many practice strategies may feel initially like you are moving further away from the goal. That does not mean it is the long way—it might be the only way, and/or it might be a way that more fully informs the final execution.

A bit of review from a slightly different perspective follows.

Ericsson (2003) links performance improvements to active efforts through deliberate practice to build increasingly complex mental representations for planning and monitoring, and another process that counteracts automation, which allows for higher levels of control of performance and continued problem solving (pp. 62–75). He also claims that the expert deliberately selects an encoding method that will fit the retrieval demands (p. 235) since memory actually involves/requires two things: learning, and the capacity to access it when needed.

The entire process forms a perpetual loop, with elements of observation and/or knowledge retrieval, planning, motor signaling, and another round of observation (of what has occurred). The elements of this loop must be carefully sequenced and accessed at just the right time in just the right order. Ericsson & Kintsch (1995) write:

> Cognitive processes can be described as a *sequence of states or thoughts* [emphasis mine]. Memory mediates between the states of this sequence. Cognitive states are dependent on each other, and memory generates this dependency, as do environmental correlations. . . . Thoughts—the cognitive states—are themselves the end products of complex generation processes. Typically, sensory and perceptual as well as conceptual operations are involved in the genesis of cognitive states, which require knowledge activation and elaboration processes at various levels. For a higher level process to use the output of a lower level process, that output must remain available for a least some minimal amount of time. This availability is achieved through process-specific memory buffers that contain for a limited amount of time the results of the intermediate processes that generate the end product, or . . . cognitive state. (p. 221)

I will put this in simpler form, using an image of the water cycle many of us learned about in elementary school. But rather than water, it's information (Figure 5.1).

Information is processed through sensory input (the cloud passing over the water), which stimulates working memory to access information in long-term memory (the water being pulled up into the cloud) to evaluate it, understand it (cognitive state), and/or employ it (the water falling back to Earth). This "cognitive" state leads to the next "episode" of pulling information from LTM, which leads to the next cognitive state, etc.

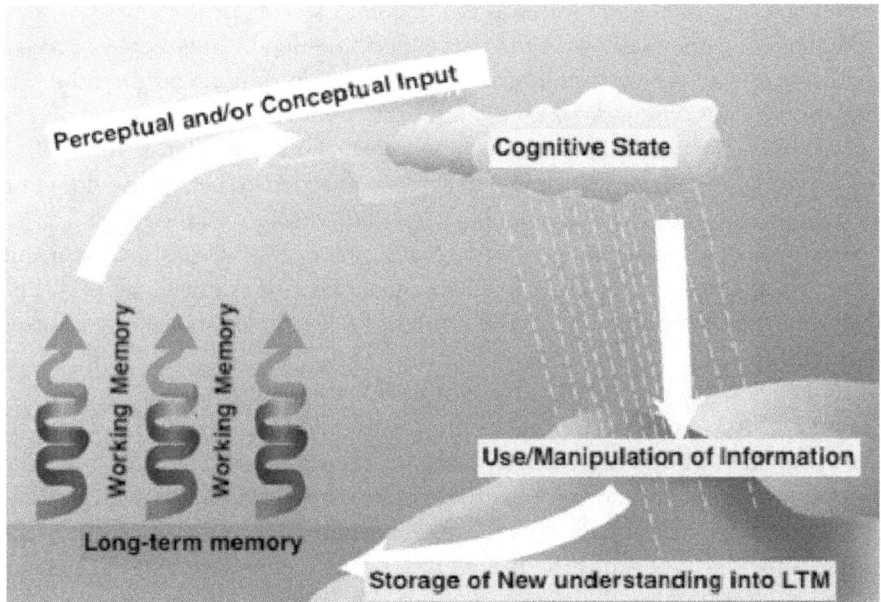

Figure 5.1. Water cycle model showing extraction of information from long-term memory by working memory, resulting in (subsequent) cognitive states.

A more detailed model is shown in Figure 5.2, tracking comparison, retrieval, action, and storage during this process.

These models demonstrate how our short-term working memory may work to retrieve information from long-term memory for use and application; the final model shows it encoding new information for storage as well as maintaining retrieval cues.

Any problems with processing new information, retrieving relevant knowledge, and/or making necessary inferences will interfere with the smooth continuation of comprehension of new material and/or of the performance of that which has already been learned.

Superior comprehension and/or performance are attributed by Ericsson and Kintsch (1995) to superior skill in encoding information in long-term memory, mak-

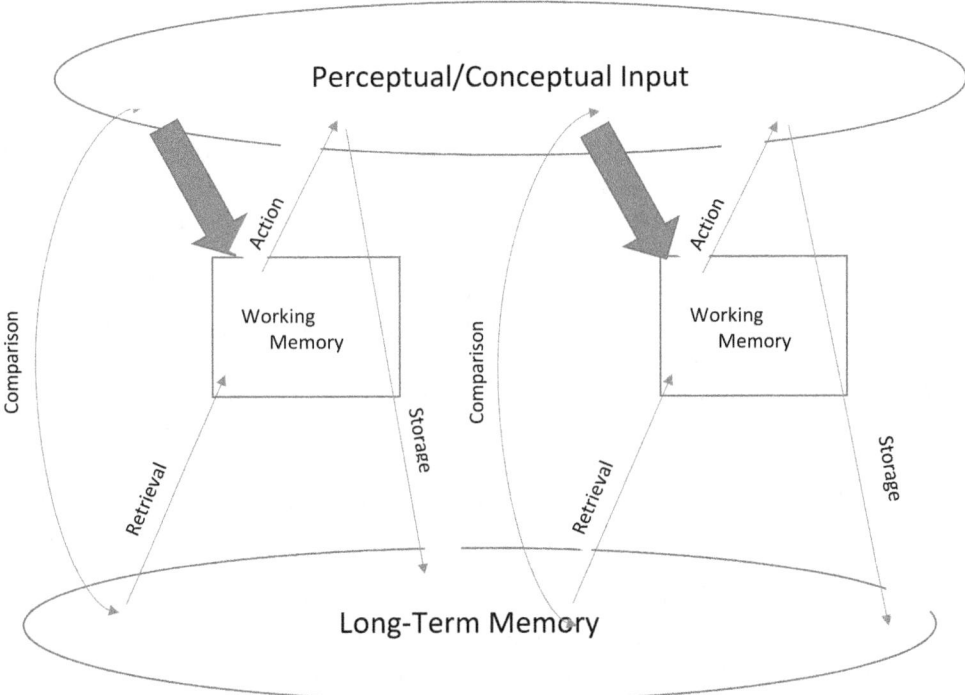

Figure 5.2. Cognitive model including retrieval, comparison, action, and storage.

ing a larger amount of information accessible through retrieval cues prompted by working memory (pp. 227–228). These encodings include, are perhaps even facilitated by, the chunking of information into meaningful units that form an important part of our deliberate practice: looking for, identifying, and encoding these chunks, *on purpose*, as early in the process as possible. This becomes an increasingly important practice/problem-solving strategy as the difficulty of the music advances, especially given that, with curiosity, investigation, and mindful chunking into conceptual units, a great deal of information may be processed as a single meaningful unit, allowing the learner to understand a measure containing forty-some notes perhaps as just two or three "things."[14]

Remember our previous discussion of long-term working memory, which serves as an intermediary between long-term memory and short-term working memory, encoding information *into* and retrieving information *from* long-term memory in a semantically meaningful and time-efficient way (Jäncke 2012a, pp. 31–33). According to this model, any highly skilled ability (e.g., music sight-reading) is attributable to more sophisticated, complex comprehension strategies. These superior procedures include:

- relatively rapid transfer of new information to storage in long-term memory, which requires a large body of previously established, relevant knowledge;

- deep familiarity with the topic so that future retrieval demands can be anticipated and become part of the encoding; and
- an organized retrieval structure.

The result is a larger effective working memory. Long-term working memory has been shown to be closely tailored to the demands of the domain so that it functions as a completely integrated, inseparable part of skilled execution of the activity itself. "In skilled activities and when subjects have had extensive experience with the task demands *and acquired stable procedures for completing the task* [emphasis mine], they can foresee retrieval demands and develop memory skills to index relevant information with retrieval structures" (Ericsson & Kintsch, 1995, pp. 215–239).

This is particularly relevant to us as advancing musicians because it highlights the importance of comprehension to learning and performance. In other words, if we don't understand what we are doing, harmonically, metrically, contextually, we are trying to do something that is mentally very demanding without the benefit of organization to aid the process. Passages such as those shown in Figure 5.3, from Mozart's "Sonata," K. 283 and Chopin's "Nocturne in E minor," Opus posth. 72 No. 1 contain a great multitude of notes and rhythmic details, a veritable flurried onslaught of tiny bits of information, and this is just a fraction of the whole. But with conscious application of comprehension strategies, as we did above with the conceptual chunking shown in Table 4.1 regarding the Clementi Sonatina, these myriad bits can be grouped into patterns of many fewer "meaningful units," making reading, processing, playing, and remembering infinitely easier.

The fact that we can get so far—say to around mid- to intermediate-level repertoire—without *needing* this type of higher level of processing can lead to musicians not learning how to do it, and therefore plateauing as they are faced with these more complicated scenarios. They might even develop severe performance anxiety as they realize that they don't really have a clue what they are doing—making the whole endeavor feel quite precarious just at the age where the risk of public failure is anathema to developing self-esteem.

In his chapter "From Cognition to Action" in the book *Music, Motor Control and the Brain*, Jäncke (2012a) points out an important aspect of visual processing that comes into play especially for advanced pianists, who are generally reading two lines of music at a time (if not more) and often need to process a lot of information quickly while also responding to intricate motor signals and demands. An important skill for advanced pianists is the ability to look further ahead in the score than those less skilled. While the *perceptual* span for skilled and non-skilled pianists appears to be approximately the same, the eye-hand span[15] differs considerably. For less skilled pianists, it is around half a beat, for skilled pianists, from two to three beats wide.

These differences in eye-hand span between expert and non-expert musicians support our understanding of short-term memory, the concept of "buffering," chunking and/or template theories, and seem also to support some aspects of Ericsson and Kintsch's theory of long-term working memory. They also accentuate the

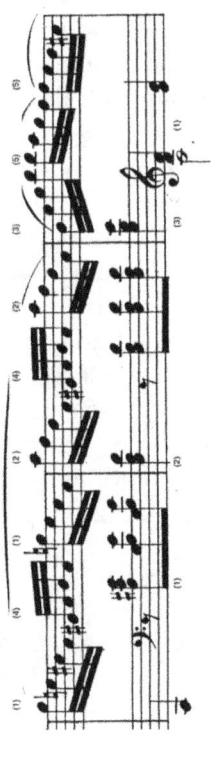

Five tonal "things": A7 (1), DM (2), Em (3), neighbor tone "noodles" (4), and descending 4-note gestures in D Major (5); and two rhythm "things":

Mozart, Sonata in G major, K. 283, I., mm. 40-42

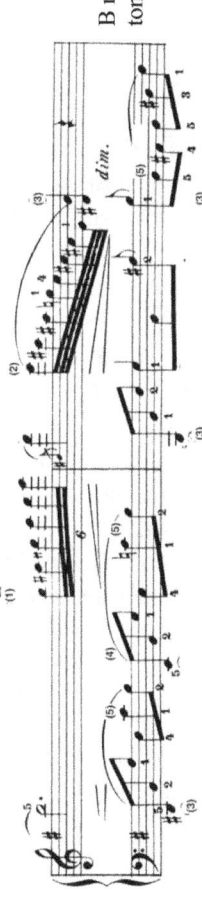

B major scale (1), A°7 arpeggio (2), V or V7 (3), Em (4), Neighbor tones and appoggiaturas (5)

Chopin, Nocturne in E minor, Op. 72 No. 1, mm. 33-34

Figure 5.3. Mozart, "Sonata," K. 283, I., and Chopin, "Nocturne in E minor," Op posth., I., meaningful units.

importance of comprehension, which allows the performer to hold and process a larger amount of information within a finite number of meaningful units.

The important roles chunking and buffering play in our learning process perhaps also explain some of the difficulty posed by Baroque repertoire, because melodically generated ideas are often more difficult to chunk. Some examples from the Baroque repertoire, such as the Preludes in C and B♭ major by J. S. Bach that are referenced throughout this book, the Invention in A minor, etc. can be chunked both mentally and physically with ease. In others, the musical structures are intricate, layered, and much more difficult to discern. I have compared passages in Bach's music to sentenceswheretherearen'tanyspacesbetweenthewords, and point out that it is our job as performers to find the "words" and convey them through careful application of characteristic articulations and subtle manipulations of note durations (while also preserving the long discursive lines that these shorter motifs form). These "chunks" are no less relevant, but will be based on motivic and musical considerations rather than obvious harmonic structures.

LONG-TERM MEMORY: RETENTION AND RETRIEVAL

> *Every time you learn something new, you change your brain.* (Brown et al., 2014, p. 7)[16]

Ericsson and Kintsch (1995) propose that the (short- and long-term) working-memory demands of a given task actually dictate which encoding method an individual is likely to choose, with superior long-term memory and increased working-memory capacity being demonstrated by "experts" within their domain of expertise (p. 220). And many researchers (Baddeley, Laney, among others), as already mentioned, demonstrate that *effective coding of information requires effective coding of retrieval routes* as well.[17] Without appropriate retrieval cues, information stored cannot be accessed. A bad hard drive provides a beneficial analogy: the information is still stored on the disc, but the computer is unable to locate it. Retrieval cues are reminders that link specific memories, and come from content, context, images, words, feelings, etc. each memory forming a retrieval cue for another. So we want not only to take in new information but to plan for how we will recall it later, and to incorporate that recall into the processing. Some cognitive scientists even say that memory[18] is reconstructed at retrieval, rather than accessed from storage, with bits of new information combined with bits of information previously gained, forming, in a type of alchemy, a new, conglomerate memory (Laney, 2013, pp. 236–237).

> One of the hallmarks of expertise is the ability to memorise with an efficiency that seems beyond the norm. These feats have been explained in terms of three principles of skilled memory: *meaningful encoding* of novel material, use of a *well-learned retrieval*

structure, and rapid retrieval from long-term memory. According to the first principle, *experts' knowledge of their domain of expertise allows them to encode new information in terms of knowledge structures already stored in memory* [all emphasis mine]. For a pianist these include chords, scales, arpeggios, phrases, and harmonic progressions, the practice of which forms an important part of every pianist's training. These knowledge structures are built up during the decade or more of training that is required to develop a high level of expertise. Their *presence in semantic memory allows the expert to recognise novel situations as variations of more familiar ones.* As a result, the expert can work with larger chunks of information than the novice, identify and remember large amounts of information rapidly, and make snap decisions about complex situations.

The second principle asserts that *expert memory requires a highly practised, hierarchically organised retrieval scheme* to provide cues to be associated with the novel information that is memorised at encoding. These cues can be used to retrieve the information when it is needed. For a pianist, the large-scale organisation for a hierarchical retrieval scheme may be provided by the formal structure of a composition.

According to the third principle, prolonged practice dramatically increases the speed with which the expert can use the retrieval scheme to access information in long-term memory. . . . This allows the expert to rely on memory in situations in which most people rely on external aids. If the pianist uses the hierarchical structure of the music in this way, then we would expect to see evidence of extended practice at using the formal structure to guide retrieval. (Chaffin & Imreh, 1997, pp. 316–317)

Boot and Ericsson (2013) claim that expert performance relies on acquired mechanisms so highly developed they may even *bypass* the constraints of long- and short-term memory, instead using complex retrieval structures that quickly and efficiently access relevant patterns and schema directly from long-term memory (p. 148).

The use of prior knowledge when dealing with new information could be modeled as a process whereby new information is: 1) perceived through various sensory means (eyes, ears); 2) attended to; 3) retrieved/recalled/compared through access to associated cues; 4) associated with, or discriminated from, similar items/events; 5) encoded; and 6) stored (Gallo & Wheeler, 2013; Baddeley, 1990).

Each process of the six above presents its own opportunities for error. And let us not forget (!) that a certain amount of forgetting is an important part of remembering.[19] We can't remember everything, nor do we want to. Imagine trying to remember where you parked your car in a lot you use every day if the most recent input were not in the forefront of your mind.

Baddeley (1990) refers to Craik and Lockhart's "Levels of Processing," a model that explains a hierarchy of types of input and associated retention. In this model, information processed superficially, in sensory terms, gives rise to relatively short-term memory traces; phonological processing produces a somewhat more durable trace; and deep semantic processing produces the most durable learning, so that longer retention comes from deeper processing within long-term memory, not from transfer from one type of memory store to another (p. 64). This surely encourages us to *use, process, and manipulate* information rather than just to observe it. Brown et al.'s (2014) recommendations of deliberate and effortful learning are based on these same principles.

The discrimination of events step (#4 above) can be more complicated than it might seem. As you may remember, the process by which we perceive, categorize, organize, prioritize, and understand musical events is a complicated one; a full investigation would move me beyond the stated purview of this book. As we move into the discussion of more advanced music and music-learning topics, the topic expands even further, including studies on harmonic priming, the impact of intonation on understandings of relatedness, and the impact of established context on how *quickly* we process and decide on things such as similarity and difference between and among events.[20]

For our purposes, suffice it to say that *stable* events (such as a harmonic progression that "behaves" as expected) and *similar* events are perceived as *more closely related* to each other, but, perhaps because of that, are more easily confused. This confusion is often made manifest in things like sonata form movements, where restatements occur in different keys or registers, or when the transition of an exposition is confused with the transition of the recapitulation. (I call this the "Candyland moment," and it is marked in my students' music with candy stickers. I always recommend learning and memorizing those transitions and second tonal areas first.) On the other hand, *distinctive* events are more likely to be recalled, with the understanding of their function and differences intact (Gallo and Wheeler, 2013, pp. 195–196). This may explain the performing-from-memory difficulties posed by music such as Bach's, where a multiplicity of patterns is derived from a single generative one, or the relative ease of memorizing a Debussy Prelude, which is what I would call an evolutionary form rather than a repetitive one.

Information *processed* in working memory is more likely to end up in long-term storage. This should encourage us to use, manipulate, and compare information rather than just receive it passively—for example, identifying patterns that recur, are varied, or contrasted; recognizing underlying harmonic structures, etc. while learning a piece, rather than sight-reading it over and over again.[21] Much research has shown the limitations of casual observations on long-term memory. We frequently "see" things repeatedly and don't notice they're there. Anyone looking for the peanut butter jar that is right in front of them, or not noticing when her husband has shaved off a moustache that he has worn for ten years, can testify to this. Brown et al. have shown that reviewing study notes (which rests firmly in the "sensory input" stage of processing) is one of the least effective study approaches, whereas reorganizing, categorizing, comparing, and other forms of manipulation—even to the point of deliberately confusing yourself so as to have to reestablish previously learned information[22]—involves both working and long-term memory, and therefore leads to deeper and more reliable memory and retrieval.[23]

New learning in either form—implicit or explicit—is built on old. In many domains, construction and mapping of new knowledge onto existing knowledge happens implicitly: language, walking, even the foundation of music audiation is learned without being "taught," either through absorption/acculturation or trial and error (or both). But as the concepts or domain get more advanced, learning requires more of a conscious effort, and those who can categorize, put new knowledge into larger contexts, and recognize structurally important information versus surface structures will learn more, better, faster. They will also use their understanding of the structurally significant to provide markers or cues for relatively unimportant information—such as using an identified and audiated harmonic progression (structurally significant) as the foundation for the figurations of a melody.

The construction of "meaningful units" in the "manipulation" and/or "comparison" processes happens when we chunk detailed information into a larger, cohesive structural model. This facilitates the making of connections between new and old information, which leads to deeper processing, and therefore better memory (Laney, 2013). Bugs et al. (2013) use the term "implementation intentions"—a systematic strategy a learner deliberately formulates during encoding to maximize his/her likelihood of retrieval upon the onset of an expected cue, bolstering linkages between cues and intentions. The best type of retrieval cue is one that includes thinking about both the target and the action at the same time (pp. 270–273). Many of the recommended practice strategies I discuss next focus on exactly this: knowing what we do when we do it, so that we can do it again, whenever we want.

Implementation intentions probably also come into play in terms of attention and performance. I used to tell my children that love was not a pie—the giving of some to one did not mean there was less for the others. But our attention, in fact, *is*. There is a finite amount, and it must be partitioned out very carefully. If we rehearse dividing our attention in a particular way, and it is completely consumed with dealing with the multitude of problems at hand, our performance will probably be degraded by unprepared-for attentional demands such as an unfamiliar instrument or audience-caused distractions (coughing, people coming in or leaving, the rustle of programs or candy wrappers, CELL PHONES). Therefore, a not inconsequential part of our rehearsal must include partitioning mental space to allow for unforeseen demands on our attention. This will be addressed to some degree in the upcoming section on motor control and automaticity, but bears anticipating here.

We must practice with awareness of the encoding and retrieval strategies of the meaningful units we plan to rely on, and develop enough mindful motor automaticity that thinking it will allow us to play it, while reserving enough mental capacity to monitor our own performance and maintain awareness of upcoming demands.

No small task!

There also seems to be a benefit from attempting to recount information in varying order, and from a different range of perspectives (Baddeley, 1990, p. 289). This will be particularly discussed in the section on memorization strategies.

Semantic coding is an important aspect of long-term learning, evidenced by how understanding and recall are superior when recall is cued by the original context. For example, if I present a list of sentences that includes one about toast and strawberry jam, the memory of having read the word "jam" is less likely to be triggered later by a reference to traffic. Musically speaking, semantic encoding would imply that, for example, recognizing a C major triad in terms of its function—as the tonic chord, the subdominant chord, or the result of a deceptive resolution—would make it more likely to be remembered, and also to lead us on more securely to the next musical event.

Coding also seems to be broadly context dependent, so that things learned in one (physical) environment are better recalled in the same environment (Baddeley, 1990, pp. 268–285). There even seems to be a connection between the formation of the retrieval cue and the type of sensory input involved in its encoding, so that sensory experiences may not be as successfully retrieved using language-based retrieval cues unless those language-based retrieval cues are also part of the early coding (Gallo & Wheeler, 2013). This encourages the conceptual chunking and mental labeling that should accompany any deliberate practice activity, especially at an advanced level of repertoire.[24]

In a broad sense, the influence of environment might also explain why performing in an unfamiliar space may pose unexpected difficulties, and why practicing performance while visualizing the space in which you will perform seems beneficial. Part of what is remembered is not the "word," or the "chord," but the *experience*.

The importance of *how*, and *how deeply* we process new information, and its influence on our ability to remember and retrieve it, makes a very strong argument for mindful learning from the very first experience with a new piece of music.

MULTIPLE INTELLIGENCES AND RULE LEARNING

In previous sections of the book I have discussed the importance of aligning the type of instruction or practice with the mode of the domain, i.e., aural skills being learned primarily aurally, etc. At the same time, there is a measurably positive impact of an adaptable, multiple-intelligence approach to *problem solving*. An example of this adaptability might be to apply innate aural skill to the study of sight-reading, since important parts of sight-reading involve making predictions, recognizing patterns, and "faking" specifics as necessary while preserving keyality, harmonic function, meter, and tempo.

As the difficulty of the domain increases, a creative approach to problem solving, and the ability to generalize as well as to build new experiences onto old models, becomes even more important. Brown et al. (2014) write:

> People who as a matter of habit extract underlying principles or rules from new experiences are more successful learners than those who take their experiences at face value, failing to infer lessons that can be applied later in similar situations. Likewise, people who single out salient concepts from the less important information they encounter in

new material and who link these key ideas into a mental structure are more successful learners than those who can't separate wheat from chaff. (p. 133)

This type of approach may occur for some as a result of their innate personality, but it is certainly something that can be learned, nurtured, and consciously pursued.

Among the many factors that should discourage consideration of "learning styles" and "talent" as a factor in how learning should be approached is the *negative* impact it can have on belief in our ability to succeed.[25] Brown et al. (2014), again:

> What you tell yourself about your ability plays a part in shaping the ways you learn and perform—how hard you apply yourself, for example, or your tolerance for risk-taking and your willingness to persevere in the face of difficulty. But differences in skills, and your ability to convert new knowledge into building blocks for further learning, also shape your routes to success. . . . Each of us has a large basket of resources in the form of aptitudes, prior knowledge, intelligence, interests, and sense of personal empowerment that shape how we learn and how we overcome our shortcomings. Some of these differences matter a lot . . . [others that] we may think count for a lot . . . actually don't. (pp. 140–141)

These authors propose two approaches that are 100 percent learnable, and explicit,[26] and that are both more valid and more effective than focusing on learning-style approaches.

They refer to the first as "structure building," through the construction of mental models, or maps. In this process, we construct a coherent mental framework by extracting salient ideas, identifying foundational concepts, sorting new information as to whether it belongs to these concepts or not, and incorporating new, nonfoundational ideas into the design. In practice this might mean identifying the underlying harmonic progression and practicing in physical and/or conceptual chunks before learning to play all of the notes hands together as written.

Their second approach prioritizes rule learning over example learning, forming an abstract representation through pattern recognition within an established context. Research has shown that structure-building/rule-learning results in more successful transfer to unfamiliar situations—an important consideration for music-learning at all levels. Comparing examples can result in rule learning, but those who focus on the latter sooner in the process fare better.

> *. . . it is [always] better to solve a problem than to memorize a solution*[27]

I will provide an example for each approach.

First, "structure building."

Say a student with strong aural skills is trying to sight-read an excerpt such as the one in Figure 5.4.

Application of his/her aural skills can be encouraged by first asking him/her to sing or play each of the Figure 5.5 tonal patterns in call-and-response fashion. At this point the learner is not reading the notation.

Figure 5.4. Iott, sight-reading excerpt.

Figure 5.5. Sight-reading tonal patterns.

You could then sing each pattern again and ask the student if he/she can find its representation in the score. This may be initially less successful with the given bassline patterns, as the structural pattern just sung omitted some of the surface elements, but with guidance and repeated attempts at such activities you should find increasing success. This practice not only encourages audiation while reading music; the singing of the *structural* bass line encourages semantic coding. After these patterns have been sung and found in the score, the student might identify each of the chord structures, tap the pulse and chant the rhythms, and then play the example.

Choosing a rule-learning approach can be deliberate through careful monitoring of one's own thought process. For example, when learning scales or arpeggios and their fingerings, rather than acquiring a book of scales and arpeggios, with page after page of notated patterns and finger numbers, the student could be guided to investigate, apply, and understand how the scales are constructed (two tetrachords made up of two whole steps and a half step, separated by a whole step), realized at the piano (a group of three notes + a group of four) and the basic fingering rules. The latter includes not just information about what finger goes where, but *why*.

For pianists, *every* scale—major and the three forms of minor—falls into one of three fingering rules. I call them the "C fingering" scales, the "Fingers together" scales, and the "Thumb rule" scales. The thumb rule is actually the most important rule we can learn; it will help us also in arpeggios and their inversions as well as in solving fingering problems in our repertoire.

C fingering scales are C, G, D, A and E major and minor, and are defined by the occurrence of the fourth finger one step "in" from the pinkies (finger 5) on the tonic notes (Figure 5.6). This means the left-hand fourth finger will play ^2, and the right-hand fourth finger will play ^7.

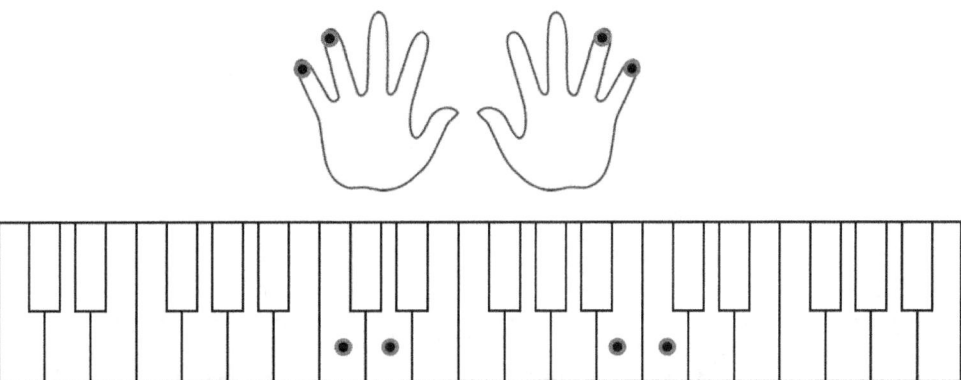

Figure 5.6. "C fingering" hands (scales), showing 5–4.

Fingers together scales are when 234/432 are played in concert (in most cases on or around the group of three black keys), 23/32 (on or around the group of two black keys), with thumbs together on the only two white keys when all five black keys are involved (Figure 5.7). It is easy to remember three of the four major keys because they involve the scales that use all five black keys: F♯/G♭, D♭/C♯, B; plus F major (the odd man out—teach it last). The other four are made up of the relative minors of the first two (D♯/E♭ minor and B♭/A♯ minor) and the parallel minors of the last two (B and F minor).[28]

If the basic principle is understood, then all that is needed is to find the first note so as to identify the appropriate starting place in the pattern. And yes, if the rule dictates starting with finger 3 or 4 in the right hand, you do so, even if finger 2 feels "easier." At this point, consistency is key.

Last are the thumb rule scales—B♭, E♭, and A♭ major, and F♯, C♯, and G♯ minor. For many, these are the most challenging, especially the melodic form of the minors, since they each require different fingerings ascending and descending in one of the two hands. These scales each start on a black key, but only G♯ minor natural form uses all of the black keys, making determination of where the thumbs go less obvious than in the "fingers together" scales.

To understand this rule, we start by noting the relative placement of the thumb on the hand—the highest finger on the left and the lowest on the right. Therefore, to facilitate crossing, the thumb of the left hand will play the highest white key,

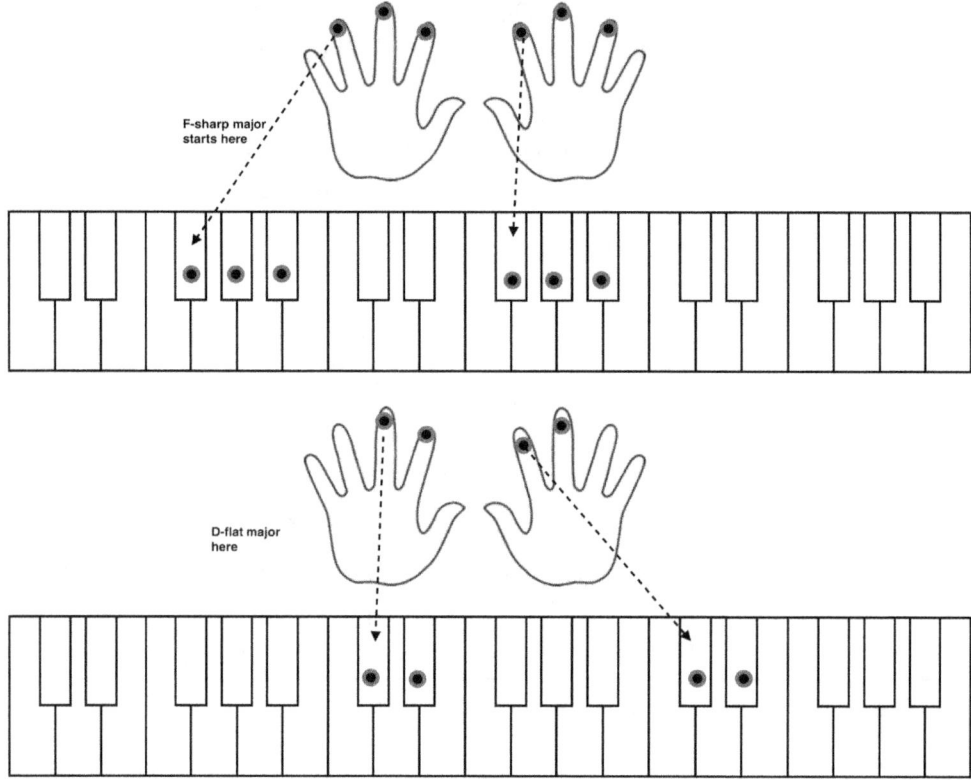

Figure 5.7. "Fingers together" hands (scales) for B, D-flat, and F-sharp major and B-flat and D-sharp minor.

meaning the white key directly *below* a black; and the thumb of the right hand will play the lowest white key, or the white key directly *above* a black. This might seem a little confusing at first, but some simple visual teaching aids can really help.

For example, you can "write" the whole scale using foam dots or pennies on a real or cardboard keyboard (Figure 5.8 [1]). Then split it for the left hand so that each group has a black key on the bottom and a white key on top (Figure 5.8 [2]). This makes it easy to see the 4-note group and the 3-note group.

The right hand is perhaps a little trickier to work out, since the 4-note group is not apparent until the musician proceeds into the second octave.[29] In any case, since the right-hand thumb is the lowest finger, the right-hand groups have a white key on the bottom and a black key on top (Figure 5.9).

In many respects it might seem "easier" just to look in the scale book, see what finger goes where, and memorize it. But we're not giving a man a fish so he can eat for a day, we're teaching him how to fish so he can eat for a lifetime. There are a lot of scales, and a lot of scale passages in our music that don't always present neatly from ^1 to ^1, meaning that understanding the principles and applications of fingerings is an important tool in the advanced musician's toolbox. Taking the time to

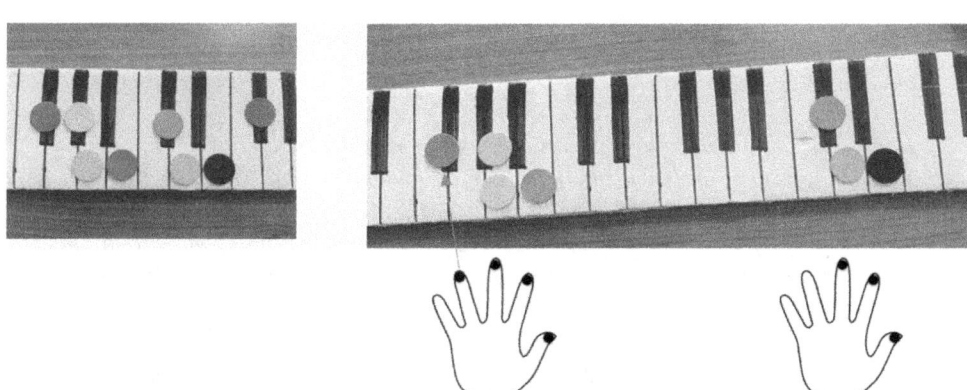

Figure 5.8. "Thumb rule," note and fingering groups for F-sharp minor scale, natural form, left hand.

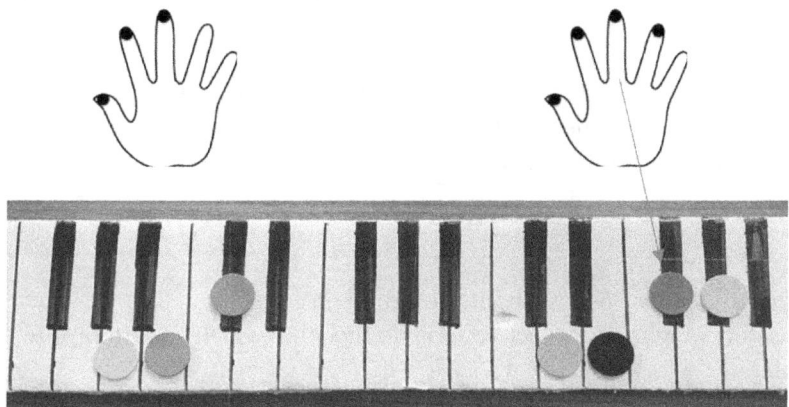

Figure 5.9. Note and fingering groups F-sharp minor, natural form, right hand.

understand, to problem solve, to work through a rule and its application, is time well spent, and will result in much *less* time, effort, and frustration, later.

As I don't play any other instruments, I am not qualified here to expand in detail on how rule learning might be used to teach scales to string or brass players. In any case, I would encourage a rule-learning, foundational approach to as many fundamental skills as possible. The more it is done, the faster you get, to the point where the fingerings and patterns seem to be memorized, but in reality are problems being solved very quickly.

In any case, deliberately accessing and using all your intelligences not only aids remembering, but is also positively correlated with more *persistent*, and more *creative*, problem solving. This is an adaptive approach, so that the mode of activity matches the mode of the task to be learned, and it also consciously accesses stored information and uses innate abilities to supplement new learning.

(CREATIVE) PROBLEM SOLVING

A problem is a goal that is not immediately attainable. (Hambrick and Engle, 2003, p. 178)

Improving performance to the level of expertise requires deliberate practice—essentially a form of problem solving, where individuals engage in tasks with goals that exceed the current level of performance. The experts and their teachers and coaches have to continue to design training situations where the goal is to attain a level beyond their current performance in order to keep improving. (Ericsson, 2003, p. 64)

Even the most talented individual probably will not get to a level of accomplishment one would call "expertise" without engaging in some form of deliberate practice and higher-level problem solving. Like all cognitive processes, problem solving is multistage, with cognitive psychologists proposing various serial models. While many differ in precisely what order each of these steps is undertaken, the gist is pretty much the same:

- We recognize that there is, in fact, a problem to be solved.
- The problem is defined and "represented" mentally, which generally includes comparisons to the final goal state.

We then:

- organize our knowledge about the problem;
- consider, weigh, and select various methods by which we attempt to solve the problem;
- allocate mental and/or physical resources toward the solution;
- monitor our progress toward the goal; and
- evaluate the chosen solution for success/accuracy.

These processes can, nay, *should*, be pursued *consciously*, through self-regulatory techniques and supportive feedback that encourage setting specific goals, focusing on relevant information, estimating the efficacy of various solutions, selecting and/or constructing strategies, interpreting the results, and modifying future efforts. Because effective problem solving—especially when the learner is faced with complex challenges or those that may require sustained effort—requires high levels of self-motivation and self-regulatory ability, these qualities must be nurtured and rewarded to the *n*th degree. Behaviors such as setting intermediary goals along the path to long-term goals can help maintain a learner's persistence during problem solving. As previously mentioned, focusing on *process* and an open-minded exploration of the problem space and potential solutions, rather than *outcome*, will encourage a learner who is facing a particularly thorny challenge to make systematic changes in solution efforts, and to attribute his/her successes or failures to the choices of strategy rather than ability. This leads to stronger feelings of self-efficacy, contributing to sustainment of discipline, motivation, and interest (Zimmerman & Campillo, 2003, pp. 245–256).

In fact, Getzels and Csikszentmihalyi[30] found that individuals who were more *creative*, and therefore more successful, in their problem solving were those who exhibited effort in problem *finding*[31] throughout the learning process, and who displayed divergent thinking, openness, tolerance of ambiguity, and intrinsic motivation. They found that divergent thinking was especially important in the early stages of solving a problem, when various possibilities and representations must be considered. According to their research, highly creative people seem to attend to more things in their environment, taking in information that other people might consider irrelevant. Creative problem solvers also tend to be autonomous, open to new experiences, self-confident, driven, and ambitious. For the most part, these are qualities that can be actively pursued.[32]

Problems in general are more easily/readily solved if the individual has knowledge and a set of expectations about the problem, and if those expectations are not violated.[33] This prior knowledge provides a scaffolding on which the new problem can be structured, which often helps lead more quickly to a solution, although prior knowledge can also cause its own problems as a result of "functional fixedness."

Functional fixedness occurs when an individual gets stuck in a particular (erroneous) way of looking at a problem, and is common in the ordinary processes of problem solving. When faced with a problem, you bring to the task previous experience with similar problems. These predictions can be helpful, but if the learner is not careful, and those predictions not checked for veracity, mistakes can be made, learned, and reinforced (Pretz et al., 2003, p. 20). An example of this given in Pretz et al. presents a vocabulary/language question as an example: "Nefarious is to Dromedary as Eggs are to (Chapel, Yellow, Bees, Friend)." This question might cause a long detour as the test taker tried to parse the semantic connection between "Nefarious" and "Dromedary," whereas "Eggs" is actually "to" "Bees" because of the number of letters in each word (pp. 10–11). For musicians it might look something like misreading an altered dominant chord as an actual dominant chord, playing passage *a'* the same as passage *a*, even though passage *a'* has a subtle difference, or the occurrence of courtesy accidentals resulting in the reader "removing" those accidentals mentally from the key signature.

Considerable knowledge in a domain helps experts "represent"[34] problems more efficiently, stripping away irrelevant details and getting at the deeper structure of the problem sooner, often through chunking information. Experts "perceive meaningful patterns" that "novices miss," and perform more quickly while making fewer errors. This is because they can "use their domain-specific knowledge" to make predictions and "take strategic short-cuts," with many of the solution strategies automatized based on prior learning. Experts are also better able to carefully "monitor their own performance," and understand "the value of strategy use better" (Zimmerman & Campillo, 2003, pp. 236–237).

Novices, on the other hand, tend to focus on surface structures, which can distract from both the source of the problem and the route to the solution. Novices also tend to represent the problem relatively quickly, moving almost immediately to working on a solution. Because novices may not notice the flaws in their initial representations, they will often head quite far down invalid paths, and need to start over and over again, forfeiting a lot of hard work and investing a lot of time in pursuing poor solutions. This can be particularly thorny for musicians because the motor-control pathways to the *wrong* solutions become just as embedded as would those to the correct ones. These errant pathways must then be corrected with even more reinforcement of the correct route than an original, correct approach might require. The metaphor I often use is that a road crew has begun building a road in the wrong place. Now not only must they start over and build the road in the correct place, they must *first* fill in the previous excavation and reinforce it because prior excavation will impact the soil around it in terms of likelihood of collapse and/or erosion. Thus work our neural pathways—once built, their influence can continue for years.[35]

This perhaps is one of the strongest arguments against the "practice makes perfect" theory, because inappropriate practice can actually move you further from your goal. (Perhaps the modern "update": practice makes *permanent*, strikes a more truthful chord.) It also confirms one of the most important tasks for intermediate and advancing musicians: constructing meaningful, practical, sequential practice approaches while cultivating active observation and involvement.

On the other hand, experts generally take longer to make a comparison between what they already know and what they need to learn in order to solve a new problem, using a well-organized knowledge base. This not only helps them represent the problem better in the first place, but also equips them better to assess the appropriateness of both the representation and the chosen paths toward a solution (Pretz et al., 2003, pp. 12–14). At this stage, advanced musicians know quite a bit about what they do and don't already know, and have an appropriately developed sensibility to determine which problem-solving strategies are most likely to get them from point A to point B.

These differences between problem representations by novices and experts are even more marked when solving an ill-defined problem, with novices jumping right in with both feet, and mindful, self-aware experts taking the time to modify the problem into a well-defined one before attempting to solve it (Bédard & Chi, 1992). Another advantage for experts is that the knowledge base on which a new problem is built also includes representations of previous problem solving. Taking a moment after making a mistake to observe the mistake, try to determine the cause, and plan a different approach before playing again might *seem* less "active," but the result of playing it right away is often the same as the prior attempt, resulting in a reinforced error rather than a correction. The "think it then play it" section in the intermediate section of the book addressed some of these strategies. They will be revisited ahead, applied to advanced repertoire.

Transfer of prior knowledge to new problems is, as would be expected, especially effective with similar problems, even more so within similar contexts. However, reliance on similarity can lead to negative transfer and/or blockage of positive transfer in the case of *functional fixedness* as described above, or because problems that appear to be similar might actually entail different solutions and vice versa (Bassok, 2003, p. 344). That being said, taking breaks in conscious problem solving for what cognitive psychologists call an incubation period can instigate a breakthrough beyond this functional fixedness, resulting in what Bassok calls "illumination": a sudden insight into a problem and its solution.

Incubation in the hopes of illumination does require adequate preparation time—the more appropriately structured the better—and then time spent away from the problem. An example of this might be observed when trying to complete a difficult crossword puzzle, feeling stuck at a certain point, taking a break, and then being able to answer the remaining clues in quick succession an hour or two later. Most importantly to our purposes, these "Eureka!" moments should be recognized not as bolts of lightning from above, but rather, often, a direct result of *careful and deliberate practice*. Perhaps the most important factor is the ability to recognize the true nature of the similarity so as to choose the appropriate strategy, some effortful work to test out the strategy, *followed by a break* (to be discussed at length in the section on distributed and interleaved practice). I can't count how many times I have practiced in a focused and disciplined manner, feeling that, while my efforts were superior, improvement was minimal, but the *next* time I approached the instrument and the passage, found that it had improved immensely. It might feel like magic, but it's not.

The process of incubation might contribute to why it is helpful to practice passages in ways that may seem to differ from the intended goals. As long as it is mindful and intentional, taking a *divergent* approach—practicing a loud passage softly, for example, or a staccato passage legato—sheds light on various elements, and seems to kindle new associations, often revealing important connections between our physical approach and the resulting execution or sound. This is related to variable priority training, discussed previously, where a set of complex goals is approached by first striving to solve one of them at a time. Since it is difficult to perform advanced repertoire with all its layers of technical demands and musical elements—clarity, rhythmic evenness, dynamics, balance, phrasing, articulation—working on attending to one at a time, then perhaps paired, combinations of three elements, etc. can help develop the ability to attend to all at once. A divergent approach also cultivates the sense of exploration and observation so important to effective and flexible performance.

Impact of Mood on Problem Solving and Success

As previously mentioned, research tells us that how a person feels emotionally during a particular learning experience directly impacts not only how they feel about the topic itself, but also *their aptitude*, their *ability to learn* the associated topic or material. What I haven't yet discussed is how our mood impacts both the type, and discipline, of our efforts in problem solving and practice. Moods are probably most impactful with musicians in preteen and teenage years, who may be a bit more susceptible to emotional swings triggered by hormonal surges along with an innate striving for both societal acceptance and independence from their parents and other forms of authority.

Positive and negative emotions as well as bodily sensations and cognitive experiences (such as fluency of recall or perception) can facilitate or inhibit problem solving, depending on the nature of the task. The same feeling can actually have different effects at different stages of the problem-solving process.

Let's take a step back for a moment, with some help from Schwarz and Skurnik (2003).

We generally refer to something as a "problem" if/when we have a goal for which we don't already know the solution, and can view "problem solving" as a search through metaphorical space. This problem space consists of the initial state, a number of intermediate states, and the goal state. Operators move us from one state to another, while path constraints may impose limits on the paths to the solution. Our ease in solving the problem will depend on how successfully we have represented crucial elements of the task environment in the problem space.

For the sake of intuitional efficiency, a problem solver who has experience in the domain will adopt a heuristic[36] approach to his/her search of the problem space, choosing and attending to a small number of alternatives that seem to be the most promising. This search for a solution will also be most effective when the problem solver has a clear goal, understands the initial state and constraints, and *knows what operators might be useful*. An ability to choose the right strategy or pathways is perhaps the most important thing that sets "experts" apart from "nonexperts." I know I'm probably not that much better a pianist than I was in my twenties, but I am a much more efficient learner, and can generally work up a piece to performance readiness in weeks rather than months. I attribute most of this difference to making much better choices of problem-solving strategies, and being much more systematic and observant in how I apply them.

We could even define "expertise" as this very ability: a basis of knowledge in a domain that allows for the organization of the problem situation into meaningful chunks, which allows the problem solver to draw on patterns of relations between the problem elements. This facilitates transfer of related knowledge already acquired to the problem at hand, preventing the need for an extensive search for appropriate solutions (see Figure 5.10).

Mood and emotion can influence whether the problem solver adopts a top-down (from general to specific) or bottom-up (from specific to general) strategy, how the problem solver represents the problem and searches the problem space, and which knowledge becomes accessible in memory to contribute to analogical problem-solving strategies.

We recognize a "problem" when we perceive a discrepancy between the current state and the goal state and it is not immediately apparent how the discrepancy can be eliminated. Being "in a bad mood" may cause the learner to see the current state as worse, increasing the distance between it and the goal state, but this dissatisfaction in the current state may serve as an instigator to searching for a solution.

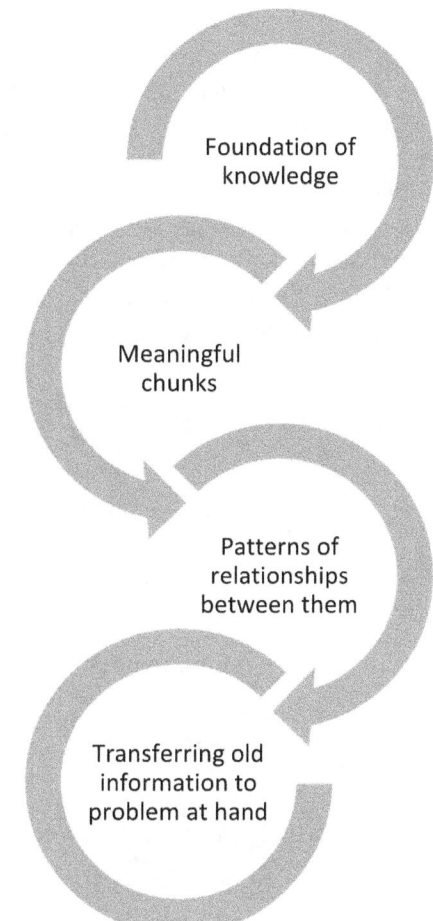

Figure 5.10. Expert's problem-solving process.

Conversely, if the learner is in a good mood, the goal state is perceived as more attractive, which may increase motivation to achieve it.

If the goal seems unattainable given the learners' current resources, they are more likely to give up. *But*, learners in a good mood will be more optimistic about their resources, which will make them more likely to initiate problem solving. "Sad" learners tend to set higher performance standards for themselves, and are simultaneously less optimistic that they can achieve them.

Clear as mud, right?

That's not all. If the performance goal doesn't have defined criteria for intermediate states, learners must draw on their apparent affective response to assess whether they are moving closer to the goal. When performance criterion is being used as the measure of whether the goal state has been achieved, "sad" individuals will evaluate their performance more negatively, but this will probably motivate them to keep searching for a better solution, while "happy" individuals will be more easily satisfied and therefore may be more likely to settle for a suboptimal result.

If an "enjoyment criterion" is used, happy individuals will keep trying and sad individuals will give up.

People are more likely to rely on their preexisting knowledge structures and routines that have served them well in the past when things go smoothly and they don't face any hurdles. When/if complications arise, they shift from a top-down processing style to a bottom-up one, paying increased attention to details. This shift can also be impacted by mood. Individuals in a sad mood are more likely to use a systematic, data-driven strategy of information processing, including considerable attention to detail, while "happy" individuals are more likely to rely on preexisting knowledge structures, with less attention to detail (see Figure 5.11).

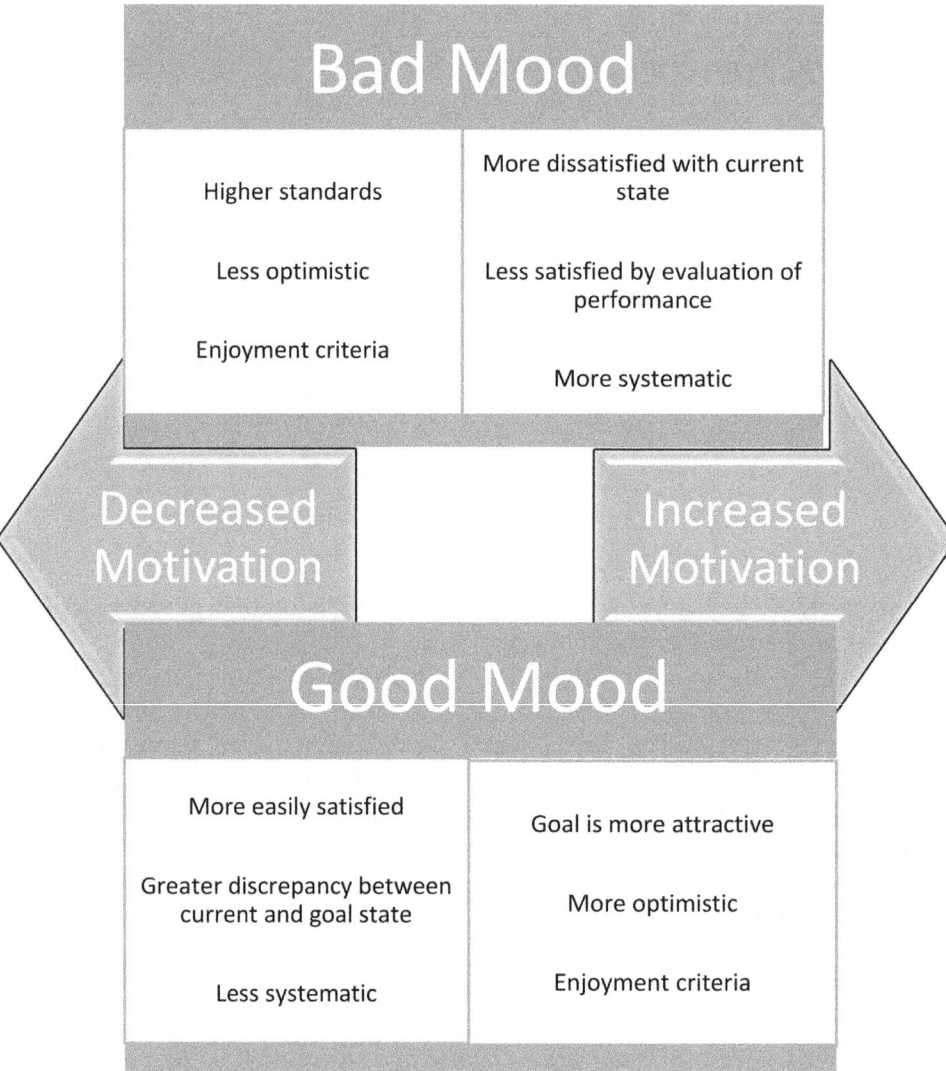

Figure 5.11. Impact of mood on problem-solving efforts.

The relevance of all of this is as complicated as the explanation. I would say that we could just go with our moods, and on our good-mood days enjoy our accomplishments, indulge our optimism about our abilities to succeed, and enjoy our current state. On darker days (say, when in the middle of a global pandemic) we might use this state of general dissatisfaction to motivate us to work harder, longer, better.[37] At the same time, if we tend toward optimism or pessimism, we may be more consistently effective if we focus on the more objective goal of "have you solved any/most/all of the problems that presented themselves today?" rather than the subjective evaluation of "that was fun," or "that was pretty." We could even, theoretically, consciously choose whether we are using a performance versus an enjoyment criterion for self-monitoring and analysis dependent on our mood.

One way to avoid mood-based decisions about progress or success is to frame observations in more objective terms. Sometimes I ask a student how s/he feels about his/her performance and s/he will start with something like, "I thought that went pretty well," or "It was better yesterday." Digging a little deeper reveals more informative details: "The dynamic range was well presented," "I really thought I brought out the melody beautifully in the second section," "That technically challenging section I've been working on so much is really improving," etc. This type of awareness, self-observation/monitoring, and objective description of what did or didn't work lends weight to the practice, the decisions made in practice, and the goals for performance in a way that seems to transcend mood. And moving deliberately from working on the big picture to the small and back again (whole/part/whole and zooming in/zooming out) is an excellent way to utilize both ends of the mood spectrum while also helping to avoid over-automatization and complacency.

Effective problem solving, especially for advanced problems, requires more than mere knowledge about a problem task. It also requires high levels of motivation, metacognition,[38] and motoric competence. The self-regulation of "forethought, performance, and self-reflection," in a continuous cycle, can heighten the learner's "sense of personal agency," preserving motivation toward "long-term solution efforts" (Zimmerman & Campillo, 2003, p. 257). *Creative* problem solving—the type required when faced with either an ill-defined problem or one that the learner has not encountered before, requires both convergent and divergent thinking, with multiple cycles of thought that restructure, reorganize, and/or combine existing information rather than "merely" recalling it or using existing categories or solution strategies (Lubart & Mouchiroud, 2003, pp. 138–139). This perhaps best describes what experts do when they practice—identify tried and true strategies from previous efforts that seem to apply to the problem at hand, monitor the effectiveness of these efforts, and adapt accordingly. A sense of curiosity can also help. Ask yourself: What would happen if you . . . played it louder? Played it slower? Brought out the melody in the lower voice? Played it legato instead of staccato? Decrescendoed instead of crescendoed? etc. and then try it, observing the result from both an acoustic and physical standpoint. These explorations provide much information that contributes not only to understanding the needs of that particular passage, but also potential for application in future situations. It is my contention that this approach is available even to beginning musicians, with proper instruction and encouraging guidance from the earliest levels.

I also like to ask myself questions about why a composer might have written something a certain way. Say in one phrase Haydn writes staccato 16ths, and in a passage that seems to be built on the same motivic material, he writes 32nds with rests in between. This may be an oversight, or it may be telling you something about how he would like you to play those sets of notes in relation to each other. Debussy often writes simultaneous chords on the two staves in such a way that makes reaching them both difficult, but that through redistribution could be much easier to play. Surely he knew how hands fit on a piano keyboard,[39] so perhaps he is distributing them in a particular way so as to reflect something regarding the voicing. Asking oneself "why" and exploring the possible answers may shed some helpful light on both technical issues and musical considerations.

Of course, all the right thinking and deliberate practice in the world can't solve problems if appropriate technical facility has not been developed. Which leads us nicely to . . .

MOTOR CONTROL AND DEVELOPMENT, AND THE RISKS OF EXCESSIVE AUTOMATICITY

> . . . *our brain does not represent muscles, but . . . movements.* (Altenmüller, 2003, p. 526)

Jerde et al. (2012) write:

> The technical proficiency that is required to play evenly and to layer nuances onto a musical phrase does assume the ability to play the notes in that phrase accurately and in the correct order, but this is in itself no small feat, as anyone who has tried to play an instrument can tell you. From a motor control perspective, the effortlessness with which experienced musicians accomplish this translation from notes on a page to a complicated movement sequence is perhaps even more interesting than the refinements and adjustments that set apart a truly remarkable performance from a mediocre one. Taking the example of a wind instrument player, step one in learning the technique of the instrument is memorizing which keys must be closed to produce a given note. But mastering these static fingerings is only the lowest level of competence. Serious music students pursue practice routines of technical exercises designed expressly to isolate the most important finger movement sequences [*and may study alternative fingerings that affect tuning*]. Musicians practice endless varieties of scales and arpeggios, because in Western music if you know them in all 12 keys [*sic; 24, actually, if you want to include minor; plus modes, octatonic, pentatonic, etc.*], you have already trained to automaticity a rather high percentage of all the note-to-note transitions and sequences you might encounter in the repertoire. It is the systematic overlearning of these transitions that allows effortless fluency in performance, like acquiring a comprehensive vocabulary of note-combination transitions. Musicians also practice these patterns with varieties in

tempo, volume, and articulation, attempting to internalize all combinations of conditions that might be required in a performance situation. (pp. 86–87)

The ease with which an accomplished musician can make spontaneous adjustments is a sign of what we call expertise. This ease is remarkable in and of itself, and a result of the fluency gained through thoughtful, deliberate practice of a wide variety of patterns, etudes, and repertoire. Spontaneous adjustments start with complex mental representations and sufficient ease to allow for continuous monitoring of the performance. The motor control we strive for and exhibit in expert performance is a *result* of our representations rather than vice versa.

Expertise in physical performance is related directly to the ability to look, and prepare, ahead. In tasks requiring rapid motor production, superiority seems to be mostly impacted by skilled *preparatory* processing (Ericsson, 2003, p. 58). Of course, there must be appropriate facility, but once this is attained, in most cases, if you can think it (at the correct time—more on that soon), you can play it.

Elliot (1991) writes:

> Knowing how to do something effectively always implies an understanding, either tacit or verbal, of the *principles* that underpin the repetition of successful actions. Our ability to do something successfully on succeeding occasions demonstrates that we are able to distinguish, select, and redo what it is that works in our successful actions. Understanding, then, makes it likely that we can both apply and extend our proficient actions in future situations which will inevitably combine both old and new challenges. (p. 27)

Playing a musical instrument or singing, even at low levels of skill, requires a highly adaptive organization of multiple submovements and the ability to make continual adjustments. The motor command itself seems to specify a movement goal rather than just identifying details of individual muscle contractions. This command is interpreted by the cerebellar-spinal system, which has learned through experience to compute the patterns of muscle movements required in order to achieve the goal over a broad range of starting conditions. The scope of the command includes a complex pattern of bodily movements, distributed in both space and time (Shaffer, 1981, p. 331).

> [T]he skilled performer has learned, over years of practice, a large variety of procedures for translating his intentions into action. In this way he can assemble representations of output that merely designate the procedures whose information is used at the next lower level of output. . . . As well as achieving flexibility, programming at this abstract level allows greater fluency of performance by enabling coordination to range over larger segments of output, and hence provides the opportunity to introduce features of expressiveness into the performance. (Shaffer, 1981, p. 337)

Three factors of interrelated movements seem to be optimized during practice: efficiency, interaction, and mechanics. *Efficiency* refers to the refinement of movement down to exactly what is required, no more and no less. If you're practicing a large leap, and repeatedly overshoot and then adjust, you will want to keep practicing until the movement is immediately precise, and in as direct a route as possible.

Interaction refers to the coordination of movements between all involved parts of the body—upper arm, forearm, wrist, hand, fingers, etc. These interactions contribute to efficiency, reducing the number of independent choices the motor system must make. Observing/evaluating the angle of the arm or how much wrist movement is needed to execute a wide broken-chord pattern, or for bowing arpeggiations across several strings, and comparing differences—sometimes subtle, sometimes substantial—between different chord structures, provides important information to both our mental and our physical memory. Conscious development of these motions and interactions plays a crucial role in effective practice strategies.

Mechanics refers to the properties of both the musician (extension and contraction of muscles, for example) and to those of the environment, such as the role and impact of gravity or the relative responsiveness of the instrument (Jäncke, 2012a, p. 30).

Repetition plays an important part in the representation and execution of motor skills. If the learner repeatedly pairs a stimulus with a response, the response takes subsequently fewer attentional resources while interfering less and less with other concurrent tasks. This results in a certain degree of automaticity, which is desirable, *as long as it is rooted in mindful awareness* (Baddeley, 1990, p. 124; Huber, 2013).

In fact, the neural circuits we use when taking conscious action are different from the ones we use when our actions are automatic. The coding of automated motions happens deep in the brain in the basal ganglia—the area that codes/recodes motor learning, sequential tasks, and subconscious actions such as eye movement. As the brain recodes, motor and cognitive sequences are chunked together to become a single unit (a "macro"), thereby requiring fewer conscious decisions, which is helpful, since the effort required for making conscious decisions slows response time.[40] To the learner, this recoding may, at times, result in a feeling that information has been moved around and is suddenly not accessible. Any advanced musician reading this has probably had the experience of observing something improve, and then having an hour or a day or even longer when it seems to have regressed. In addition to some of the forgetting that's a natural part of learning, this may be a result of this recoding, where the brain has "decided" that it has processed this information enough at a certain level and has embarked on a process of recoding it elsewhere. Also, our brain likes to deal with new, unfamiliar information in the right hemisphere, and familiar information in the left (McGilchrist, 2009), so that certain types of processing literally change sides. Any of the above may result in you feeling that the information has been lost—it has not been, but you may have to look for it in a different way—like when you rearrange your kitchen, and it's better organized, but it takes you a few days to remember where the silverware is.

The coordination of movements is made more difficult by the fact that for many instrumentalists the two hands must move different distances or in different manners, or hand and finger must be coordinated with embouchure, yet all must arrive at their targets synchronously. For string players the coordination of the fingering hand with the bow hand involves motions in different planes; for pianists it almost always involves playing different voices/lines simultaneously, and results in different problems of movement trajectory, different levels of intensity, different manners of striking the keys, and different patterns of timing.[41] These movements require a highly functioning internal clock and careful sequencing of a mental plan, resulting in synchronous and coordinated movements for sustained periods of time (Baddeley, 1990, pp. 120, 336; Shaffer, 1981, p. 338). This coordination can be made even more complicated when interpreting performance styles such as slow movements of Mozart Sonatas or much of Chopin's writing, which is customarily performed with the two hands slightly dissociated in time for expressive purposes; and I have always imagined things like that chromatic slide in the clarinet at the beginning of "Rhapsody in Blue" are probably a lot harder to execute than non-clarinet playing people realize. Shaffer theorizes that these coordinations are possible because an advanced representation maps motor output onto two different command arrays, each of which has its own clock translating timing into movement. Obviously, this isn't going to just happen, but must be *practiced*.

Motor learning has also been shown to be related to *adjustments* of mental plans—with the cognitive representations of the movements being independent of the limbs with which the movements will be performed. Studies have found that, as skill increases, mental representations of performance may become dissociated from the movements required, which may show that the mental plans of advanced performers are based on more abstract concepts, independent of the notation, or of hand/finger/embouchure movements. This suggests that the motor and conceptual dimensions actually become more distinct as learning progresses (Jäncke, 2012a, p. 31), and aligns precisely with my experience. For example, when I was first learning advanced repertoire, I could only play the piece with the fingering I had planned and rehearsed, and a change of the score edition would create reading difficulty because of differences in engraving font size or measure placement. Now I write in very few fingerings, can generally play many passages with a variety of fingerings, and find there is no impact at all of what edition I am reading from—unless the edition is full of unnecessary courtesy accidentals or inelegant fingerings, which, contrary to my younger and less-enlightened self, I now seem unable to ignore. This suggests almost an intermediary filter of sorts, where the sensory input or memory of a passage becomes a concept, and the motor signals seek for stimulus from the concept rather than from the input. I have also found that small finger slips have much less impact in performance, probably because I am thinking in larger structures, a bit further ahead, and am more focused on the physical and musical *process* than on individual note or finger details.

As the musician advances, motor movements are more and more effectively transferred, helping the musician master new repertoire more and more quickly. This reflects an ability to generalize, and to transfer movements not only from one piece to another, but from one hand or finger combination to another (Palmer, 2012, pp. 42–43). There is also an important difference observed in expert performance, where less time is spent in a "home" position and more time spent in continuous,

Figure 5.12. Hindemith, "Sonata for viola and piano," Op. 11 No. 4.

prepared movements (Shaffer, 1981, p. 327).[42] An important consideration that's often overlooked is that how we play something is affected by what comes next. For example, the octaves of the first boxed gesture in Figure 5.12 will feel different from the second set of octaves, partially because of the differences in the intervening voice in the same hand, and perhaps even more so because of differences in where some of the octaves go next.

Musicians performing from memory are relying on visual, aural, physical, and mental/analytical memory. But Jerde et al. (2012) claim (and I agree) that analytical memory is the most important. Knowledge of harmony plus chunking processes allows for rapid categorization of domain-specific patterns, and analytical memory is often able to efficiently trigger assembled musical-motor-vocabulary sequences.

MULTIMODAL IMAGERY AND MUSICAL MEMORIZATION

> *Actions will be more effective if they are planned in terms of their intended outcome or effect rather than in terms of the specific movement patterns.* (Wulf & Prinz, in Davidson-Kelly et al., 2015)

Both the perception and the production of music require various interacting memory structures. Information about the form and structure of musical events is represented by a perceptually organized musical memory system. As musical sounds unfold over time, the auditory system remembers and integrates the sequentially ordered sounds into a coherent musical line. This mechanism occurs in working memory, which temporarily stores auditory units and combines them into a single precept. Recognizing or producing a musical selection either with the score or from memory requires storage of many invariant properties in long-term memory. In addition, expert musicians have developed a memory system that utilizes their existing knowledge structure in semantic memory in order to store new information during skilled performance, and to incorporate cues, item information, and associative information into a specific memory mechanism used to facilitate encoding and retrieval of information in and from long-term memory—all done in less time (Jäncke, 2012a, pp. 31–32). If these forms of storage as a result of organization are going to happen anyway, we can make them happen more quickly by being deliberate about it.

> For fluent expert performance with or without a score, multi-modal mental representations of the music need to be securely encoded in memory in order to be recalled under performance conditions. Auditory, motor, conceptual, structural, visual, and linguistic images may all concurrently contribute to performance. The manner in which performers attend to different aspects of a musical image is likely to be context-dependent and idiosyncratic. Individual performers report conscious reliance on certain mental images more than others; for example, some musicians report vivid visual recall of the score, while others have no conscious access to a visual image of the text. . . . [T]he depth of processing of different types of image may vary depending on the performer, the nature of the task, and the stage of learning—and potentially irrespective of the degree to which the mental representation of the music is consciously accessed by the performer. (Davidson-Kelly et al., 2015, pp. 83–92)

These authors also point out that beginning pianists often rely on motor memory, since it seems to develop almost automatically through sheer repetition, but it often appears to be the source of the classic failure scenario. When a failure occurs in what I call "autopilot" performance there is literally nowhere to turn. This becomes more and more risky as the repertoire lengthens and becomes more difficult. On the other hand, conceptual representation of the formal structure and memorization via various sensory and organizational pathways provides retrieval cues that can be used as impetus for reliable performance.

Successful memorization is a result of a complex multimodal representation consisting of visual-spatial, aural, physical, and analytical elements built up in meaningful chunks through accurate processing of each component. Efficiency of movement brings clarity to this representation through close connection of the physical and mental aspects. This would imply that identifying patterns and their interrelated meaning(s) and using these identifications to categorize the material can, even should, take place *before* any specific motor programs are extensively rehearsed and therefore stored. One or two "play-throughs" can be used as the first stage of that important initial learning phase, in order to provide auditory information and to consider the demands and appropriate strategies, not yet in efforts to store physical/motor information. The intention of this approach is actually to *reduce* the cognitive load required through a higher-quality understanding of the piece—knowing more leading to needing to think less. An integrated representation reduces the cognitive load, allowing the performer later to focus on the expressive goals of the performance rather than "just" the technical or mechanical aspects. In fact, studies have shown that attending to the external effects of motor actions as well as the actions themselves enhances both retention and recall. I can personally attest to this; I notice that I perform much more securely from memory when focusing primarily (but not completely) on my musical intentions.

The thing is, as with so many aspects of learning at an advanced stage, this multimodal representation is going to be attempted by the brain whether we do it intentionally or not. If we are deliberate about it, that representation will be better and more useful, in its construction and in its retrieval. Creating higher-level chunks—which involve myriad musical elements as well as many of the aspects of learning and processing—into coherent meaningful units results in fewer chunks that need to be retrieved. Davidson-Kelly et al. (2015) and Varela et al. (2017) refer to this phenomenon as *embodied cognition*, reflecting the connection between movement imagery and body awareness, and express belief that the body is directly involved in the representation of movements rather than a passive perceiver or actor serving the mind. By creating a clear mental representation that includes structural, auditory, visuo-spatial, *and* movement information, an integrated image of the music is stored, and recalled, during performance. Like many of the most useful approaches, this may seem like it will require an increase in initial effort, but this type of learning facilitates learning over the long term, bringing body and mind together, and allows cognitive resources to be more fully allocated to musical expression during performance.

Benefits and execution of mental imagery practice have been previously discussed as they relate to the intermediate musician. To take these ideas further, consider the work of Alexander Technique expert Nelly Ben-Or with musicians learning and *memorizing* their pieces prior to *any kind* of physical rehearsal, using multimodal imagery (Davidson-Kelly et al., 2015). This imagery is reliant not on a visual memory of the score but on a mental map constructed by the learner, with a detailed structural image, probably in multiple layers, and including a deep sense of the *physical* structures involved. Chunking musical materials, identifying manageable subunits within complex material, clarifying each subunit, and reconstructing them into a whole are important features of this multidimensional learning.

Obviously this approach takes practice(!), and would be particularly difficult for those who don't have experience with imagery rehearsal, or who are deficient in any of the supporting abilities such as aural skills, technique, and/or understanding of theory. That makes a very strong argument not just for being sure that musicians of all levels are learning everything they should,[43] but also for the potential benefit of the practice strategy I refer to as "think it then play it." This mental picture-taking can be incorporated into practice from the earliest stages—first as the audiation pause, later in practicing to repair small sections: play, pause, observe in memory—

What did I *do*? What did it *feel* like? How did it *sound*? How do I want to do next time?—play again.

Therefore, rather than thinking of memorization as something separate, done after working on the piece for a while, we are preparing for it from our very first experiences with the piece. Hearing, recognizing, and analyzing harmonic structures, form, and melodic/motivic interrelationships as well as technical challenges and how we want to meet them should be an important part of our earliest observations, and the focus of all of our practice sessions. Awareness of the physical motions involved in successful and musical execution are incorporated into the representations of the piece along with the concepts behind the notation and our musical goals. With this approach, memorizing is just one more step on the road you've been heading down for a while.

DELIBERATE, DISTRIBUTED, INTERLEAVED PRACTICE

> *Frequent repetition does not guarantee learning, except perhaps of simple messages. What is most important to learning is what the learner* does [emphasis mine] *with the material s/he will be asked to remember.* (Baddeley, 1990, p. 160)

> *Skill acquisition, even in what may seem to be an initial encounter, always involves transforming or modifying existing behavior and skills. Improvements in skills involve idiosyncratic changes to various knowledge structures and complex acquired mechanisms, according to each individual's already acquired mechanisms and representations. This view of skill acquisition as a series of* deliberate *adjustments requires that performers* actively *construct their skills.* (Ericsson, 2003, p. 68, emphasis mine)

> *You can get a good deal from rehearsal,*
> *If it just has the proper dispersal.*
> *You would just be an ass*
> *To do it en masse:*
> *Your remembering would turn out much worsal.* (Neisser's Law, in Baddeley, 1990, p. 158)

The benefits of deliberate and distributed practice are much touted in the latest on music learning and learning in general, including by prominent cognitive scientists such as Ericsson, Boot, Baddeley, and Brown. Addressing this topic in the most detail in one source would probably be Brown et al.'s *Make It Stick*, one of the books I have already mentioned, and recommend highly to anyone who is interested in learning more about how we learn and how to learn effectively.

When it comes to efficient, effective practice, it is the type and construction of that work that is actually most important. As mentioned in the introduction, Ericsson et al. (1993) define deliberate practice as "a regimen of effortful activities designed to optimize improvement" (p. 363). I expanded this definition to *a regimen of effortful activities designed to optimize improvement by being age-*[44] *and level-appropriate, structured in alignment with the processes by which we learn music, and reflective of the thought and physical processes we will want to draw on in performance.* Coming at the same thing from a slightly different angle, we recognize it as *time spent in mindful, carefully-constructed, pedagogically-sound activities in order to problem solve and/or reinforce execution of appropriate solutions toward a goal of easeful, secure, musical performance.*

To that end, deliberate practice for advancing musicians may involve specific activities such as score study and formal analysis, practicing associated technical patterns such as scales, arpeggios, etc. and working on the demands of the piece itself at the instrument. The most important elements of deliberate practice are that it is mindful, observant, disciplined, routine, distributed,[45] and effortful. In fact, the distribution and interleaving[46] of practice is much more important than many people realize, partially to provide opportunities for incubation, and also since effort expended in order to retrieve knowledge or execute a skill will more deeply entrench the learning (Brown et al., 2014, p. 79).

In other words, "easier" isn't better. The most efficient practice will, especially at first, often feel like more and more difficult work[47]—even though it will almost always get you to your goal more quickly and securely. Even if you have already become proficient with an earlier-stage solution to a related problem, progressing to new problems that will lead to higher levels of accomplishment may at first make the performance of the task feel less comfortable, less efficient. New motions must be found and learned to the point of sufficient comfort and ease through management of attention and rehearsal. Working on problematic combinations in isolation can help embed them into increasingly complex constructs, especially if recognizing how they will fit into those constructs is part of the work, which increases generalizability and encourages transfer. Alternating them with contrasting or similar constructs embeds them more firmly.

Practice that pushes performance beyond reliable limits may initially lead to mistakes as old habits are broken, misconceptions identified and dealt with, and adaptations rehearsed. Noticing you made an error is really, really important to beneficial progress, and to help avoid reinforcing it. Being able to identify *why* you made that error gets, literally, to the root of the problem, helping even more. It's especially informative if something goes "wrong" in the same way over and over—perhaps the passage resembles a previous or subsequent passage or behaves in an unexpected way. For example, a memory slip at measure 26 of the Aria from the Goldberg Variations might be because of its initial striking similarity to measure 6 (shown in Figure 5.13).

These moments happen constantly in music from the Western canon—parallel antecedent/consequent phrases, Sonata-Allegro forms, sequences—where we must know where we are and what comes next. Being able to compare, recognize, identify these similarities and differences long before muscle memory starts to take over is the best route to security. I think that the main reason Bach's music is so hard to memorize is that everything is melodically generated, and almost compulsively interconnected—inherently interleaved, if you will. I often refer to Bach as the first minimalist composer. The reiterations, reimaginations, and manipulations of a small

Figure 5.13. Bach, "Goldberg Variations," Aria, mm. 6–8 and 25–26.

bit of material over the scope of the whole work is part of his genius, and the source of much of the difficulty for us as performers.

Making the right choice about what to practice, how, and when, is a crucial aspect of a beneficial approach. Deliberately organizing and forming intentional mental chunks early in the process helps ensure that what you are observing and what you are doing is appropriate, applicable, and consistent with prior learning.

As discussed in the section on rule learning, organizational principles are actually of key importance to learning in general. Research shows that *organized material is easier to remember*[48] than disorganized, and that organizational attempts will be made subconsciously and spontaneously if not deliberately. If you haven't guessed already, my argument is that deliberate is—always—better. So why not do it early, consciously, and well? How much more efficient might our learning be if we systematically did this intentionally from the very start, maximizing each exposure and experience? Compare reading over notes from a class (the equivalent of what many do when they "practice" by playing through their piece from start to finish) to reorganizing them. Rather, constructing, organizing, and then shuffling flash cards, or explaining a concept to someone who has a bit of background knowledge but missed class that day or is a little confused will more firmly establish the knowledge and strengthen retrieval routes to it.

Just the fact that effort is made to organize information contributes to learning. The process of looking for a solution, even the act of retrieving knowledge that is subsequently discarded as unrelated, strengthens routes connecting to material made fresh by efforts to retrieve it. Those in public school education know about the benefit of the pretest—neither designed nor employed to test existing knowledge, but to "prime the pump," so to speak. Students who are pretested on something, even if they have no recollection later of having been pretested on it or of what they were asked, will have learned related material better than students who were not.

Distributed, interleaved practice also allows for more versatile application of the learning in later settings. This is of utmost importance to us as performers. Putting different learning experiences into play and coming at something from as many different angles as possible aid both learning and flexibility. For example, children who practiced throwing beanbags into baskets that were two feet *and* four feet away were ultimately more successful throwing beanbags into a basket that was three feet away than children who practiced an equal amount of time throwing beanbags only into a basket three feet away.[49] An important part of learning what something is, is learning what it's not. Part of learning to become successful at a skill is mastering skills that are on either side of it, while observing and evaluating different results of different actions. Mix up the problems, practice just until you start to feel like you have a handle on it—I usually aim for about three to five mindful, subsequent repetitions that feel secure and at least somewhat easeful—then move on, coming back to check in again at varying intervals.

Intuition may tell you to focus on many, many reiterations of a solution to a single problem, but mixing up problems or problem types (in balance with sufficient mindful reinforcement) actually improves your ability to group, discriminate, and form mental models, which improves the possibilities of success in performance. Massed practice may show rapid gains, but there is nothing to forestall the rapid forgetting that follows all learning.[50]

As pointed out in Brown et al. (2014), we can be poor judges of when we are learning and when we're not. When the going is more difficult and slower and doesn't feel productive we can be easily drawn to strategies that feel more fruitful—playing this passage five hundred times, for example—unaware that the gains made from these strategies are often temporary, and risky (both mentally and physically). We are also more likely to put in more work if there's a result we can see, or if we can understand the importance of what we're doing, and we'll place a higher value on what we produce if we had to work harder at it. Therefore, if you know *why* you're practicing something in a certain way, you're going to be more likely to do so; if you recognize that you might not see progress right away, that might help you persist; and if you invest in it, you will value it more.[51]

Massed practice, which is single-minded and involves rapid-fire repetition, might *feel* like a preferable strategy, but it's actually among the least productive. Retrieval practice, however, is much more effective. "*While the brain is not a muscle that gets stronger with exercise, the neural pathways that make up a body of learning do get stronger when the memory is retrieved and the learning is practiced.* Periodic practice arrests forgetting, strengthens retrieval routes, and is essential for hanging on to the knowledge you want to gain" (Brown et al., 2014, p. 49).[52]

German scientist Sebastian Leitner proposes a set of four "boxes" to help calculate the ideal amount of time for distribution of practice, based on unfamiliarity, difficulty, and ease of retrieval. In the first box is the stuff that is the newest or most difficult, practiced most frequently; in the second is the stuff you feel you've made some progress in, but is perhaps still a bit tenuous; in the third is that which is known quite well, executed or remembered with relative facility and ease, so reviewed less often; and in the fourth that which is mastered but warrants review/maintenance rehearsal, perhaps for an upcoming performance (Figure 5.14). If something "in" one of boxes 2 through 4 has deteriorated since the last time you worked on it, it is moved up a box, but never completely removed if it's important to retain, and practiced in various ways even if it's in the fourth box to avoid over-automaticity.

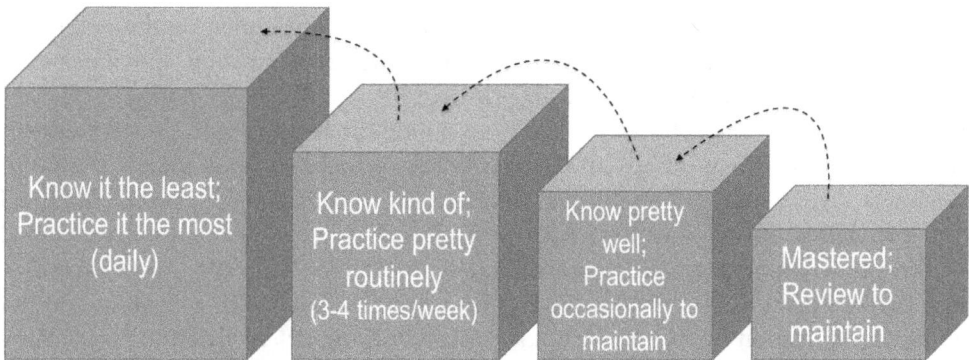

Figure 5.14. Leitner's boxes.

Being confused, working out of order, or working on something in a different way (practicing from memory at half tempo, chunking Alberti bass patterns into blocked chords, say, or practicing downbeat-notes only, etc.) changes our experience with the same material. A change from the typical or expected presentation of information introduces a difficulty—Brown et al. call it a disruption of fluency—which then forces the learner to work harder to construct an interpretation that makes sense. This makes new associations and links them to old ones, creating interconnected networks that bolster, support, and multiply cues for retrieval, increasing versatility and applicability. Repeated effortful recall or practice integrates the learning, so that interrelated ideas or sequences of motor skills become fused into a coherent whole, which can then be adapted and applied in later, differing settings. In the process of building skill, motor actions already acquired will take on special importance, as they provide the foundation for future adjustments (Ericsson, 2003, p. 69).

You also learn best when drawing on every aptitude and resource, rather than limiting the approach to a favored learning style. Whether you're a visual, aural, or kinesthetic learner, making use of all these aspects built on a foundation of mental/analytical understanding will lead to the deepest and most adaptable learning and secure memorization and performance. Neuroimaging shows that different types of practice use different parts of the brain. Employing as many processing routes as possible encodes the information more deeply, leading to consolidation and adaptability.

In all cases, our goal is to create, utilize, and reinforce the same mental processes in "practice" as will be used when "doing."

*Practice like you play
and you will
play like you practice*

Baddeley distinguishes between two types of rehearsal: maintenance (which we might consider "review") and elaborative.

Maintenance rehearsal works to hold the information at its current state, aiding recognition more than recall, but does not contribute to deepening the coding. It prevents forgetting but does not lead to better long-term learning. For musicians, maintenance rehearsal would be a play-through. You are still attending to the task at hand, playing mindfully and with awareness, and there is certainly benefit to this type of rehearsal, perhaps interleaved between the more elaborative, problem-solving types. This is also beneficial as the time of performance approaches, when all the "problems" of the piece have been solved, and appropriate solutions rehearsed to the point where they are familiar and comfortable. This type of rehearsal is merely practicing the process of playing from front to back with reliable execution and communication of your musical ideals. It is still important that you are, always, attending to what you are doing. Westney (2003) writes, "In the world of practicing, every choice we make has some effect. If we play through a piece rather idly, with nothing particular in mind, the effect is not neutral . . . in other words, *if you're not actively making things better, chances are you're making them worse*" (pp. 93–94).

*If you're not thinking,
you're not practicing*

Elaborative rehearsal, on the other hand, truly deepens the semantic processing, constructing various pathways to the material, which leads to better learning and easier retrieval. This type of rehearsal refines the mental processes you want to reinforce for reliable and musically flexible execution.

I would like to take this opportunity to stress the importance of continuing to pursue elaborative types of rehearsal even when pieces are mastered and ready for performance, and of maintaining mindfulness always. Besides the somewhat vague artistic goal of keeping our performances "fresh," there is great, and justified, concern over the potentially disastrous results of over-automatization. As noted earlier in this chapter, automatization comes with an associated loss of control of many relevant aspects (Ericsson, 2003, p. 75), as well as leaving mental space for the mind to wander, which rarely ends well.

Rather, even at an accomplished level of performance, musicians can continue to challenge themselves to pursue elaborative rehearsal in various ways:

- Practicing from memory starting from various points, out of order, or each hand alone (with*out* the other hand "doing its thing" on the fallboard or music

rack or knee; this creates intertwining interdependencies that can lead to outright disaster)
- Practicing at half tempo, especially if approached in a "musically saturated" way, so that every desired musical element is present and closely observed
- Working backward and/or in sections[53]
- Continuing to explore interpretive alternatives[54]
- Paying close attention to the thought process as well as making the connection between when-I-play-it-like-this-it-sounds-like-this
- Practicing memorized pieces mentally, away from the instrument
- Annotating a score based on a variety of interpretations from recordings (using a different colored pencil for each performer) and then trying to imitate each interpretation before returning to your own
- Practicing in layers (covered in more detail in chapter 6)
- Shaping middle or lower voices alone
- Practicing in different registers dynamics, articulations, etc.

Each of these approaches can also shed light on various elements that may have heretofore been overlooked, such as a countermelody buried in a middle voice or a timbral quality not yet considered.

I would like to go back and address one of the above bullet points in particular—when-I-play-it-like-this-it-sounds-like-this; the practice of self-monitoring and observation is of critical importance to effective practicing.

SELF-MONITORING AND SELF-EVALUATION

> *The design of situations in which individuals can receive immediate feedback is one of the essential prerequisites for deliberate practice activities that generalize across widely disparate domains.* (Ericsson & Towne, 2013, p. 894)

> *[R]eflection is not just on experience, but . . . is a form of experience itself. . . . When reflection is done [where mind and body are brought together], it can cut the chain of habitual thought patterns and preconceptions such that it can be an open-ended reflection, open to possibilities other than those contained in one's current representations of the life space.* (Varela et al., 2017, Loc 1712 of 7672)

"Self-observation of one's own performance, especially in informal contexts, has been shown to lead to systematic self-discovery. . . . Systematically varying certain aspects of functioning" can engage this aspect of learning, even when "vary[ing] effective performance tactics [so as] to enhance . . . concentration and creative solutions." In addition, self-monitoring (including self-recording) and setting of learning goals have been shown to increase persistence and achievement, and to improve problem solving, self-efficacy beliefs, feelings of self-satisfaction, and intrinsic interest in the task. Problem solvers *without* the ability to self-monitor and/or self-regulate will have "difficulty focusing on key elements of problems, envisioning solution goals, and self-monitoring their progress." These can lead to "faulty self-evaluative judgments, . . . [undermining] . . . self-motivation." On the other hand, a clear sense of the end point of a problematic task helps the learner self-monitor and accurately evaluate the effectiveness of various attempted solutions (Zimmerman & Campillo, 2003, pp. 243–255).

Self-observation is not important only to effective performance, as we may need to make adjustments within the performance itself, but crucial to effective practicing, although the areas of focus differ somewhat. Self-observation in practice involves noting the physical parameters of our executions and the effectiveness thereof. In performance self-observation focuses on the acoustic results of our actions, while we consciously avoid contemplation of anything in the past that bears no impact on future demands.

The two are inextricably linked. Self-observation in practice makes it much more likely we will notice our own mistakes, choose appropriate adaptations to correct those mistakes, and encode the appropriate thought and movement sequences to execute intended actions correctly. The observations of those movement sequences and their results become the focus of our self-observations in performance, allowing us to make almost instant adjustments in voicing, dynamic, pedaling, to meet our expressive goals.

In practice, making an error or producing an undesired sound can be just as informative as playing it correctly, *if we're paying attention* and take the appropriate steps to *ensure that that same mistake doesn't happen in the same way again*. And even despite all of our best efforts, *practice won't make perfect*. However, beneficial practice will increase the likelihood that the performance will be correct, and easeful, and minimize attentional demands so as to provide the mental space required to attend to your musical goals.

Often, the first stage of beneficial practice is *finding* the mistakes. If you operate under the assumption that the only practice that is going to help your performance improve is that which focuses on avoiding mistakes, you may find that either you are creating different types of interference with continuity and/or understanding, or that the mistakes just get better at hiding.

Rather than practicing so as to *avoid* mistakes—Westney (2003) says "a suppressed mistake is unfinished business" (p. 68)—practice so as to *find* them, through a free approach to the passage and a highly observational mind, and *fix* them. If you are paying attention, and take time immediately to process the mistake, learning will be more thorough, comprehensive, and long-lasting. Wrong notes "reveal hidden truths" (p. 102), and "honest mistakes save a lot of time . . . revealing the underlying, specific reason for a particular glitch—a reason the conscious mind may not have considered" (pp. 61–62). And don't be surprised if fixing one thing causes a new mistake to happen just after. As we learn to play a passage, each input and movement is programmed into a sequence, so that sometimes solving one thing makes something else wrong. Just keep fixing; eventually the mistake will "fall off" the end of the passage, and you're good to go.

The goal is to be *proactive* rather than *reactive*, in just the right amount, at just the right time. If you think about the solution to a problem too soon, you may make a different error in the passage leading up to the spot you are trying to fix. Too late, and the problem occurs again just as usual. Often the trickiest part of the solution is figuring out *what to think about when*.

In practice, all this self-observation and self-evaluation—not just of what you are doing, but what you are *thinking*—must be going on *the entire time* you're playing. On one hand is your observation of any mistake or difficulty, determining why you think the mistake happened, and deciding what you want to do differently. On the other hand is your observation of success—what you were actually *doing* during that success, then taking a kind of mental picture of this thought process plus its physical execution[55] so as to have a better chance at doing it the same way again. This type of attentional and executional security can result in a performance that, while still mindful and aware, is operating from a place of trust. This feels perhaps a bit more like a surfer riding the perfect wave, in perfect form. You're watching, you're steering, and you're enjoying the ride.

It is important in practice that we are (a) being completely honest with ourselves, and (b) refraining from judgment or negative self-talk. Consider adopting a somewhat Buddhist, yogi-like approach, coming always from a place of self-acceptance and playful self-discovery. If the mistake was a result of careless mindlessness, then by all means, *pay attention*. But if you *were* paying attention, and you were *playing* with intention, and the mistake happened anyway, then welcome it, never ignore it, thank it for showing up in the practice room instead of on stage (on stage just ignore it), and evaluate how it challenges prior actions or beliefs. For a while I had the joy of working with a fabulous yoga teacher. When you met a pose that was challenging in some way, she invited you to view it as an opportunity to say "hello" to a part of your body that maybe you hadn't been paying a lot of attention to. Forward bend is feeling a little less than friendly today? Say "hello" to your hamstrings. You're practicing and made a mistake that you haven't made before? "Hello there, missed chord, thank you so much for showing me that I don't really know you as well as I thought I did."

The result of all this thoughtful awareness is that we know what we're doing when we do it, and all (!) we have to do is remember where we are and what's next, and if the action has been properly reinforced, it will be there for us when we need it, like flipping a switch on a wall. This perhaps explains the biggest difference I have seen since revolutionizing the way I practice. I seem to be aware of where I am, and of my thought process just ahead of my hands, as if I'm that surfer riding that perfect wave. And just like a master surfer can change the angle of the board depending on the vagaries of the wave, I can adjust to the demands of the piece with security and focus.

This awareness also provides crucial adaptability for those times when perhaps things are not going as planned. Say you're performing on an instrument that has a stiffer action than the one you're used to. Your efforts to practice at home with a light, fleet touch in fast sparkling passagework would hopefully have included some practice with slow, ponderous weight as well as "ghosting," where you strive to touch all the correct keys in the correct order and rhythm, yet keeping your arms so light that there is actually no sound. Exploring a range from pure silence to the goal *pp (leggiero)*, and beyond (maybe even to *mf* or *f* and richly legato) while observing the physical movements and sensations as well as the result, gives you the capacity to make adjustments in touch and weight on the fly, producing more reliable results in less-than-reliable circumstances. It also forms foundations for later learning of passages that contain similar patterning but a different color or timbre.

In summary, we want practice to be *deliberate, effortful, distributed, goal-oriented, problem-solving in nature, and interleaved*, while observing and evaluating the mental processes, details of physical execution, and the acoustic results. The kind of practice that works will often feel like it's taking longer than the kind of practice that seems easier, but ultimately will have quicker and more reliable results. Resist the urge to take what seems like the easier way, and remember the graph earlier showing linear vs. exponential progress (Figure 4.21). Important elements include setting goals, asking yourself questions, finding the right spacing and distribution (which may vary on a given day as well as over the course of learning a piece), making sure to take the time to find meaning, and practicing with awareness and understanding. Having a plan; thinking before doing; anticipating problems, questions, and their answers; prioritizing and ordering new concepts; and continually evaluating one's organizational paradigms makes all of the chosen actions intentional, mindful, and that much more productive. Make opportunities to re-view and re-learn, coming at information from as many angles as possible. When it starts to feel like the returns are diminishing, take a break and/or work on something else. Remember: "Taking the time to learn something in the proper way not only saves time later, but allows the learner to be better able to solve more complicated problems, more quickly, and in a more effective/successful way" (Brown et al., 2014, p. 47).

NOTES

1. Ericsson (2003) even claims that, once a *sufficient* level of experience and knowledge have been achieved, attaining what he would call the level of "expertise," a relationship between additional experience and performance is relatively weak (p. 74), although an increase in efficiency of progress in surmounting the challenges of a new situation may continue to develop.

2. A Piageten approach, where meaning is generated through the interaction between experience and concept.

3. This and the following found and paraphrased/expanded from Huber, 2013.

4. With the implication that more refined or specific activities would/might take more time, which certainly seems to be the case with the development of instrumental ability for most.

5. We've all witnessed catastrophic errors in the final chord, or the last few measures. This perhaps explains why many of them occur.

6. This can actually present a bit of irony when considering brain imaging results of experts performing acts within their domain of expertise, where it looks like they are "thinking," mentally "doing," *less*.

7. Multiple authors and studies demonstrate superior chunking ability and an associated improvement in memory of said chunks within the expert's domain, *when the information being processed is meaningful rather than random* (Simon & Chase, in Ericsson & Towne, 2013, p. 892; Vicente & Wang, 1998, p. 34).

8. K. Anders Ericsson, Malcolm Gladwell.

9. This connection between thinking and doing, automatically, has become painfully aware for me in some unusual ways. For example, learning to play from a tablet using a pedal turner took much practice to coordinate the timing of my left foot on the pedal turner in a separate time-plane from what my feet are used to doing at the piano. And tapping the side of the screen to "turn" a page sometimes now results in me tapping the right margin of an actual score and then wondering why the page isn't turning. Also, I seem to have no problem when using music notation software typing 1-2-3-4 for right-hand fingerings (using fingers 5-4-3-2 in the left hand), but all kinds of problems when typing them for the left hand.

10. Such a strong argument for how we should, nay, must, involve beginning musicians in evaluation of their own progress and strategizing their own solutions.

11. Such as in variable priority training, discussed above.

12. Another way in which we are often misled is in our evaluation of our own musicality during performance. A common experience is believing you are projecting a much more varied expression than you actually are. It seems that the *thought* of playing louder, or softer, or slower, means that we believe our playing to be louder, or softer, or slower than it actually is. Truly listening and observing requires a level of objective observation and the ability to project our listening ear out, in a way, into the room. One strategy I have found to be particularly helpful is to listen to and react to my sound as if it were a second musician in the room with whom I am collaborating. Sounds a little bizarre, maybe, but it has proven quite effective. Of course, this is me thinking this is so, so it's hard to know for sure. :-)

13. A really good metaphor for "deliberate, effortful" practice that ultimately does nothing to facilitate learning or progress. That dog is working awfully hard to bark and bark and bark at that bone, and might do it for hours, but none of the barking will bring him any closer to that bone.

14. Of course this depends a great deal on the musician, and the context. Many more specific manifestations of this as a conscious practice is discussed at length below.

15. The eye-hand span is the distance between the note that is being looked at and the note that is being played; the perceptual span is the region around the note being looked at from which useful information is being extracted.

16. I'm tempted for this section, and the one on "deliberate practice," just to send you all to read Brown et al.'s *Make It Stick* (2014) first. Go ahead. I'll wait.

17. Memory errors can result from errors of omission (failures to initially encode information) and/or commission (failures to correctly retrieve it; Laney, 2013).

18. My use of the word "memory" here is referring to our ability to learn and remember new information; not necessarily in terms of memorized performance, which will be addressed later in the book.

19. Brown et al. (2014) actually assign an important role to forgetting, which will be discussed at length in the section below on distributed practice.

20. Tillman et al. (2000) is worth investigating if you find this topic interesting. Some interesting tangents: 1) An established musical context generates expectancies for the passages that follow, and expected chords are more quickly processed (understood) than unexpected ones. 2) Certain chords seem inherently and surprisingly related; for example, C major and E major triads will stimulate "phasic activation" in both top-down and bottom-up activations, more strongly than C major and D major, probably because the C major and E major triads share a tone and C and D don't. It would seem that composers were intuitively aware of this connection; there will be tonal pieces with mediant relationships (Beethoven Waldstein, for example) much more frequently and sooner than tonal pieces with secondary relationships. 3) These authors also claim that listeners are more aware of modulations that move counterclockwise on the circle of 5ths than those that move clockwise—which triggers curiosity on my part if composers were aware of this as well, and move clockwise when they want the modulations to sound smoother, and counterclockwise when they want them to be more noticeable (Tillman et al., 2000, pp. 888–903).

21. So, thinking *and* playing.

22. Distributed and interleaved practice are the two best methods for what might be called "deliberate forgetting," and the subsequent reconstruction of information so as to deepen both retrieval and recall structures. See Deliberate, Distributed, Interleaved Practice, below.

23. I have often wondered whether the ease of information input on ubiquitous laptops and other devices interferes with long-term learning. Back when I was an undergraduate—a long, long time ago—I spent a lot of time rewriting and reorganizing my handwritten notes from class lectures. This took a fair bit of time, but also helped me to sort out and process the information, which seemed to go a long way toward my remembering and successful retrieval of it. The mere movement of a cursor and typing in of information does not seem to make the same contribution, especially if you're a good typist, which means you are not thinking about what you're typing as much as if you're a poor one.

24. It might be helpful just to adopt a strategy of the harder the piece, the more you need to know about it.

25. Like the old adage: Whether you believe you *can* or you *can't*, you're right.

26. Meaning, the type of learning of which you have conscious awareness (thefreedictionary.com/explicit+learning).

27. Brown et al. (2014), p. 88.

28. D♭ major is actually the first scale I teach, often to young beginners; B major the second. They are the easiest for students to recognize fingering patterns. F♯/G♭ don't cause problems for young beginners if they are learning them by rote, which they do. Peter, Peter Pumpkin Eater (see Appendix A) is actually a favorite for students in their first lessons and presents no cognitive dissonance whatsoever. Understanding these rules also makes some of the more bizarre constructions much more accessible, such as the left-hand fingerings for E♭ harmonic and melodic minor, since the chunking is the same as for the natural form.

29. For this reason, I always insist that students start with the "correct" finger (in this case, 3) so that when they go on to play multiple octaves the fingering is the same.

30. Pretz et al. (2003), pp. 21–23.

31. I have been known to call practicing "looking for mistakes."

32. They also claim creative thinkers to be somewhat impulsive, even hostile! These characteristics perhaps are not as desirable.

33. Violations of expectations will cause delays in navigating to a solution, which explains why for most people it's harder to learn the notes to a piece by Debussy than one by Mozart, and harder to learn the notes to a piece by Schoenberg than by Debussy.

34. "Represent"—short for "knowledge representation," a common term in cognitive psychology referring to the method used for encoding knowledge and/or semantic information.

35. I learned a note wrong in a Debussy prelude in 1987. When relearning this prelude in 2011, I memorized it in a day. Feeling quite proud of myself, I reconsulted the score to make sure I had memorized all of the musical markings, and noticed a note was circled. Upon closer consideration, I realized that I had just relearned the same mistake . . . twenty-four years later.

36. Strategies devised from previous experience with similar problems; this "mental shortcut" can form a path and ease the cognitive load required in solving a problem.

37. My new favorite hashtag is #CovidRuinsEverything; but without it I might still be at the beginning of the third chapter. So maybe not *everything*.

38. Awareness and understanding of one's own thought processes.

39. Something I'm not always sure about when talking about Tchaikovsky.

40. Learning and memory is consolidated in the hippocampus, which is able to generate new neurons throughout a person's life (called neurogenesis). Neurogenesis actually starts before the learning activity starts and continues beyond the end of the activity, showing that just the *intent* to learn generates new neurons, and suggests that it also plays a role in the beneficial effects of spaced, effortful retrieval toward long-term retention (Brown et al., 2014, p. 171).

41. For example, producing a projected melody against a softer accompaniment, three or four rates of simultaneous rhythmic motion, incorporating before-the-beat ornamentation, managing multiple voices of independent articulation patterns in multiple-voice fugues, etc.

42. I've also seen this preparedness cause interference, such as an intermediate or early advanced musician learning a piece with more shifts of position than they are used to, and they start playing simple constructions in the piece in a more complicated way unnecessarily.

43. Some examples of integrated lessons and practice plans are provided in Appendix C.

44. Developmental, especially important when this differs from chronological age.

44. Meaning you don't try necessarily to solve each problem 100 percent before you move on to the next one and that you come back to it over and over again in short- and long-term time distribution.

46. In effect, leaving the task at hand and weaving in the practicing of other challenges before returning, etc.

47. And perhaps be more than a bit annoying to listen to, hence the rumors of my "bashing around" referenced in the introduction.

48. Baddeley (1990).

49. Brownet al. (2014, p. 49).

50. Brown et al. (2014) theorize around 70 percent is lost fairly quickly.

51. Guy Raz talks about how value judgments inspire extra effort at https://www.npr.org/transcripts/443433645, and then there's Dan Ariely's Ted Talk "What Makes Us Feel Good About Our Work": https://www.ted.com/talks/dan_ariely_what_makes_us_feel_good_about_our_work/transcript.

52. This is important to remember for all learning, but really comes into play for us when memorizing a piece for performance, addressed in more detail below.

53. This is how I actually have my students learn and memorize almost everything. If we only start from the beginning, we will inadvertently practice the beginning more, and be more "fresh" while doing so, meaning our work will be more focused and productive. The result is what I call *EOPD* (End of the Piece Disease). Better, rather, to practice that which is harder, or rarer, first and most.

54. I actually do this quite systematically for repetitive forms, where I come up with a few subtle variations in terms of shaping, dynamics, timing, etc. but don't "decide" which I'm going to do when until I'm actually performing.

55. Westney's "feelmage"; more on this in chapter 7.

6

CONCEPTUAL SOLUTIONS TO TECHNICAL PROBLEMS

(They Are All Technical Problems)

Musical problems are technical problems. (Iott, 2014)

PRACTICE TOOLS AND STRATEGIES FOR MORE CHALLENGING PROBLEMS

Much of the learning we do at the beginning stages of many domains is implicit, where we learn much just through exposure. The learning of our native language and of our culture's musical syntax falls under this category, where acculturation and the individual's self-directed attempts to move from "babble" to understanding happen spontaneously. Initial progress for beginners embarking on learning to play a musical instrument, especially if they have benefited from broad and deep early-childhood music acculturation experiences, can seem effortless, almost magical. As learners progress, though, in any domain, improvements will almost always become more gradual and require increasingly disciplined efforts. Without adjustments in problem-solving and practice efforts, many learners will, usually around the intermediate stage, reach some kind of plateau.

At the same time, our enjoyment of a pursuit is usually best sustained if both the challenges and expertise become increasingly complex, with a clear structure and logical, well-paced progression from one stage to the next. Opportunities to stretch current knowledge must be bolstered by developments and refinements of our problem-solving strategies coupled with increased discipline and reward so as to preserve motivation. How we sequence and pace these challenges is perhaps the most important consideration. I've mentioned the positive impact of a desirable level of difficulty—a challenge that can be overcome through increased effort, which triggers encoding and retrieval processes that support learning and comprehension. On the other hand, if the difficulty is too excessive—when the learner feels s/he does not have sufficient background knowledge, skill, or the resources with which to meet the challenges—these effects are not seen, often resulting in frustration, disengagement, even withdrawal from the domain. This can be countered both through careful selection and sequencing of repertoire and through equipping the learner with appropriate preparatory and practice strategies to help him/her feel empowered and capable of meeting the challenges.

Of course, there are learners who thrive when faced with highly challenging situations. This is a good example of when personality and motivation play an important role.

This is probably as good a time as any to point out that just about anything we are working on in a practice room is a "problem." Some of these can be easily identified as such: Where are the subject entrances in our fugue, how do we want to bow this passage, how does rhythm x interact with rhythm y, etc.? We might even try to categorize problems as technical (physical) versus mental (conceptual) and overlook *musical* problems entirely.

The thing is, every problem is in *some* way a technical problem, and many solutions originate in how we understand and plan for them. Phrasing, balance, voicing, inflection, rhythmic vitality, articulation, the slight adjustments in pitch or timing we might make to highlight a particular expressive element; these might be considered *musical* problems but require physical mastery and finesse—technique—to execute and convey. It really comes down to (a) this is what you want and (b) this is how you do it.

I had this book well under way a couple of years ago, when I was asked to teach a seminar on practice strategies for intermediate and high school pianists at Interlochen Arts Camp, where I am a member of the piano faculty. A result of that class was my realization that I needed to reorganize the book, in no small way due to the insight revealed by the following activity.

We began the class hour brainstorming, with the students calling out situations or problems they have encountered that required systematic practice. Next we went through the list of problems and determined whether each of the problems was primarily conceptual or physical. At this point many realized, much to their surprise, that a great majority of the problems were much more conceptual in nature than they had thought. Even those requiring efforts to increase dexterity, facility, and accuracy have structures and elements that can be aided by mental chunking, deeper understanding, and/or well-divided attention and planning. One could almost see the lightbulbs popping on all around the room.

A long time ago I read Eloise Ristad's *A Soprano On Her Head*, and was first exposed to the idea of mental practice. I was intrigued, so decided to try it. If I encountered a difficulty in whatever I was practicing, I would stop, close my eyes, and try to "play" it in my head. I almost always *made the exact same mistake*. Talk about lightbulbs! Our fingers, hands, arms, breath, tongue, lips, *only do what we tell them to* [insert mind blown emoji here]. *And*, if we are not providing them with adequate information, they will, in fact, just make something up. Sometimes we get lucky and our hands find the right notes as if by magic—which can be informative in its own way and will be something I discuss in the section on gesture » detail—but if we cannot think it, or hear it, it's probably a good idea not to put any trust in it.

I also found that finding my way to a viable, *personally convicted* interpretation generally involves careful analysis and a fair bit of experimentation. Understanding the implications of harmonic progression, dissonance and consonance, motivic development, and stylistic norms helps the musician make informed decisions that can be justified through a comprehensive understanding of the music itself. Extending a sequence by a few more iterations, or transposing a chord progression that is persistently giving you trouble, deepens your understanding of what is in the score. Score study—where the musician analyzes elements of form, harmonic progression, motivic development—and listening to recordings with heightened musical discernment are beneficial prepractice activities. They also lay a groundwork for mental and physical chunking, conceptual mapping, and think-it-then-play-it practice strategies to be outlined in upcoming sections.

Mental imagery practice has already been discussed in chapter 2, the introduction to the intermediate musician. It can be a bit more expansive, and rigorous, as the musician develops. The importance of a solid technical and aural foundation cannot be overstated. The most productive practicing happens if you can hear whether you played what was on the page. And if you cannot play arpeggios and alternating chord patterns in 16th notes at quarter = MM. 120, how are you going to play Prokofiev's Prelude in C major? If you can't build a dominant 7th chord, how are you going to play a series of successive ones as you might find in the music of Debussy? At this level, if you can't *hear* it, *play* it, *identify* it,[1] how will you even know what "it" is, much less remember it or be able to perform it reliably?

An important and somewhat nuanced set of considerations an advancing musician needs to know and be able to apply are the elements of stylistic performance. Baroque repertoire is replete with recurring melodic and motivic structures and is assembled through the layering of fairly equal voices. A successful interpretation requires phrasing and thematic identification through careful application of articulation patterns and oh-so-subtle manipulations of time, and incorporates terraced dynamics rather than graduated ones. The stylistic forms of expression for Classical-era repertoire are quite different. Here the musician ideally focuses on elegant phrasing, subtle accompaniment figures, dynamic contrasts and gradations without excess, rubato only at structural moments, etc. As musicians we must bring all types of information to the score while gleaning every detail it has to offer, always striving to move beyond the notes and rhythms and playing with understanding of form, harmony, *and* style. I have heard young, beginning musicians play "Old MacDonald" with subtle phrasing and a beautiful ritardando at the end, and advanced musicians playing Mozart's "Rondo in D major" like they are late for a movie date with their friends and have cotton wool in their ears. And yes, some musicians are just naturally, well, *musical*, and some are not. But these subtleties can be taught, from the beginning, and reinforced at every stage.

Because the majority of the "problems" we need to solve in the practice room seem to be more of the mind than of the body, we will start there. Practice strategies that support our conceptual understanding of the piece and how to play it include practicing in layers, refining what we want to think about when, think-it-then-play-it chunks, scaffolding, and specific mental practice strategies as they relate to mapping and memorization.

LAYERS

Much music, in one way or another, involves layers. In contrapuntal music, these layers are inherent and obvious, with all voices being generally melodically driven and intricately intertwined. In pieces like the Bach suites, or even intermediate-level minuets or polonaises, these layers are perhaps not exactly equal, but the strata are still clear. Taking them apart and practicing in individual voices gives us the mental space to make important, informed decisions regarding articulation, tone color, and each voice's relative role. At the same time, if we want to present those myriad voices in a way that is discernible to the listener yet still idiomatic, slight manipulations of tone, generally through articulation[2] rather than dynamic, are of crucial importance. When working on inventions, sinfonias, and fugues, attention to each voice and recognition of the thematic and motivic relationships drives articulation decisions, which might also drive fingering choices. But we can work on individual voices, and then voice pairs, without making those fingering decisions just yet. This helps place them in our "mind's ear"—audiation. If we can audiate these voicings and their characteristic articulations, it is much easier to realize them with the appropriate hands when it comes time to put it all together. And while we certainly want to design a plan for consistent fingerings—perhaps most especially in Baroque repertoire, where the inherent intricacies can cause all kinds of difficulties without careful planning—spending some time using alternatives, especially in these exploratory stages, is not a waste of time or even a deterrent, *as long as we are not practicing in such a way as to be reinforcing them to the point of automaticity.* We have all made fingering mistakes in performance, and we want to recover from them seamlessly, without them being audible to the listener. This type of flexibility, to the appropriate degree, is an aid rather than an impediment, as long as it is *mindful*.

It is also a good opportunity to link our analysis goals with practice goals. If you are working on a fugue, a good place to start is to mark up two copies of the score, one according to voice, and one according to subject, countersubject 1, and countersubject 2. (See Figures 6.1 and 6.2.)

Some examples of how we might practice this "in layers":

- Practicing each voice alone,
  - then in voice pairs with one voice in each hand (Soprano/right + Alto/left; Alto/right + Bass/Left; Soprano/right + Bass/left);
    - finally in voice pairs with the voices in the hands as written (considering the full texture);
- Practicing all the way through playing just the subjects or subject-driven voices,
  - then subject + one or the other of the countersubjects.

These approaches help us work on the entire piece in some form hands together right from the start, while developing awareness of how the voices and subject/countersubject material are being deployed. By the time all the voices are put together, the formal process of the piece is well understood, laying a reliable foundation for memory and performance. If you add, to your identifications of the subject, analysis

CONCEPTUAL SOLUTIONS TO TECHNICAL PROBLEMS 147

Figure 6.1. Bach, "Fugue in B-flat major," *WTC I*, BWV 866, mm. 1–12, by voice.

Figure 6.2. Bach, "Fugue in B-flat major," *WTC I*, BWV 866, mm. 1–12, by subject, countersubjects.

of the key areas and cadences, your understanding of the process and piece is even more thorough and multilayered.

This leads to an important tangent—reinforcing the already-mentioned benefit of practicing hands together as much as possible, as early as possible, at every level. Remember, brain imaging shows that the areas or degree of activity in the brain when playing individual hands are *not* the same as the areas or degree of activity when both hands are playing at the same time, even when the imaging for each hand is overlaid. And while we all probably know that the right side of the brain "talks" to the left side of the body and vice versa,[3] to play both hands at the same time requires the two sides of the brain to "talk" to each other. If we learn one hand of a piece to a certain level of completion, and then the other hand, and then put it hands together, we will often find that it is not really any easier to put it hands together than it might have been at the beginning. Practicing hands separately is certainly valid and can be beneficial, but it should be considered *a strategy toward attaining a primary purpose* beyond "practicing hands separately." And then we must find a way to put it hands together *in some fashion* as soon as possible. This might mean playing one hand while chanting or tapping the rhythm of the other, which is an excellent intermediary, as it requires us to read both parts, but only needing to atend to around half the information of one of those parts.

Salvucci and Taatgen's theory of threaded cognition could also perhaps be seen as contributing to this philosophy, as playing hands together may force us to move from declarative processing to procedural processing sooner, allowing for more efficient multitasking with less cognitive interference.

Perhaps this can be achieved by a general goal of trying to spend as much or more time hands together as hands alone in a single practice session. If you practice something in one hand, put it together. Then practice the other hand, and put it together again. The put-together times might not go particularly well, and we want to be sure that we are not inadvertently reinforcing errors, but they do serve important functions in teaching our brain to attend to both at once.

Linear analysis also helps students see the bigger picture. Stepwise motion governs the sequences shown in Figure 6.3, and lays the foundation for the disjunct melodic motion on the surface of Bach's first duet, shown in Figure 6.4.[4]

Consciously seeking out the groupings of the Gestalt—especially simplicity, similarity, and continuation—over long-term lines makes these encodings deliberate, earlier in the process, contributing to musical and secure performance. You might practice structural notes only to highlight the longer phrase lines, play them an octave above or below in conjunction with the full figuration,[5] or even try to sing the structural line while playing. This not only informs musical interpretation,[6] but leads and guides memory.

In Classical-era repertoire layering practice might involve chunking accompaniment figures into chord structures first while learning the piece hands together, then working left hand alone[7] to refine the ease or facility required to play the Alberti or arpeggiated patterning with appropriate weight and voicing, and then putting it all together again. Practicing chord patterning with recurrent notes over-

CONCEPTUAL SOLUTIONS TO TECHNICAL PROBLEMS 149

Figure 6.3. Bach, "Invention No. 1," structural realization.

Figure 6.4. Bach, "Vier Duetten," Duet 1, first subject statement.

held (tied) as shown in Figure 6.5 can help draw attention to the longer line and encourage reading through comparison and context rather than in isolation.

We can also find and practice layers with many Romantic-era, Impressionistic, and contemporary pieces.

In the Brahms Romance, Op. 118 No. 5, we can identify at least four layers: melody, bass, and middle voice(s). Practicing each layer alone, so as to focus on dynamic, weight, and phrasing, and then pairing the voices, working on attaining

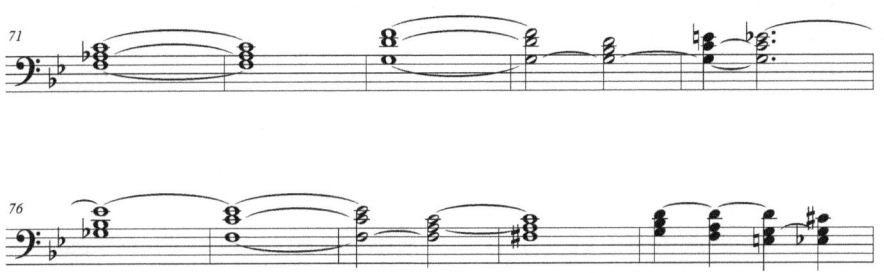

Figure 6.5. Mozart, "Piano Sonata in B-flat major," K. 333, mm. 71–80, Alberti bass in chunked chord patterns, common tones tied.

optimal balance according to their relative roles, can give us access to the detailed hierarchy and supple phrasing required to convey the musical elements of the piece well when performed in its entirety. Asking the student to rewrite in four-part score notation (as shown in Figure 6.6) can be a valuable exercise, revealing the invertible counterpoint and interplay of voicing.

Figure 6.6. Brahms, "Romance," Op. 118 No. 5, mm. 1–4 and 9–13, open score, showing parallelisms and invertible counterpoint.

While layering is an obvious and excellent practice for learning Baroque music, you can see that much of the repertoire is often contrapuntal on some level. The process of copying out as in Figure 6.6 requires making decisions about what belongs to which voice, exposes parallelisms and/or invertible counterpoint, and also reveals some of the intricate phrasing that might otherwise be overlooked. While it is a time-consuming process (you may have noticed that I skipped rewriting measures 5–8 because they behave much like measures 1–4 with just a little added figuration in the middle voices), it is time well spent. It was practicing according to this layered approach that led me to discover the countermelody in this well-known passage in a different Brahms piece, the Intermezzo from Op. 118, shown in Figure 6.7.

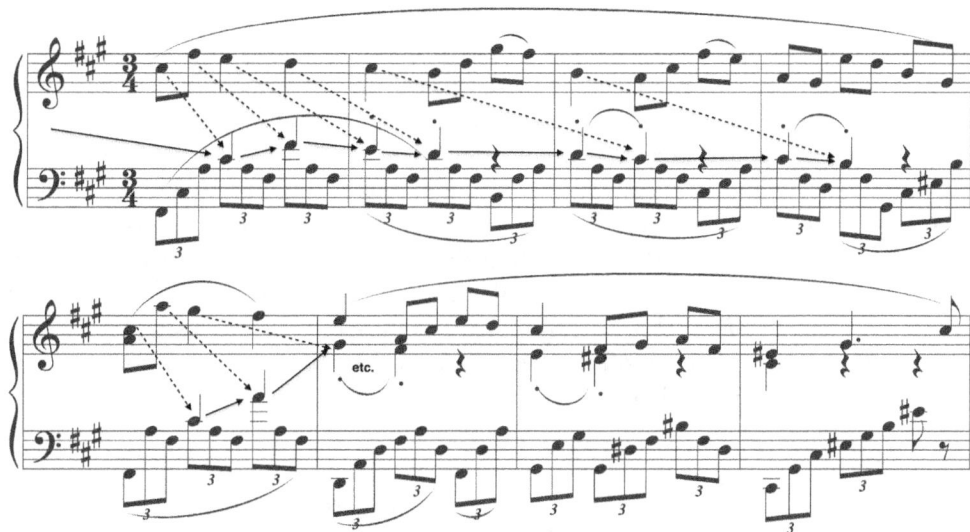

Figure 6.7. Brahms, "Romance," Op. 118 No. 2, mm. 49–56, melody/countermelody canon.

WHAT TO THINK ABOUT WHEN

One of the things we are figuring out as we learn a piece is what we need to think about when so as to execute effectively and reliably. Intentionally chunking these elements into meaningful units mentally and, whenever possible, physically, will help this learning take less time and be that much more secure. Our goal is that when performing we will be able to "follow" a piece like we follow a well-traveled route—we know where we are, where we came from, and what we need to do next, and also have a sense of the big picture, which includes future turns, durations, and alternatives if we encounter a roadblock or a detour. Not a GPS-directed version, where we can see only our car in our driveway and one house on either side, but a route with deep familiarity and alternate possibilities if needed. If we follow this well-traveled route with too much automaticity, we might find ourselves in the musical equivalent of driving to work when we meant to go to the grocery store, such as playing the Recapitulation of a Sonata form movement when we are supposed to be in the Exposition.

★ *You Are Here*

Rather, you know where you are going, and you have rehearsed the execution of each twist and turn along the way as responses to mindful cues, so that the performance itself feels almost like flipping a series of switches as you walk down a long hallway, and the lights behind you turn themselves off as you pass so that you don't need to worry about them anymore.

If the "going" is level and clear, we can look a bit further ahead, more toward the horizon; if we find ourselves on uneven terrain, perhaps riddled with rocks and tree roots, we might be watching a bit closer to each step, as when crossing a river by stepping from rock to rock.

In a passage such as the opening of the first Prelude from *Book I* of the *Well-Tempered Clavier*, shown in reduction in Figure 4.20, it is easy to see that a meaningful unit is one chord per measure, so we read, and think, a measure at a time. In a passage such as the one from the Dussek Sonatina in Figure 6.9, we are perhaps reading/thinking in half note chunks. And in the first movement of Schumann's "Kreisleriana," disjunct surface figuration disguises a complex compound melody. The result is we will probably have to work a little harder to find and keep track of the horizontal voices. This plus the technical difficulty of the passage means we may be reading/chunking an 8th note at a time at first. Melody + countermelody in parallel motion shown with arrows in Figure 6.8.[8]

Figure 6.8. Schumann, "Kreisleriana," Op. 16, I., mm.1–5, layering.

Once we have established our chosen rate of observation (which will most likely vary over the course of a piece according to varying mental and physical demands), we can practice accordingly, striving to chunk visually and mentally even when we cannot physically "hold" the chunks in our hands, although in some cases, such as for the first Prelude, we can.

A meaningful unit might also be understood as conceptual chunking, and includes things like recognizing/identifying scales, recurrent patterns, and/or arpeggiated or disjunct chord structures. The conceptual chunks shown in Figure 6.9 then serve to provide a type of map to the piece, discussed a bit further below.

Even when reading irregularly contoured scale passages, noticing on what beat or what part of the beat the change of direction occurs, or on what scale degree, is both easier and more conceptually relevant than counting 16ths, identifying specific note names, or even counting iterations. This is shown in the annotations of Figure 6.10.

CONCEPTUAL SOLUTIONS TO TECHNICAL PROBLEMS 153

Figure 6.9. Dussek, "Sonatina in E-flat major," Op. 19/20, mm. 19–23, conceptual chunking.

Figure 6.10. Kuhlau, "Sonatina in C major," Op. 20, No 1, III., mm. 14–35, conceptual chunking.

More complicated repertoire and more difficult challenges require higher-order thinking and will benefit from carefully constructed and sequenced practicing strategies. For something like the "Kreisleriana" excerpt, we can build the piece one layer at a time (Figure 6.11), and then work on mental chunking through think-it-then-play-it practice (Figure 6.12).

This type of practice helps the musician untangle the threads of an intricate or complex texture, establishing a hierarchy of melody, bass, and accompaniment, which can serve as an important foundation for memory. I will return to this concept in a few pages in the section on scaffolding.

mm. 1-5, structure building stage 1

mm. 1-5, melody + countermelody rhythmically displaced

mm. 1-5, melody, countermelody and bassline

Figure 6.11. Schumann, "Kreisleriana," I. structural points and layering.

CONCEPTUAL SOLUTIONS TO TECHNICAL PROBLEMS

THINK IT THEN PLAY IT

The benefits of mental imagery incorporated into physical practice were discussed in chapter 2, and think-it-then-play-it practicing has been presented already with some intermediate-level examples. It seems worthwhile to revisit it here, with a few more challenging excerpts.

Depending on the harmonic rhythm and surface difficulties of the passage, we might work in single beats, in tempo (or close), thinking each group before we play it, then in two-beat groups. Because the pickup is so important to the physical gesture, it is included in each group.

mm. 1-2, one-beat groups

mm. 1-2, two-beat groups

Figure 6.12. Schumann "Kreisleriana," I. "think-it-then-play-it," one- and two-beat groups.

A couple of really important things to emphasize here: First, you *"think"* each gesture *before you play* it. This "thinking" is imagining yourself playing it, no finger wiggling or tapping or physical motions at all, but your brain processing the input and imagining the motions. Only after you've "played" it correctly in your mind do you play it. (You may even find yourself needing to think it two or three times before you think it correctly.) You can work from one-beat groups to two-beat groups to four-beat groups,[9] thinking each group before you play. You will hopefully notice, when you put it all together, that you are now reliably thinking ahead, just the right amount, and the gesture has been programmed in to respond to the thought. (And there's probably no need for eight-beat groups, although there might be; the specifics of the situation and what you are observing dictate these kinds of decisions.)

Second important thing: notice the overlap. Each group starts where we previously stopped so that we don't practice a gap into our mental- or muscle-memory.

It is also important whenever possible to link our analytical awareness with thinking-ahead strategies, working in clearly defined and predetermined sections.[10] After the thought and then the execution, the final step is to observe the result in audiational memory and determine whether the execution was effective. If it was, ask/remind yourself of what you thought, what you did, how it felt, how it sounded.[11] If not, ask yourself why you think it didn't work, come up with how you want to try it again, "think" that, then play it again. This loop is shown in Figure 6.13.

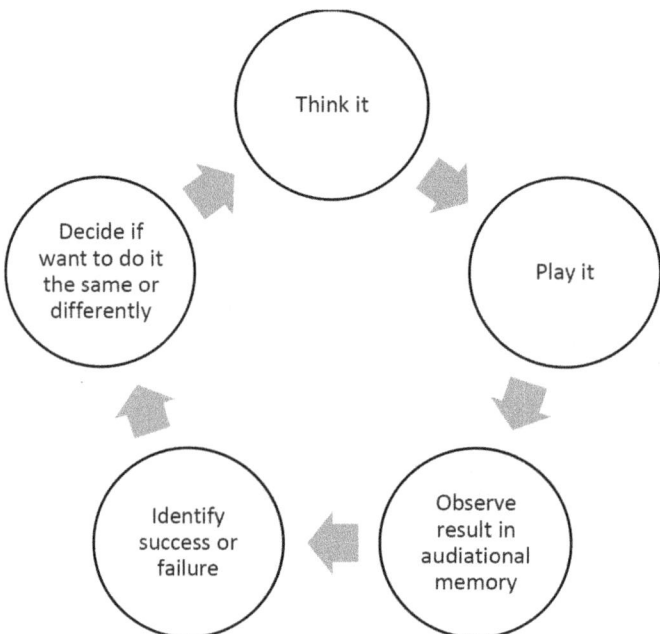

Figure 6.13. Think-it-then-play-it-loop.

You will notice that this practice:

- expands on the earlier-discussed audiation pause, and the theory that we learn in the "gap";
- gives you an opportunity to remember what went well and strategize to improve on what didn't;
- avoids excessive, mindless repetition, which only builds tension and may reinforce errors; and
- teaches you to think ahead, which helps enormously when putting it all together.

And rather than needing to repeat ten or fifty or five hundred times, a few mindfully prepared and observed repetitions will often provide sufficient reinforcement.

My feeling is that if I got it right, it felt comfortable, and *I knew it was going to be right even before I did it*, that's enough for the moment. If you got it right but weren't sure that was going to be the case until after the fact, do it again.

You don't know it 'til you know it

Alternating these think-it-then-play-it strategies, at tempo, with slow deliberate practice is an especially good approach for solving problems that stem from needing to process a lot of information quickly.

Bugs et al. (2013) refer to this type of approach as practicing with implementation intentions, discussed in the previous section on long-term memory and retrieval. To review: a person can systematically formulate a strategy or plan *during encoding* to maximize the likelihood of retrieval upon the onset of an expected cue. In fact, implementation intentions can produce automatic initiation of a desired action, bolstering linkages between cues and intentions. *The best retrieval cues are those that include both the target and the action* (Bugs et al., 2013, pp. 270–273). So, at the risk of repeating myself, what we are thinking isn't just reading the notes on the page, but *imagining ourselves playing them, with all of the musical elements included*. Again, we turn to cognitive studies and brain imaging to support this approach.

When observing someone do something that we ourselves can do, our brain will trigger signals in many of the same areas of the brain as if we were doing it ourselves. This is why you might find yourself kicking when watching a soccer game or moving as if to apply the brake as a passenger if the driver needs to stop suddenly.[12] Mental rehearsal results in motor imagery, providing an opportunity for your central nervous system to evaluate the consequences of imagined action, and to prepare properly for execution thereof (Bangert, 2012, pp. 175–176). Practicing *mentally* that which we want to perform *physically* not only helps save your chops if you're a brass player, your lips if you play oboe, or your hands and arms if you're a pianist or a string player, it also ensures that when we *do* something, it is done mindfully. Palmer (2012) also shows that mental practice is particularly beneficial for tasks with a higher cognitive load and has a positive impact on memorization as a result of analytical pre-study. The benefits include helping the musician memorize unfamiliar music, facilitating creation and storage of auditory and/or motor images, and aid in forming a mental representation as the piece is practiced (pp. 44–45).

One of the theories about why good readers are poor memorizers is that the connection between what they see and their means of execution is so efficient they almost don't need to think about what they are reading. I think this is especially true if musicians are taught to read music too early, before they have developed proper audiation skills, and approach notes-to-instrument in a purely digital way.[13] No matter how strong our reading ability, if we *analyze, understand, and think before playing*, our awareness of what is going on in the piece and our rehearsal of planning before executing can only stand us in good stead when it comes time to memorize or perform.

I have found that this practicing strategy (think-it-then-play-it) contributes greatly to secure memory, and really helps for passages or pieces that are going to be performed at a fast tempo. Rather than only practicing from half tempo and working up with the metronome painstakingly 3–4 bpm at a time, we can also practice small bits *in tempo*, learning how to think ahead and move with efficient accuracy. There are many situations where practicing slowly for a while works *against* playing at a fast tempo; it may allow for inefficient motions or fingerings (which we don't notice until it is time to speed up), and does not teach us how to think in meaningful units large enough to allow for execution at a fast tempo. Altenmüller (2003) actually provides a neurological explanation for the difficulties posed by extensive slow practice in his article on focal dystonia:

> Another unsolved problem is the neuronal basis of the transition from guided slow movements, which are performed under steady sensory control, to fast, ballistic movements, which have to be performed without online sensory feedback. It is assumed that different brain regions produce these two types of movements and that the transition from one type to the other may be incomplete. This might explain why practicing guided movements while slowly and systematically increasing the tempo may finally hamper the execution of this movement at a very fast tempo. (p. 530)

While slow practice has its benefits, it must be balanced by other types of practice that will help prepare us for thinking in larger chunks, monitoring larger chunks, and making decisions that will ultimately facilitate playing at a faster tempo.

Another example of beneficial think-it-then-play-it came up in my teaching as I was writing this section, with a student working on Liszt's "Un Sospiro Etude." There are many crosses and shifts in this piece, a musical need for supple technique in the middle voice, easeful yet controlled broad movements, and careful voicing of bass notes and the top notes of large chord structures.

First, we had decided to play the top note of each measure's second arpeggio with the left hand as the desired suppleness of sound seemed easier to create with an extra hand cross than it would be with the extension in the right hand suggested by the editor's fingerings. (Fingering changes shown in Figure 6.14.) This allowed the musician to keep her right hand loose throughout—a really good example of why you want to have your musical goals in mind right from the start. This does perhaps create a bit of added difficulty in terms of accuracy of the crossings, but it seemed like a good trade, and there is plenty of time.

Our think-it-then-play-it approach spanned the half measure, as shown in Figure 6.14, since that was the lower arrival point for each cross, and the uppermost note was not presenting any great difficulty for my student.

If trouble arises with getting to the top note, the think-it-then-play-it groups can be shortened to each beat, as shown in Figure 6.15.

When the half-measure groups are mastered, accurate, easeful, and secure, you can then expand the group to a full measure, continuing the think-it-then-play-it approach, as shown in Figure 6.16.

CONCEPTUAL SOLUTIONS TO TECHNICAL PROBLEMS 159

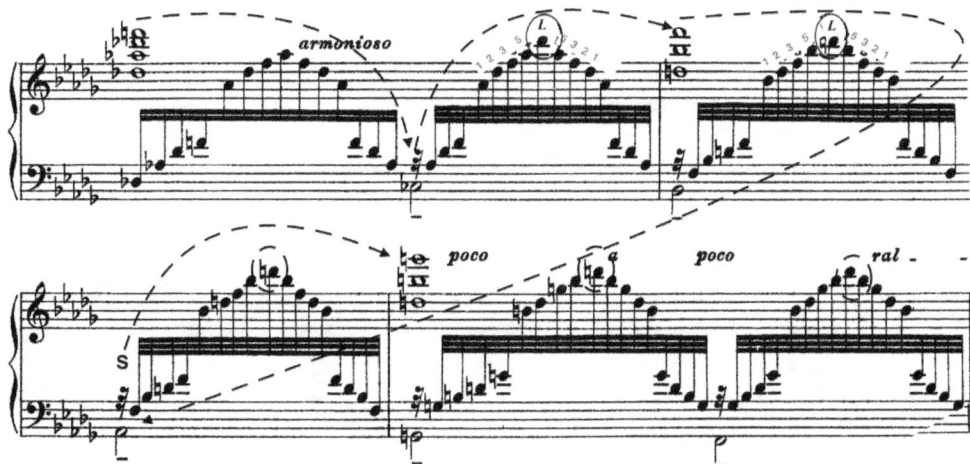

Figure 6.14. Liszt, "Un Sospiro," from *Three Concert Etudes*, mm. 63–65, think-it-then-play-it, two-beat groups.

Figure 6.15. Liszt, "Un Sospiro," mm. 63–64, think-it-then-play-it, by the beat.

At this point you're probably ready to put it all together.

Alternating between slow, careful practice sessions when you strive for appropriate, consistent fingerings and perfect note security with deliberation, and at-tempo days in smaller bits working up to ever larger ones (or smaller ones again if some trouble arises, or to revisit cognitive or associative stages so as to avoid excessive automaticity) seems to strike a beneficial balance. Checking in at tempo also helps us make sure we are choosing and reinforcing the fingerings we are going to need to use in order to play at a fast tempo. Nothing like practicing something slowly for three weeks, then starting to work it up to tempo and realizing that a great many of your fingering choices that are now so carefully and thoroughly imprinted are not going to work.

I do want to issue a caveat here. While at times it might sound like I'm issuing a series of directions: do this, then do that, now! so much of what the practicer should choose to do depends on the needs and challenges of the moment. I once was working on the second movement to Chopin's "Sonata in B minor," getting close to tempo, but just couldn't get those last few clicks. Out of curiosity, I tried to play it

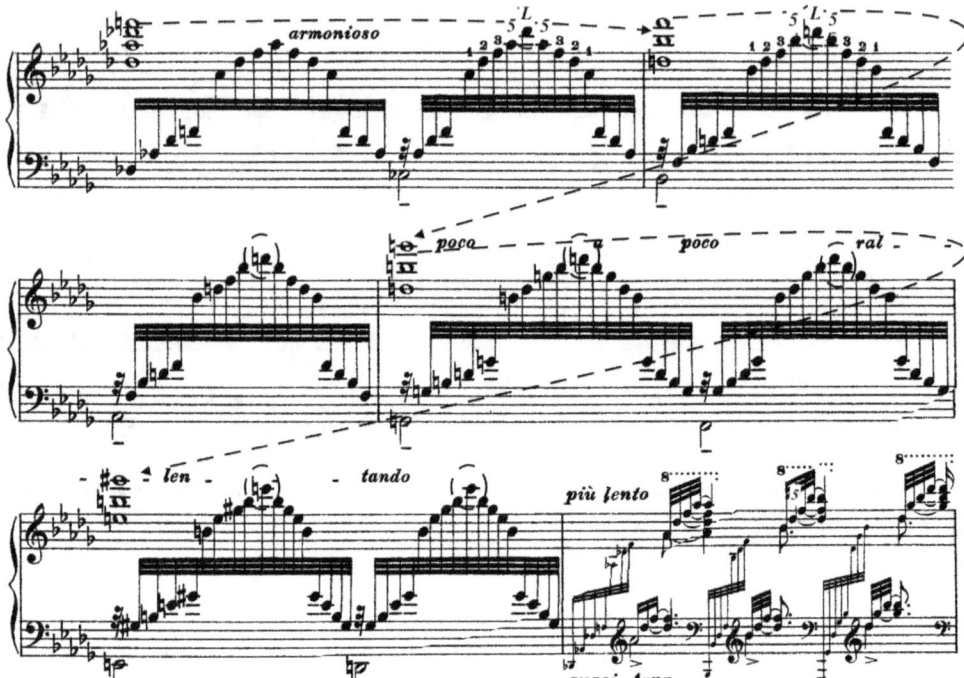

Figure 6.16. Liszt, "Un Sospiro," mm. 63–67, think-it-then-play-it, by the measure.

at half tempo, which turned out to be semi-disastrous. This actually seemed to imply that, as I was playing closer to tempo, I was actually *en route* to many wrong notes, but was *running out of time*, so was playing the right ones *by accident*! A couple of days at a slow tempo, a couple of days with The Chart (upcoming), and *voila!*

Ultimately, one of the most important skills, in practice as in life, might be the ability to recognize what is needed at any given moment.

Think-it-then-play-it strategies can also work well for instrumental music.

I will use a brief excerpt from the clarinet part of the Brahms Clarinet Trio, Op. 114, to demonstrate a few of these applications, shown in Figures 6.17 and 6.18.

We might start by going through the excerpt and identifying the most obvious meaningful units (first excerpt in Figure 6.17). Next we might look for short patterns that recur and/or are related to each other (second excerpt in Figure 6.17). After those have been found and practiced—each one thought, played, and compared—we might look for longer recurring patterns and practice/compare those (first excerpt in Figure 6.18). Finally we work from downbeat to downbeat (always overlapping), and then, so as to imitate Brahms's groupings, from first note of a slur to the first note of the next slur, incorporating the breath (second excerpt in Figure 6.18).

If, when this is all put together there are still difficulties with execution or breathing, we might work through The Chart, as demonstrated in Figures 7.20 and 7.21 below.

Figure 6.17. Brahms, "Trio for clarinet, cello, and piano," Op. 114, III., mm. 114–142, clarinet part, meaningful unit and short similar patterns.

It is generally better to practice like this without marking the groupings in the score, so that you have to keep observing and making decisions, although for many in the initial stages of learning how to practice like this it can be helpful to practice from a marked-up score for a week or two. You can always print up a copy, mark it up like crazy, practice from that for a week or two, then return to the original and add only necessary fingerings[14] and musical decisions such as articulations or dynamics, although sometimes not even those.[15] But returning to a minimally marked score is of utmost importance so as to encourage attention, observation, and remembering rather than encouraging dependence on extraneous markings, which often duplicate what the notation is already telling us, and, when numerous, are just overlooked anyway.

similar patterns (longer)

from slur to slur

Figure 6.18. Brahms, "Trio for clarinet, cello, and piano," III., mm. 114–134, clarinet part, longer similar patterns and slur-to-slur.

SCAFFOLDING AND HYPERMETER

Scaffolding/structural practice provides an excellent foundation for understanding long-term harmonic and phrase structures, leading to informed interpretation and secure memory. I will use the Prelude from the B♭ Major Prelude and Fugue, *WTC Book I* for a further exploration of this idea.

Say we have practiced the first page of the Prelude in blocks, and then investigated and identified the underlying harmonic structure. Next, we "scaffold" by practicing only what's on the downbeats, then what's on beats 1 and 3. These steps are shown in Figure 6.19.

Reducing and adding back helps reveal foundational levels of harmonic motion, some of which is perhaps disguised by figuration. Downbeats only (2nd excerpt in Figure 6.19) reveals long-term harmonic motion, adding back layers will reveal the embedded expansions of I, shown in Figure 6.20.

Figure 6.19. Bach, "Prelude in B-flat major," *Well Tempered Clavier* I, mm. 1–8, harmonic structure and first two steps of scaffolding.

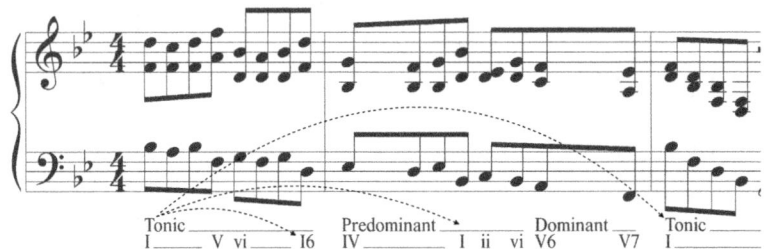

Figure 6.20. Bach, "Prelude in B-flat major," mm. 1–3, expansions.

After all this careful study, we have probably noticed (we hope) that the first three eighths of each half note are their own expansions, and what's interesting harmonically actually usually happens on the "ands" of beats 2 and 4. Therefore, we might finish our scaffolding practice by practicing as shown in Figure 6.21

Figure 6.21. Bach, "Prelude in B-flat major," mm. 1–4, harmonic scaffolding.[16]

The musician now better understands the harmonic structure of the piece, which helps develop awareness of the bigger picture and lays the foundation for long-term phrasing and secure memory. It is really helpful to do each of these steps at the final/goal tempo, audiating the stuff in the middle. You could even play just these structural parts along with a recording, if you can find one that is suitably steady and not too fast for these early experiences. Moving from the blocked dyads to a bit of work on forearm rotation connects awareness of a general hand shape and of various angles of approach from the elbow to the wrist with the necessary facility in order to execute the alternating 32nds with evenness. Add to that some scale passage practice, and you're well on your way to having the first section mastered. (I will talk more about working on the evenness in the subsequent section on horizontal grouping and practicing "to the thumbs.") This approach also helps develop a strong sense of pulse, establishing a firmer foundation while you add back the rhythmic details and technical figurations.

I have actually used this beats-only strategy precisely for students who struggle with a sense of pulse across changes of rhythmic content. There is a wealth of examples, but I will use the second movement of the Haydn "Sonata in C major," Hob. XVI/50; its rhythmic complexity is problematic for many.

CONCEPTUAL SOLUTIONS TO TECHNICAL PROBLEMS 165

This movement, or a section thereof, could be practiced downbeats-only for the sake of understanding the long-term harmonic structure, but since it is in a slow tempo and our purpose for this practice strategy is to establish sense of pulse through rhythmic complexity of notes of shorter durations, such as 16ths and 32nds, it is perhaps more appropriate to practice the beats (with the metronome if desired), and then beats and "ands." Both are shown in Figure 6.22.

This can be done playing beats and "ands" while chanting the rhythms of the melody, singing the melody, or playing along with a recording. Any of these should help acculturate the musician to the placement of these complicated divisions above a steady pulse before attempting to play everything as notated. (If it is a recording of a particularly free performance, it can also help inform his/her developing sense

mm. 1-6, beats only (in dashed boxes)

mm. 1-6, beats and "ands"

Figure 6.22. Haydn, "Sonata in C major," Hob. XVI/50, II., beats, and beats and "ands."[17]

of rubato. More on that momentarily.) This foundation can go a long way toward avoiding learned rhythm errors or accidentally changing the tempo with changes of rhythmic content, while also encouraging a sense of line and long-term structure. It is also a good way to practice with a metronome, since you are playing just in coincidence with the "ticks," at least at first.

Scaffolding practice will often reveal hypermeter, particularly in triple-meter movements, where four measures felt "in one" end up feeling like and being shaped as four beats in common time. For example, practicing the *Allegretto* from the "Sonata in E major," Op. 14 No. 1 by Beethoven downbeats-only reveals the conceptual hypermeter shown in Figure 6.23.

mm. 1-16, downbeats only

mm. 1-16, hypermeter

Figure 6.23. Beethoven, "Sonata in E major," Op 14 No 1, II., mm. 1–16, downbeats and hypermeter.

We can then strive to preserve this awareness of long-term harmonic structure and phrasing when we fill in all the details again (Figure 6.24).

While we are talking about rhythm and hypermeter, this seems like a good time to readdress that, in musical performance, rhythms are not counted, *they are felt*. I stumbled onto a confirmation of this through encounters with two different

CONCEPTUAL SOLUTIONS TO TECHNICAL PROBLEMS 167

Figure 6.24. Beethoven, "Sonata in E major," II., mm. 1–8.

editions of the Kent Kennan's "Sonata for trumpet and piano." As a collaborative pianist, I had actually played the piece several times from the second edition (second excerpt in Figure 6.25), although I hadn't realized that it was a "second edition" at the time. This edition utilizes multiple time signature changes in the third movement. A few years ago I was given a copy of the score by a student I was working with, and discovered the first edition (first excerpt in Figure 6.25).

It is clear from the two experiences that Kennan either discovered or was warned about the difficulties for the performer when notation does not align with audiation, motivating a revision to a much clearer presentation. The fact that I had already learned it from the notation that supported audiation meant that I was able to play it pretty easily from the first edition, but I was also quite aware of audiating the shifting meters as if I were reading the version with which I was more familiar. I did go and dig out my own copy anyway, just to avoid any unnecessary cognitive dissonance.[18] The written-in counts were from a previous user of that copy of the score—you can see the difficulties.

In fact, I think a bit of tweaking with the beaming might make the groupings even more clear, leading to even faster learning, shown in Figure 6.26. I have also written in some different counting systems. You will notice the 1-2-1-2-3-1-2 and Du-Be Du-Ba-Bi (pronounced Doo-Bay-Doo-Bah-Bee) syllables between the two lower (rhythmic only) staves. The notes in the second stave from the bottom indicate the note values of the beats; the lowest staff and syllables show how those beats are divided. When rhythms get complicated, sometimes counting *can* help solve problems of what's on/in what beat, etc. But counting does not usually lead to musically inflected performance. To be performed musically, *rhythms must be felt*. Gordon's rhythm solfège system helps do just that.[19] And you will see that if you can feel the big beats and the divisions into two or three, the placement of the 16th does not generally present a problem, and probably does not need to be chanted or counted. Written between the piano right hand and the trumpet part is the realization of a more traditional counting system; you can see how complicated it is—the different meanings of "a," for example. This lack of consistency can lead to lack of understanding, establishment of context, and efficiency. Rather, the first bar in the example is 2 + 2 + 3 + 2, the next 2 + 3 + 2, the next 2 + 2, etc.

Take a few moments to compare the interpretations in Figure 6.26, with the indications of the divisions of pulse into two- and three- (lower staves) versus the more

first edition

second edition

Figure 6.25. Kennan, "Sonata for trumpet and piano," III., mm. 92–100 comparing 1st and 2nd editions.

CONCEPTUAL SOLUTIONS TO TECHNICAL PROBLEMS   169

Figure 6.26. Kennan, "Sonata for trumpet and piano," III., mm. 92–100, comparing counting systems.

traditional counting system (upper staves). Tapping the pulse (the quarters and dotted quarters) and chanting the rhythm of your part on "Bum" or any other neutral syllable will place the rhythm pattern into context and help you learn and *feel* it.[20] This is one shortcoming of the metronome. Having it tick all the 8th notes might be a common solution, which works fairly well at slower tempos, but it is hard for us to process input when it is coming at us that quickly.[21] If only we could program the piece into a digital metronome of sorts. (Maybe next year.) Until then, we can be our own metronomes. This is probably more useful anyway.

As previously mentioned, practicing downbeats-only with a metronome or recording can also be helpful for musicians learning how to use rubato. In fact, a foundation of playing the piece as a whole with a metronome is an excellent starting point for learning to use rubato effectively. In this way, the foundation of a steady pulse is firmly established before the musician begins to experiment with pulling back a little, and then pushing forward to regain the next "tick" in time, which helps ensure that *rubato* does not end up meaning *meno mosso*.

I have also used beats-only practice in collaborative situations. One that comes to mind is putting the trumpet and piano parts together in "Légende," by Enesco (Figure 6.27), which moves to fast, flowing passagework in both parts that only coincide on beats and "ands." If the two musicians practice alone and together playing only what lands on those rhythmic scaffolds, the ensemble is established with a

as written

Simultaneities, scaffolded

Figure 6.27. Enesco, "Légende," trumpet and piano, mm. 20–25, scaffolding.

sense of the overall line and a steady tempo. The figuration then is the responsibility of each musician's technique, but the coordination between the two parts is much more secure.

In all cases, our honing of these important analytical and observational skills will make the learning deeper and more readily accessible. For developing musicians especially, the purpose is not just to learn the current piece, but to ease the learning of the next one. And remember Brown et al. (2014): the best learning is effortful. Writing out harmonic or melodic scaffolding can also serve as the basis of maps for the piece as an aid to memory.

MENTAL PRACTICE, MAPPING, AND MEMORIZATION

When we talk about "memory" in cognitive terms, it is often in reference to what we might call "learning" or "remembering" rather than to how we use the term "memory" when it comes to preparing to perform a piece of music without a score. As just discussed, though, how those learning experiences are structured affects how they are encoded, which can in turn contribute to, or impair, our efforts to memorize a piece of music. At this point, the establishment of retrieval cues becomes of utmost importance, and it is the pursuit of those that we talk about now.

When it comes to memorizing music, there are four systems in play: muscle, visual, aural, and analytical. Muscle memory—the first type of memory to come for many, and the first to abandon us at the slightest distraction or finger slip—is probably the cause of many typical failure scenarios, and therefore, worth going to great lengths to avoid overreliance on. Aural and visual memory do connect us to the sounds and notation, although aural memory often focuses on melodic structures, surface rhythm, and perhaps (if we are lucky), foundational bassline/functional moments, leaving us guessing as to details of the harmonic progressions and at the mercy of luck in altered recurrences of material. Visual memory tends to focus on surface structures and middle-ground elements.

Mental memory—based in analysis, conceptual mapping, and mindful awareness of the physical paths of execution—is the most important, and the most reliable, and should serve as the foundation for the other types. Chunking certainly plays a role, and should be considered a subcategory of conceptual mapping. This priority has been very deliberately reflected in that I have chosen to write about all of the myriad mental practice strategies, and memorization, before I discuss practice to solve physical problems of execution. It is extremely beneficial if the basis of these *conceptual* foundations is laid early in the process, long before any muscle or even aural memory begins to establish itself. Utilizing mindful practice strategies, including those that involve scaffolding and reduction, can lay an important groundwork for secure memory. Writing out various representations of these mental structures provides a map of sorts, such as in the scaffolding, rhythmic reductions, and conceptual mapping discussed for Figures 6.9, 6.19, 6.20, and 6.23, and discussed further below. It is also really helpful if any clearly defined musical elements (notated dynamics, articulations, etc.) are memorized at the same time as their associated notes and rhythms—a yarn-dyed approach to musicality and memory, say, rather than a silk-screened appliqué painted on after the fact, which then functions as *an-other* thing to think about.

Think-it-then-play-it strategies also help memorization because they involve our observing, audiating, and imagining requisite mental signals to initiate movement. Remembering the advantages of multimodal imagery to memorization, and of laying a strong foundation, it can help to begin the study of a piece with some analytical work and mapping perhaps at multiple layers. I recommend moving back and forth between the notation and the map(s), gradually weaning yourself from the more detailed layers until you are playing from the most rudimentary version, which you then memorize to remove the need of notation altogether.

An elementary example of mapping can be seen in the learning of "Broken Record Boogie," Figure 2.10 above, which the beginning student uses as an aid to "memory" as he/she plays his/her twelve-bar blues piece that has been learned by rote.

For an intermediate student memorizing "Minuetto" by James Hook, you might begin by analyzing the form of the piece, learning each four-bar phrase according to its designation of a, a', a", and b. When it is time to memorize, make a copy and cut it apart (see the dotted-line boxes in Figure 6.28)—if you want it to be truly challenging cut the bar lines off on the right margin to remove the inadvertent clues provided by the repeat signs—and the first thing the musician does each day before playing the piece from memory is to put the slips of paper in their proper order. Then we graduate to four 4" x 6" note cards, with a, a', a" and b written on them; mix them up, put them up on the music rack, and play the version of the piece that results with the sections played in whatever order has occurred. Then put the cards back in the proper order and play from memory.

Dickinson provides the reductionist map seen in Figure 6.29 for the "Minuet in G minor" from the *Anna Magdalena Bach Notebook*.

In this case you might memorize by doing a bit of score study and practice, then play using the *b* map, then move on to playing it from the *c* map, and then play from memory entirely. This might take one practice session, a few days, or several weeks, depending on your technical facility, your level of audiation ability, and your ability to reconstruct missing information.

As you can imagine, as the music gets more complex, the maps will also, or several might be made over several weeks as the piece becomes more well-known. I sometimes model mapping, or have had students map the same piece and then trade maps with each other and try to play from each other's. This requires filling in other people's conceptual gaps, and also stimulates a reevaluation of what you may have included or omitted.

Maps might show the overall harmonic progression and form and/or interesting motivic observations, as seen in Figure 6.30 (from my own personal library).

Figure 6.28. Hook, "Minuetto," basic analysis.

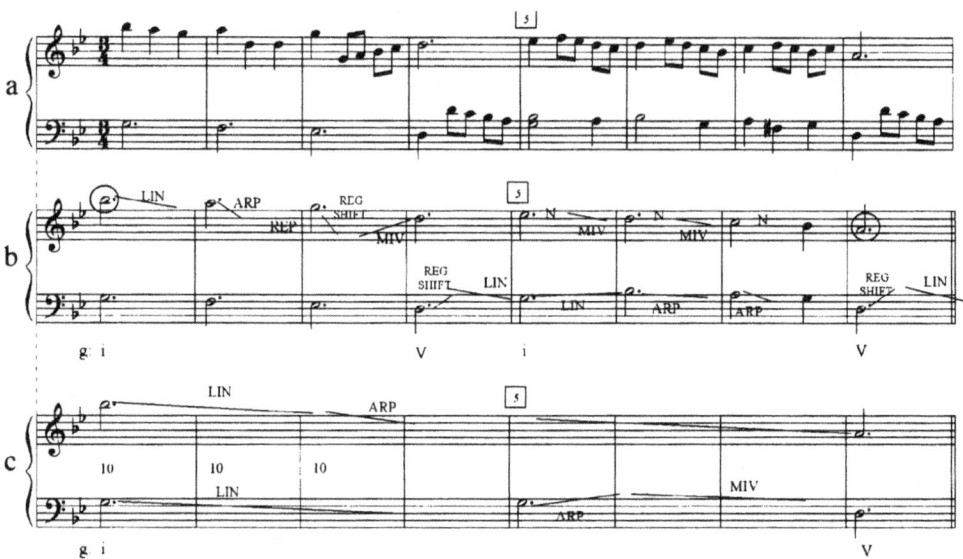

Figure 6.29. Dickinson, reductionist map of Bach's "Minuet in G minor," mm. 1–8.

Figure 6.30. Brahms, "Intermezzo," Op. 118 No. 1, general "map."

They might include more detailed harmonic and/or melodic information as we saw in Figure 6.20. Or they might be primarily pictorial, as seen on the right half of Figure 6.31.

Or maybe you construct a general map (Figure 6.32), and then a very involved thematic/formal comparison (Figure 6.33), such as seen in my map of the last movement of "Kreisleriana," trying to compare a melody that returns *almost* verbatim (twice), with a bass line that is quite similar but enters on different beats, posing all kinds of memory challenges.

Our maps might be written out even before we start practicing the piece at the instrument. Figure 6.34 shows a student's map of the subject entrances of the B♭ major Fugue from *WTC I*. A second map might show just the first note or gesture

CONCEPTUAL SOLUTIONS TO TECHNICAL PROBLEMS 175

Ex. 8-10. Brahms: Capriccio in G minor, op.116, no. 3

The excerpt below shows meas. 1-9 of this piece.

The excerpt below (representing meas. 1-8) was from a map drawn by an adult amateur pianist as an aid in learning and memorizing this work for a recital.

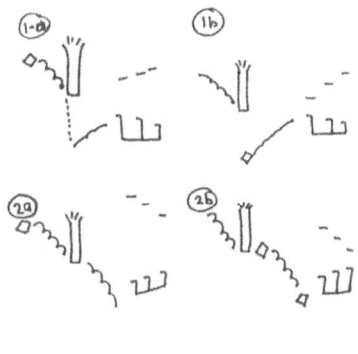

Figure 6.31. Shockley, map of Brahms's "Cappriccio in G minor," Op. 116, No. 3.

of each subject (S) and countersubject (CS), placed appropriately in the measure to show its rhythmic relativity to the downbeat. A third map may show just "S" and "CS" and key areas and cadences.

The first steps toward a map of Prelude No. 1 from the first volume of the *Well-Tempered Clavier* might have been undertaken as described earlier, with the student writing out a whole-note reduction of the figuration before beginning work on the piece. At the memorization stage, that reduction might be reduced even further,

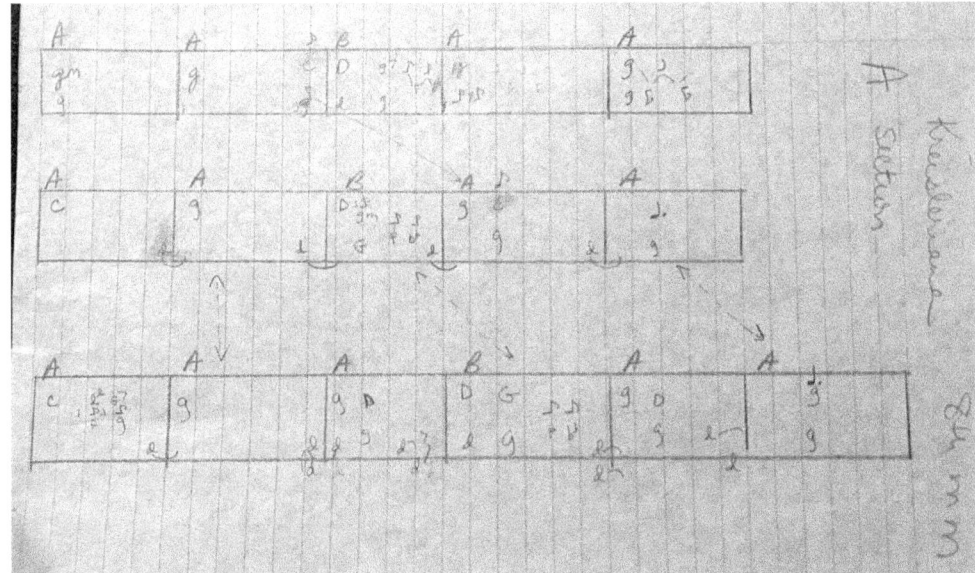

Figure 6.32. Iott, map of Schumann, "Kreisleriana," VIII.

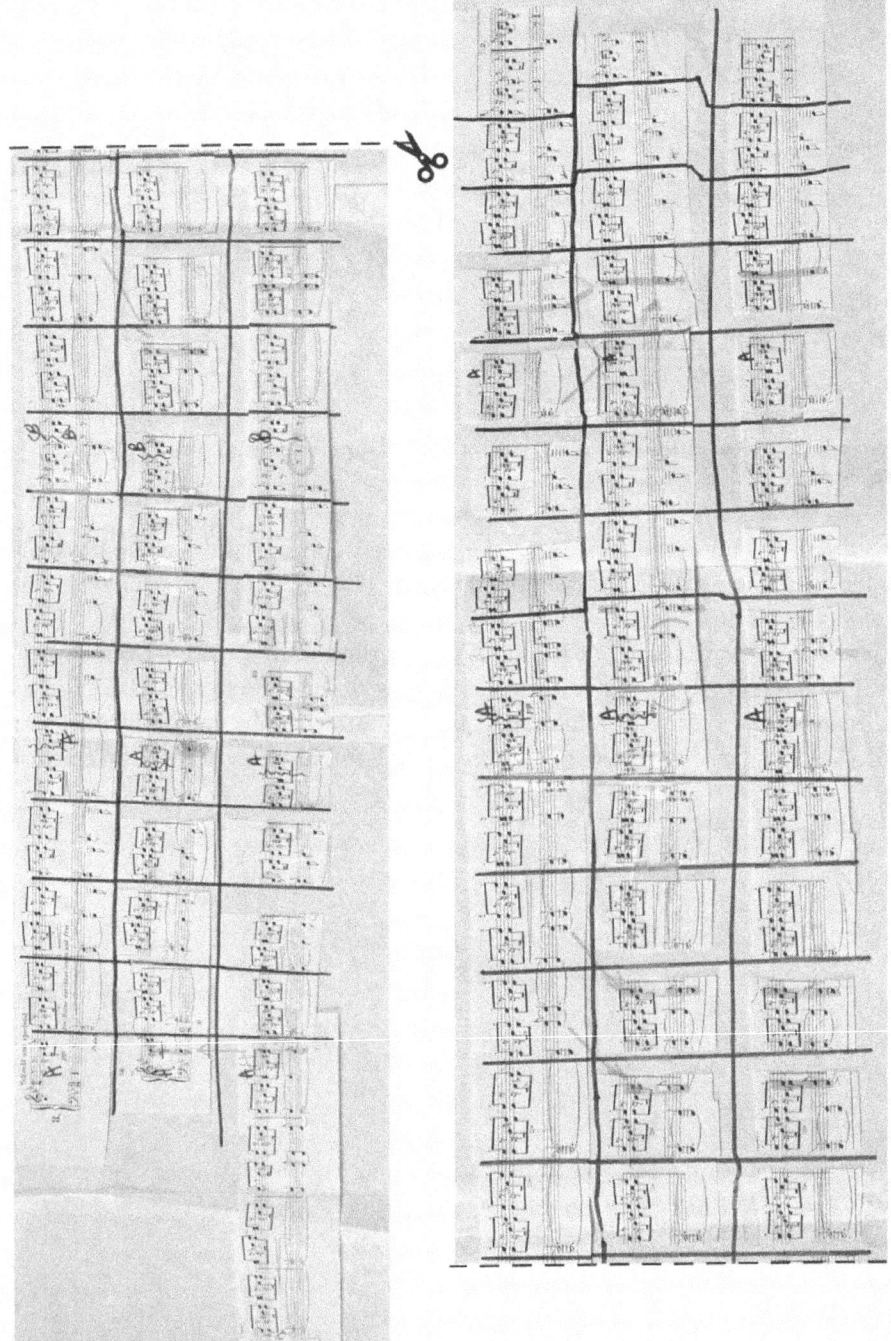

Figure 6.33. Ilott, map of Schumann, "Kreisleriana," VIII., comparing melodic material and bass line entrances.
Original map is one continuous sheet, "cut" here at the dashed line to allow for a larger image; and what appear to be greyscale markings are actually made with various colored highlighters to show exact parallelisms vs. rhythmically displaced parallelisms vs. anomalies. If you'd like to see the in-color version, just contact me through my webpage: www.sherylilott.com.

CONCEPTUAL SOLUTIONS TO TECHNICAL PROBLEMS 177

Figure 6.34. Student K. R.'s first map of first subject statements, Bach's "Fugue in B-flat major," *WTC I*.

to a bassline and Roman-numeral analysis, as shown in Figure 6.35. It's a simple step from playing from this map to memorizing, and avoids the common occurence of wandering confusedly starting around measure 24 or 30, as is far too likely if the harmonies are not understood and encoded for mindful retrieval.

For the actual final steps of memorization, an excellent approach is to study the score and play from memory, phrase by phrase, either working backward in sec-

Figure 6.35. Iott, map of bassline and harmonic progression for Bach's "Prelude No. 1," WTC I.

tions, memorizing similar but not identical passages, or working outward in either direction from the most unusual or unique passages, and memorizing the most obvious or repetitive places last. For example, you may memorize the transition and second tonal area of the Recapitulation of a Sonata-Allegro form first, then the transition and second tonal area of the Exposition, then the Development, etc.

Baddeley (1990) discusses the benefits of distributed practice, and of recounting memorized material in different orders, and Li and Lewandowsky (1995) write about the advantages of forward versus backward recall. According to the latter, if "recalling forward," you will remember early list items better; and if "recalling backward," you will recall the more recent items better. (So far pretty obvious.) But there's more:

- Forward recall seems to be based on paired interitem associations and visual-auditory processes (left brain), whereas backward recall relies more on visual-spatial (right brain) representations.

- Forward recall is more likely to be disrupted by distractors, whereas backward recall seems relatively impervious to distractors.
- Forward recall is conceptually driven and schema-based, backward recall primarily data-driven and nonschema-based.
- Backward and/or free recall are not as likely to be impacted by the order of memorization of each event.
- Forward, serial recall is more impaired by high similarity between events, but free recall *benefits* from similarities (Li & Lewandowski, 1995).

These factors all make strong arguments for some nonsequential memory work, albeit with ongoing awareness of how the parts fit into the whole. Remember also that memory does not all have to be done at the instrument. In fact, memorizing away from the instrument has a huge advantage, solidifying the structural elements in a foundational way on which the musical details are built. Mental memory work might include studying a score away from the instrument for several days and then trying to play from memory, studying a score by section at the instrument and playing each section by memory, and/or mental practice away from the instrument of passages or pieces that have already been memorized. This might include memory/mental practice on a treadmill, during a run or bike ride, doing dishes, etc. My belief is *if I cannot "play" the entire piece in my head*, away from the piano, *it is not memorized*.

This also seems a good time to return to Brown et al.'s (2014) points regarding learning that "sticks": that which is a result of *distributed, interleaved* practice and repeated, *effortful retrieval*. This is helpful for all types of learning, including memorization of a piece for performance. Repeated retrieval can embed knowledge and skills so well that the body may seem to act almost reflexively in response to thought. Strength of knowledge and ease of access also contribute to more nuanced creativity in addressing new problems. Revisiting sections, having myriad starting places, practicing hands separately, at slow tempos, etc. *still from memory* all move the learner from automatic levels of learning to cognitive and associative stages and back again, strengthening learning and reinforcing numerous pathways to the same material.

Because fluent musical performance demands this type of reflexive response, you must have memorized not only the music, but the series of steps that you will most likely take (remember "implementation intentions"?), so that you can execute those steps quickly and efficiently, and/or make adjustments as the situation warrants. I would even argue that practicing for those circumstances is invaluable—being prepared to adjust your tone or pedal for the piano or hall, to follow the spontaneous timing and nuance of another musician, or to recover from an error of either your own or a collaborator in your ensemble can and should be a part of the practice paradigm. As will be discussed in terms of mindfulness of gesture and details of physical approach in the next section, this type of awareness allows not only for consistency, but for flexibility and adaptability as well.

On the other hand, doing it any which way and paying no attention at all will only create difficulties.

"Be mindful, young Padawan."
Source: Lucasfilm Ltd. / 20th Century Fox / Photofest

Distribution of practice results in some forgetting, and the effort then exerted for retrieval more firmly encodes the information. If you are practicing something you memorized yesterday and you are stuck, don't necessarily go right to the score. Try again from a little before the moment of difficulty; if you still cannot find it, place your music several steps from the instrument, walk over, study and audiate and mentally memorize (no finger wiggling!), then return and try again.

Spreading it out, interspersing it with something else, leaving it for varying lengths of time and then retrieving it, never taking the easy route—these are the paths to security and ease necessary for musical performance. All of the above approaches reinforce the mental processes and fortify the routes to success. The next, and final, chapter on optimal practicing strategies will address solution paths for when we encounter physical obstacles to facile execution.

NOTES

1. NB: this is for the advanced musician at the advanced stage. At this point, the musician should have the aural, technical, and theoretical foundation to understand what is going on in the music s/he is playing. If s/he *can't*, s/he should be playing easier repertoire.

2. By which I mean any adjustment to the length of the note, from a full legato to a short staccato and everywhere in between. If you play five staccato 8th notes in a row, with each one a bit longer than the one before, the listener will hear a crescendo, but the idioms will still adhere to Baroque performance practice and the texture will still be clear and legible.

3. Putting this very simplistically. Recent brain science shows that both hemispheres are involved in almost everything we do, albeit in different ways and to different degrees. We also have the dichotomy of the left hemisphere, which is focused on the objective identification of individual structures, and the right hemisphere, which wants to observe/create/manipulate the whole and understands everything in terms of how it relates to everything else. The right hemisphere also deals better with new information, no matter which side of the body is perceiving or dealing with it, moving it to the left hemisphere once it seems familiar (McGilchrist, 2009). Hard to imagine which of these is more important to learning a piece of music (left brain) so as to play it beautifully (right brain). All of these factors contribute to my already firm belief that hands together, sooner, is generally better.

4. Iott (2014).

5. Ibid. Includes audio examples that do exactly that.

6. The long-term structural line of the melody in the first tonal area of Mozart's "Sonata," K. 333 not only returns in the second tonal area, but also becomes the basis for the bassline of the Development. Awareness of this reveals the lengths of the phrases in the Development as well as which of the V^7 chords is cadential and which is an "accident" born of a motivically generated bass line. Cool, right?

7. If you're going to tackle something hands separately, it's often a good idea to learn the left hand first. First of all, due to the nature of most beginning methods and intermediate repertoire, our right hand is probably more highly developed, so why not give the left hand an opportunity to catch up? We also tend to listen to and learn our right-hand parts aurally much earlier in the process. Then add that it is the right hemisphere of the brain that wants to deal with new information. You can help this along by having beginning students play everything in their left hand that they play in their right hand and vice versa.

8. This passage is fascinating. There are further embedded/overlapping levels of melodic motion that I could just as easily prioritize—for example, the intervening accented notes that actually land on the beats, and which would be just as valid to explore as a countermelody voice. What I suggest is just one of many ways to layer and deconstruct; exploring various solutions can only deepen the understanding and musical conviction of the performer.

9. Or, if you're working on something in a fast triple meter, say the Scherzo movement of Chopin's "Sonata in B minor," in one-measure, two-measure, then four-measure groups.

10. This is really, *really*, important. If practicing in 2-beat groups, resist the urge to keep going the first time it goes well. This is actually important with any practice strategy. If you have a goal, and have identified a strategy by which you hope to meet that goal, meet it more than once, and be sure that it has happened as planned each and every time.

11. If you can't answer the question "do you know what you did when you did it well?" how do you expect to be able to do it again?

12. NB: a child, or someone who does not drive, *will not* do this; an experienced driver will, completely reflexively.

13. There is also a theory that learning to read music before a vocabulary of music is established leads to perfect pitch, which is not necessarily the blessing many think it is; it often means that relative pitch is woefully underdeveloped.

14. More on fingerings upcoming.

15. Westney (2003) encourages refraining from inserting musical decisions too early in the process so as to approach each practice session with an open mind and open ears. I have found that practices such as coming up with multiple interpretations for recurring phrases but not necessarily deciding which I am going to do when keeps me musically open and appropriately focused in performance.

16. And which could also serve as the beginnings of a map, discussed more in a few paragraphs.

17. For the sake of space and clarity I did not put boxes around the "ands" that were sustained quarters or rests; of course we must take great care to give those values their full worth, or all of this is for naught.

18. Avoiding "cognitive dissonance" could make up a book all its own. Giving yourself positive messages ("Play F natural!") rather than negative ones ("Don't play the F#!"), whiting out unnecessary courtesy accidentals, making sure every fingering number in the piece is the one you want, etc. is extraordinarily helpful in eliminating counterproductive distractions. There is enough to think about already, don't you think? Plus, positive ("yes") messages are more easily learned, and negative ones more emotionally impactful.

19. According to this system, in all meters, "Du" is the big beat. In usual meters, the small beats are Du-De ("Day") in duple; Du-Da-Di in triple. "Ta" is used for divisions.

20. People play beautifully in 6/8 and have trouble dealing with triplets; or wonderfully in 2/4 but can't figure out how to "count" duples in 6/8. You are merely dividing a beat into 2, or 3. I have never actually encountered anything that does not behave thusly. If you can play in 6/8, you can play a triplet. *It's the same thing.*

21. Our brains can only deal with so much input so quickly. Forde Thompson and Schellenberg (2006) argue that we are born with an innate preference for 60–120 "events" per minute, which could be equated with a setting on a metronome (p. 107). Faster or slower than that, we adjust the hierarchy, so that in slow tempos we feel the 8th as the pulse, and in fast tempos we pair, or feel triple "in one."

7

PRACTICE STRATEGIES FOR SOLVING PHYSICAL PROBLEMS

While conceptual chunking, mapping, thinking-then-playing, and the other "mental" practice strategies just discussed are important and helpful to actual physical execution, there are obviously going to be problems of execution that require specific physical adjustments or refinements. It is my belief that the strategies and processes outlined in the previous chapter help us approach things in the best possible way *cognitively*. There are also ways to use those cognitive processes to solve more specifically mechanical problems.

PHYSICAL PRACTICE: CHUNKING, GESTURES, *THE CHART*, AND FINGERINGS

CHUNKING » GESTURE

I have written at length about mental chunking and the benefit of seeking out and processing "meaningful units." This included suggestions for physically chunking these conceptual units, such as playing the structures of the compound line in the first Prelude from the *Well-Tempered Clavier* Book I as vertical chord structures before playing as written.

There are other methods of grouping that can help solve challenges of execution. For example, the opening gestures of Debussy's second "Arabesque" can first be practiced as three-note chunks, shown in Figure 7.1. This helps establish a good fingering plan for each chord structure as well as learning how to get our hand from one to the next. Observing the distance of the shift and the angle of the arm for each of the chunked chords is helpful and informative. Linking the chunked chord pairs to rotational practice, as shown in Figure 7.2, will connect the group to the gesture and teach the hand to be prepared for the shifts and chord changes while building familiarity with the wrist and arm motion necessary to execute the notes as written.

Figure 7.1. Debussy, "Arabesque No. 2," mm. 1–4, chunking.

Figure 7.2. Debussy, "Arabesque No. 2," mm. 1–2–3–5*, chunk-to-gesture.

*Notice that I omit repetitions of identical measures. Because you are practicing a gesture, if it can be done in measure 3 it can certainly also be done in measure 4. I also divided measure 5 into two so that the practice of pairing two-chord groups with their gestures was consistent. In measures 1–3 this pairing is inherent to the piece itself.

At the same time, some of the chord shapes are similar, and use the same fingerings, which might cause some error of either omission (not noticing the differences) or commission (not executing them properly). If that happens, it is helpful to practice back and forth between the two "competing" shapes and gestures, as shown in Figure 7.3. In all instances, we are being mindful of the remembered chord shape and feel, the shape and size of the gesture, the angle of the approach, and a comparison between them—both mentally and physically. We can move back and forth between chunking all of them, chunking and gesturing in pairs or measures, or reinvestigating and comparing similar chord structures as needed. There is no need to do all of this everywhere the same gesture happens. If each chord and gesture is thought, felt, and executed with ease and the desired resultant tone and shape, practicing like iterations can be a waste of time—unless one of your challenges is maintaining focus, in which case, carry on!

But perhaps something has intervened that makes a later iteration of a recurrent pattern feel different. Again, this is where the importance of mindful observation comes in.

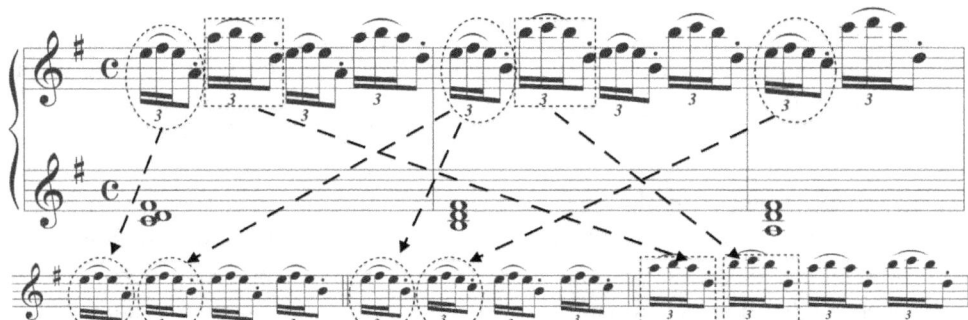

Figure 7.3. Debussy, "Arabesque No. 2," mm. 1–3, comparing similar gestures.

PRACTICE STRATEGIES FOR SOLVING PHYSICAL PROBLEMS 185

For the excerpt shown in Figure 7.4, we see the same gesture in the right hand at the beginning of measure 2 that we find again at the beginning of measure 9, but the left hand as well as the preceding and subsequent gestures differ. If trouble ensues in one of these moments, it is perhaps not the gesture itself that needs attention, but making appropriate predictions and executing accordingly. In this case we might alternate between practicing from the beginning of m. 1 to 3rd beat of m. 2, and from the beginning of m. 9 to beat 3 of m. 10, alternating as needed (boxes in upper portion of Figure 7.4).[1]

mm. 1-3 compared to mm. 9-10, larger practice groups

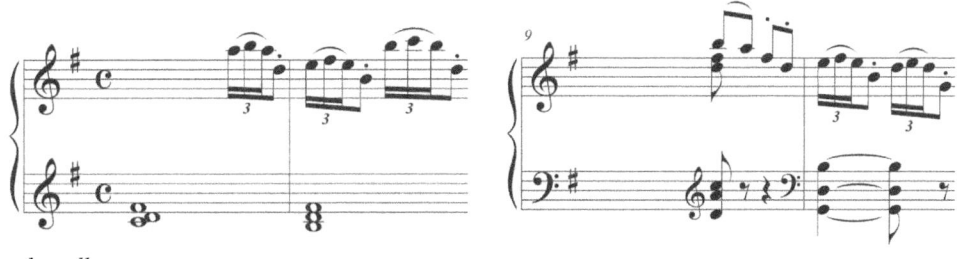

and smaller ones

Figure 7.4. Debussy, "Arabesque No. 2," mm. 1–3, compared to mm. 9–10.

If difficulty persists, we could make even smaller groups (as shown in the lower part of Figure 7.4), such as, m. 1 to m. 2, 2nd beat (LH playing and holding the chord, RH starting on beat 4 so as to also have the opportunity to practice the chord change in a manner that more closely imitates what will happen in the piece itself but eliminating some of the distractors), compared to m. 9, beat 3 to m. 10, beat 2. If success is achieved, yet difficulty persists when starting at the beginning of m. 1, you can work your way backward by starting at beat 3, then beat 2.

Another piece by Debussy, the *Prélude* from *Pour le Piano*, provides a wealth of opportunities to explore types and benefits of grouping practice.

Figure 7.5. Debussy, "Prélude," from *Pour le Piano*, mm. 6–12, right-hand blocks.

We can practice chunking the right-hand alternating pattern in measures 6 and following, which helps us read in larger meaningful units (which will help us scan further ahead), and note the horizontal motion that bridges the vertical structures. Tying the note that stays the same, as shown in Figure 7.5, helps bring our attention to the lateral movement of each voice and think about a good fingering plan.

We can also move from blocking » gesture for challenges such as those posed in mm. 41–42 (Figure 7.6), starting with blocked chords, then the 16th notes to refine the slightly circular wrist motion (swirling dashed arrows in the bottom excerpt of Figure 7.6), and then put it all together, preserving the feeling of the wrist drop motion for each thumb/beat note, and the wrist circles for the 16ths.

mm. 41-42, blocks

mm. 41-42, 16th notes only

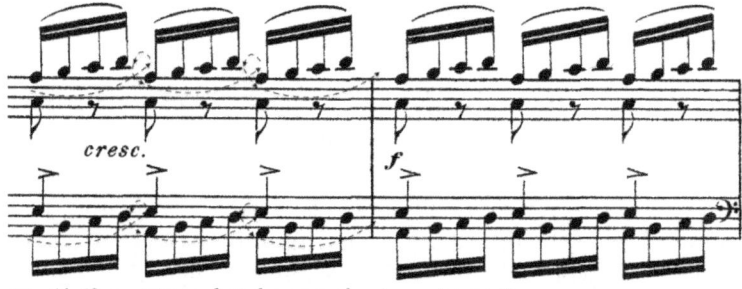

mm. 41-42, as written, dotted arrows showing wrist rotation

Figure 7.6. Debussy, "Prélude," from *Pour le Piano*, mm. 41–42, blocks » gesture.

Blocking in pairs would help to learn the notes and coordinate the hands during the intricate interplay of mm. 66–69, shown in Figure 7.7, which we could then practice with one hand in blocks and the other as written, and vice versa. When playing the left hand as written, we can focus consciously on leading the stepwise shifts alternating between pinky and thumb to help maintain the pattern and contour from a strongly recognizable physical approach.

If the closeness/overlap of the hands is causing coordination difficulties, it may help to move the right hand up an octave and practice until even and appropriately articulated. Then move back to the written position. This gives us the opportunity to feel and listen for evenness and to investigate the appropriate dynamic and tone in a slightly easier but very similar context.

Blocking » gesture practice also helps create meaningful units out of the chord patterns formed by the triplet 8th notes in mm. 78–81 and 86–89 can focus consciously (Figure 7.8), so that the brain is thinking the chords while the hand/wrist/arm practices the gesture so as to convey the articulations.

Moving between the blocks and the gesture, hands alone or hands together, helps us make sure we are reading and thinking in meaningful units while also encoding intentional motor signals—including execution of desired articulations—on that foundation. We are combining *analytical mapping* with *pattern reading/visual chunking* and with *implementation-intentions* for each individual gesture, as well as how we move from one to the next. Attending simultaneously to the vertical shape of each chord structure, the lateral motion of each voice, and the physical sensation of each gesture provides a saturated learning experience. This not only establishes these patterns firmly in conceptual, auditional, and physical memory, but gives us something concrete to attend to in performance, helping ensure that our performance of the piece or passage presents our best understanding and execution.

Moving from grouping to gesture can also help us deal more efficiently with problems in later sections, such as comparing the conceptual and physical execution of the alternating patterns of mm. 126–132 and those of mm. 159–164 can focus consciously (Figure 7.9).

In this case, we can move from scaffolding practice, where we hold rather than replay recurrent pitches (Figure 7.10, a), to a simplified rhythmic arrangement focusing on the feel of the slurred-staccato chords (b), and then add a bit of rotational (right hand, c) and alternating-hands (d) practice to establish the physical coordination of the passage as written. The process of moving from blocked chords to as written for mm. 159–161 might even reveal that bit of hemiola suggested by the alternating patterning that perhaps we weren't noticing beforehand.

And think-it-then-play-it helps us be ready for each hand-unit of the two cadenza patterns (did you realize there are only two?) before execution (Figure 7.11).

GESTURE » DETAIL

Many of the previous examples talk about working from some kind of chunking/grouping to the gesture. There are times when it may be better to work first on the gesture, and then refine for accuracy. For example, the large leaps in the second

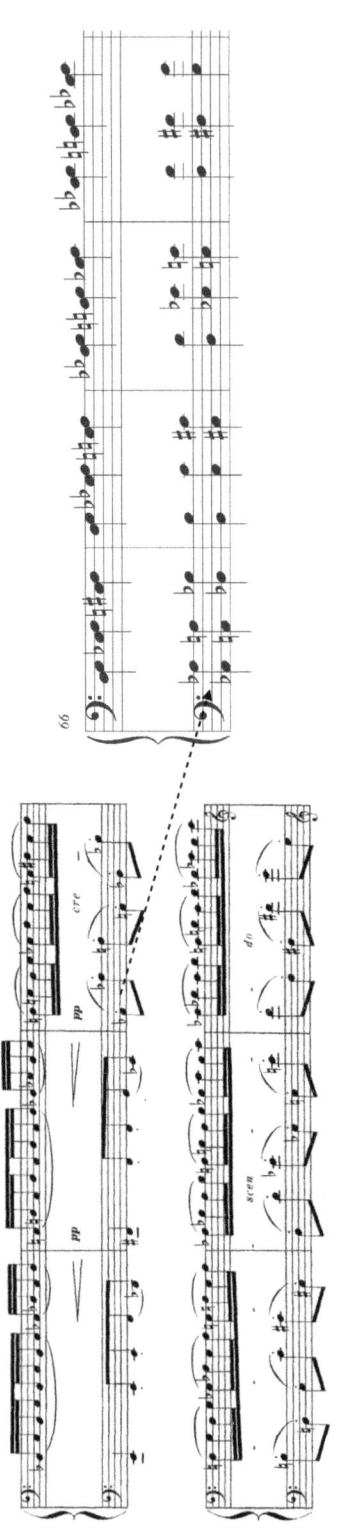

Debussy, Prélude to Pour le Piano, mm. 64-69 - - - > *mm. 66-69, Chunks*

Figure 7.7. Debussy, "Prélude," from *Pour le Piano*, mm. 64–69, chunking.

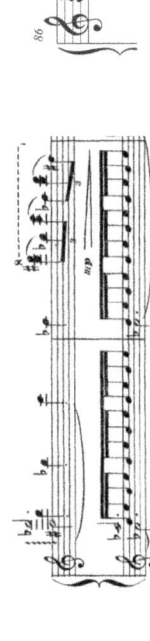

Debussy, Prélude from Pour le Piano, m. 76. . . . group → gesture

Debussy, Prélude from Pour le Piano, mm. 85–86. . . group → gesture

Figure 7.8. Debussy, "Prélude," from *Pour le Piano*, mm. 76, 85–86, group » gesture triplets.

mm. 124-132

mm. 157-165

Figure 7.9. Debussy, "Prélude," from *Pour le Piano*, mm. 124–132, 157–165.

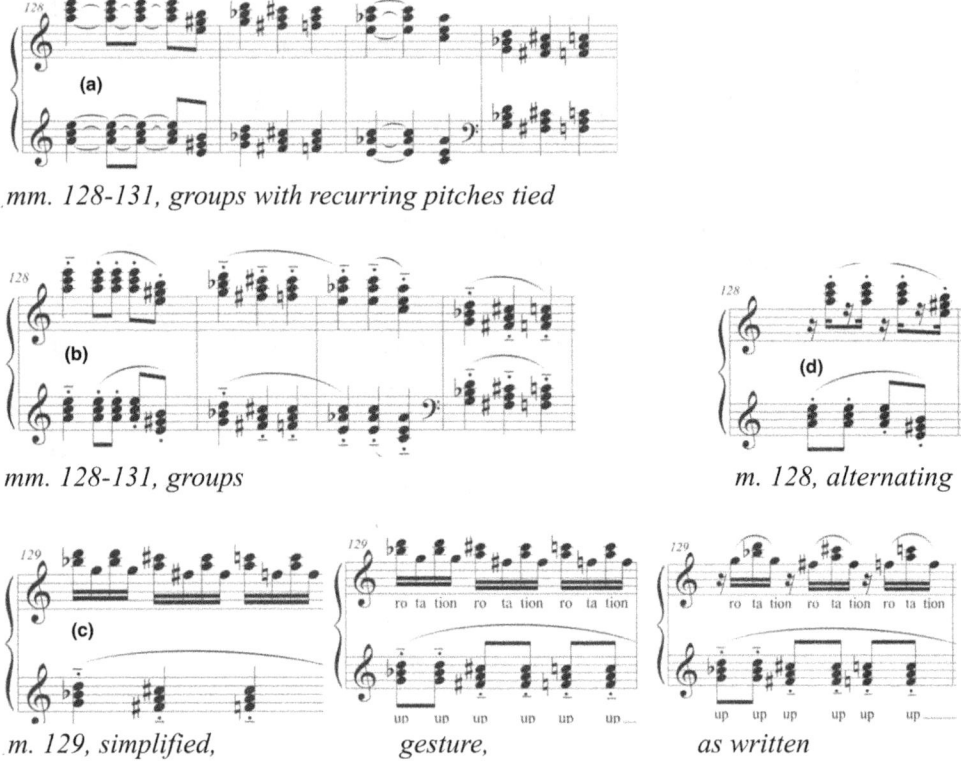

mm. 128-131, groups with recurring pitches tied

mm. 128-131, groups

m. 128, alternating

m. 129, simplified,

gesture,

as written

mm. 159-161, blocked chords

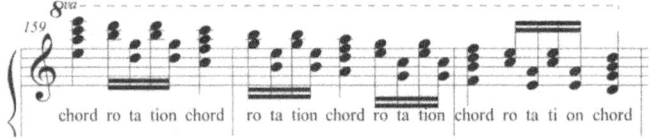

mm. 159-161, chord and rotation gesture

mm. 159-160, complete gesture

Figure 7.10. Debussy, "Prélude," from *Pour le Piano*, mm. 128–131, 159–161, evolution from simplified structure to gestural realization.

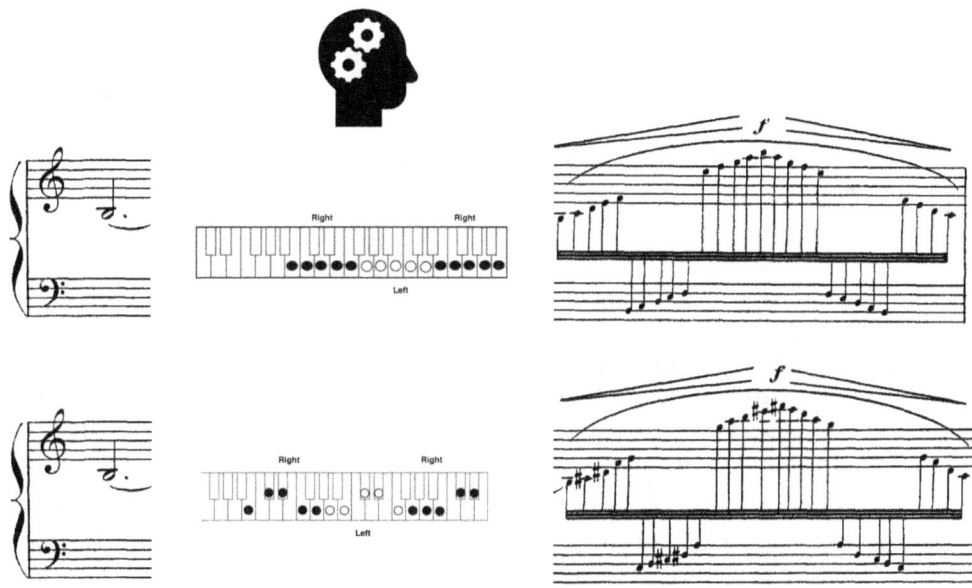

Figure 7.11. Debussy, "Prélude," from *Pour le Piano*, cadenza planning.

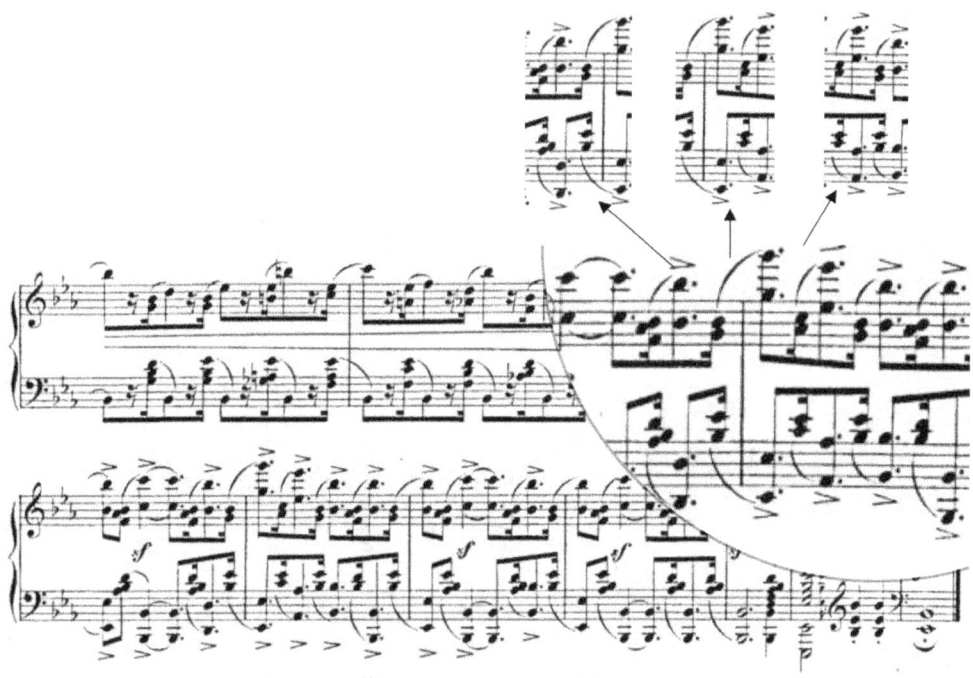

Figure 7.12. Schumann, "Fantasy," Op. 16, II., final eleven measures, think-it-then-play-it.

movement of the Schumann Fantasy (Figure 7.12) might be practiced in the think-it-then-play-it approach, with each individual leap gesture thought (mental imagery practice), played, observed in auditional memory, and corrected as needed. This always seems to be a bit like testing to see what your arms/hands/fingers *want* to do, and then making small adjustments as needed. Again, mindfulness is of key importance. Sometimes guessing helps—but guessing over and over again, not so much. If it was correct, can you remember the signals and how it felt?[2] And do it again? If it was wrong, what was the nature of the error? Too close? Too far? Missed note in a middle voice? Use mental imagery to make the correction, and then try it again. Once each *individual* leap is played accurately, comfortably, and felt as a single gesture, expand the think-it-then-play-it to two in a row, overlapping.

Many will practice sections such as this slowly; this is not wrong in and of itself. Slow practice provides certain benefit, especially in the initial stages as notes are learned and fingering decisions made, or later in the process to check for consistent accuracy and to experiment with processing all of the musical elements simultaneously. But one must be careful that, with all the extra time slow practice provides, one is still maximizing efficiency. If it is being used to rehearse your hand "looking" for the next chord in an "Is it here? Here? Oh, there it is!" sort of way, you are practicing using time you just will not have in at-tempo performance. This is why I encourage quick, direct movements even within slow practice for problems such as the Hindemith example shown in Figure 5.12. What seems to be almost miraculous is if the passage is practiced slowly, *getting to the leapt-to chord directly, and early*, the early arrival seems to persist when you return to the goal tempo. The trick is that when you *play* the short chord, you already know where you are going for the next one—especially in this kind of rhythm, where the 16th note is basically being "grabbed" on the way to the dotted 8th in one fell swoop.

Back to the Schumann. Next we can practice the same passage but with the groupings reversed (see Figure 7.13) so that the 16th note becomes the dotted 8th, and the dotted 8th the 16th; or you could even practice them both as 8ths, but still, always, getting to each one as early as possible. Rehearsing these moments, alternating between a free gesture + observation and adjustments, and a slower gesture but

Figure 7.13. Schumann, "Fantasy," Op. 16, II., rhythms reversed.

with quick, direct, early arrivals, seems to combine into a free motion that is musically exciting, technically free, but still well-prepared and accurate. And if you are thinking and playing at the proper buffering interval, missing one should not affect the ones that come after.

Another step to this approach can include alternating between five repetitions of a problematic leap in even 8ths, looking and preparing ahead, being precise in movement and "measuring" the distance of the leap; then five without looking at the keyboard—if you miss more than one, return to looking/preparing. Then repeat with the rhythms reversed, five looking, precise and measured, five not looking; then as written.

A very clear example of how practicing gesture first, then detail can avoid literal physical injury can be seen when working out the arrival at the top of the glissandos from Debussy's *Prélude* from *Pour le Piano*. In this section, glissandos are "ghosted" (skim the back of your hand along the notes without pressing) until the arrival on the top note is accurate and the left hand is appropriately timed, and then play the actual glissando once or twice, which saves you from shredding your cuticles unnecessarily (Figure 7.14).

TO THE THUMBS

Since the human hand is built of fingers that are inherently uneven both in length and in independence/dexterity, striving for an even touch, both rhythmically and acoustically, is a challenge for performers of many instruments. For pianists, there is a tendency for thumbs to "thump," and for fingers 4 (ring finger) and 5 (pinky), to be a bit less facile than fingers 1, 2, and 3. Many developing musicians will brace their fourth finger with their third, or their pinky with their fourth, and/or go to great lengths to avoid using the fourth finger at all (like a tennis player running around the ball to avoid having to hit with his/her backhand), which just exacerbates the problem. Trying to play with a "high" finger and lots of lift from the first, "major" knuckle (the one at the base of the finger/top of the bridge of the hand) can result in a lot of tension, if not injury. Instead, the pianist should cultivate motion from the length of the finger, which actually begins at the wrist with the metacarpal bones (inside the hand). (See Figure 7.15.)

I could probably go off on a book-length tangent on this topic alone, but will limit myself to practice strategies to help develop evenness, and point to Doug Johnson's work on body mapping and appropriate instrumental technique, with a few videos available on YouTube.[3]

The strategy that I call "to the thumbs" is, actually, grouping *to* the thumb if ascending in the right hand or descending in the left hand, and *to the note after the thumb* in the opposite scenarios because this forms groups that move fluently to the note immediately *after* a cross. In this case, we are forming meaningful units based on the demands of execution, and making sure that the group arrives evenly at the note that is most likely to be uneven.

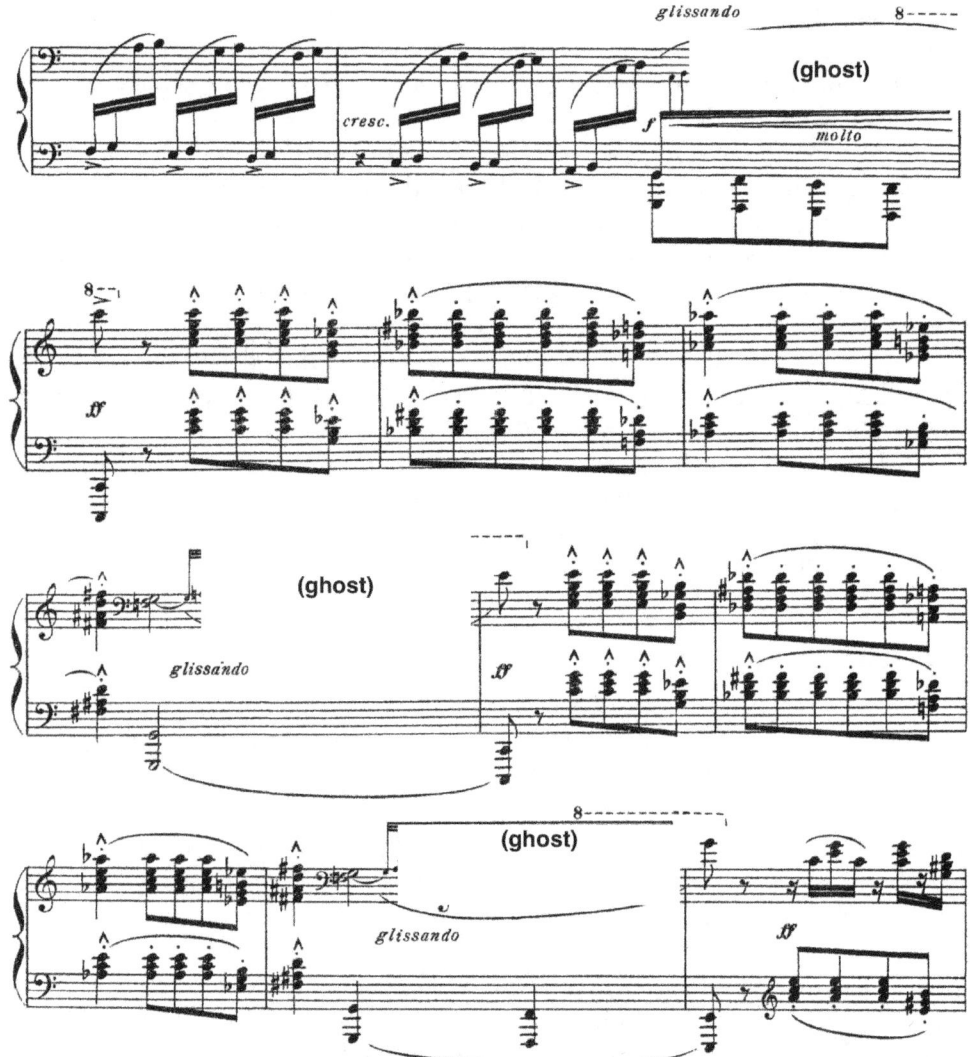

Figure 7.14. Debussy, "Prélude," from *Pour le Piano*, mm. 115–126, ghosting.

The groupings in the excerpts shown in Figures 7.16, 7.17, and 7.18 would all be practiced according to the arrows, each group starting on the last note of the previous group to avoid reinforcing gaps. These meaningful units make the processing of the passagework more cognitively-sound while allowing us to focus on the evenness of physical execution.

THE CHART[4]

Passagework that extends over many measures benefits from practicing in different rhythmic groupings. It is common to hear groupings of four, moving the "long" note to each position as shown in Figure 7.19.

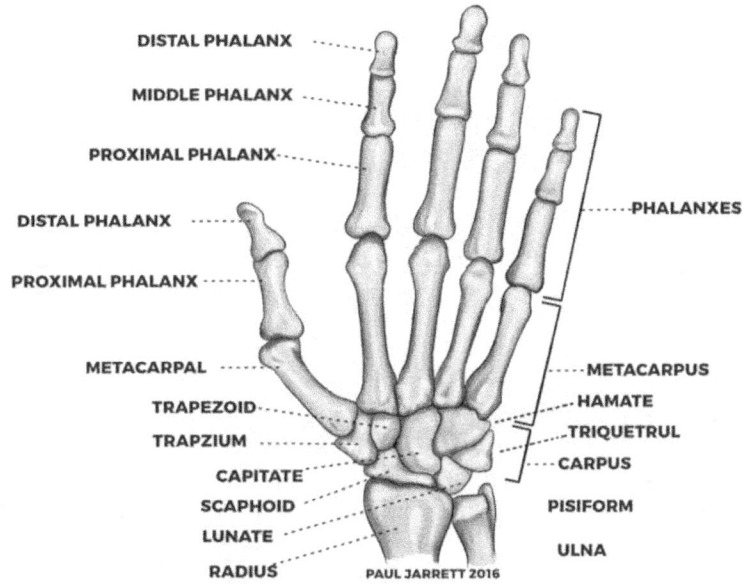

Figure 7.15. Hand anatomy diagram.
Source: https://pauljarrett.info/hand-therapy-awareness-week-2018/

Figure 7.16. Bach, "Prélude in B-flat major," *WTC I*, mm. 10–15, "to the thumbs."

Figure 7.17. Liszt, "Un Sospiro," mm. 34–35, "to the thumbs."

Figure 7.18. Chopin, "Nocturne in E minor," Op. posth., mm. 33–36, "to the thumbs."

Figure 7.19. Shifting groups of four.

This can help to some extent—and is certainly preferable to two-note groupings (short-long short-long short-long and long -short long -short long), which seems to involve practicing unevenly in an effort to get better at playing evenly. The four-note version does move the "fast" groups around, helping find where any hitches might be, although everything is still always in groups of four.

An even more beneficial approach is to practice passagework using *The Chart*, a system I was introduced to by Bonnie Blanchard at a Music Teachers National Association conference many, many years ago. The passage needing work for facility, evenness, and ease is practiced in its entirety according to each of the nine rhythms, in order, shown in Figure 7.20.

For example, the right hand of the Scherzo from the "Sonata in B minor" by Chopin would be practiced as seen in Figure 7.21. Because this type of rhythmic group-

PRACTICE STRATEGIES FOR SOLVING PHYSICAL PROBLEMS 197

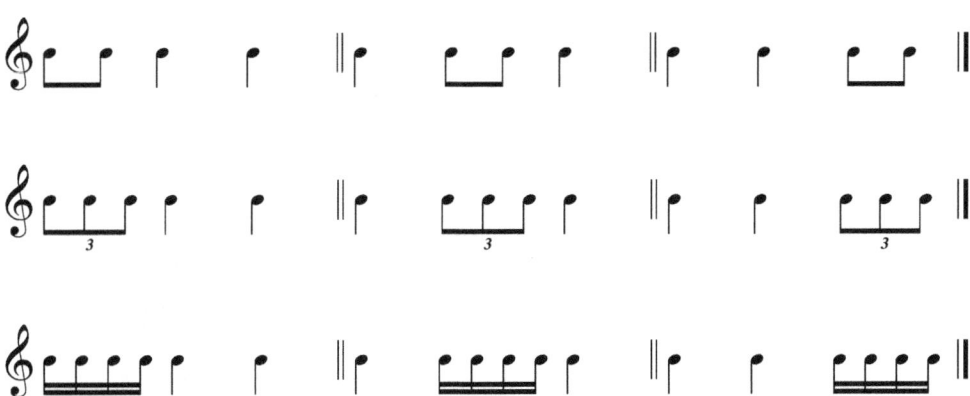

Figure 7.20. The Chart.

ing generally will, in six of the nine patterns, confound the inherent groupings of the meter, it is very difficult to recover even after small errors, requiring you to practice the entire thing correctly from start to finish—which has its own benefits. If the passagework is relentlessly continuous, though, it may be helpful to break large swathes into smaller segments, perhaps 16 or 32 measures especially while getting used to this approach. For many this is very challenging, but well worth it! Once mastered, a few practice sessions will usually remedy most if not all problems of unevenness. Sometimes alternating practice sessions using The Chart with sessions consisting of half-tempo deliberate practice is also beneficial, or you can work through The Chart with the metronome, working up by day to get closer to the goal tempo.

This practice, done conscientiously and with careful observation, aids in both rhythmic and acoustic evenness. In addition, because they are first four-note groups, then five-note groups, then six-note groups, and where the fast notes appear in each group changes from one pattern to the next, you are gradually forming larger, shifting, meaningful units. Additionally, you will find that during the two quarter notes of each pattern it is perfectly accessible to think ahead through the upcoming quick group, resulting in a practice of deliberate buffering and anticpatory motor signaling. Don't be surprised if one or two of the nine seem to be a lot more difficult than the others. Because the grouping shifts, it will reveal the specific location of breaks in the evenness. And don't be discouraged by the ones that are giving you trouble—that means you've found the source of the problem and are that much closer to the solution! This has become one of my favorite and most productive practice strategies for any passages with more than a few beats of continuous passagework.

It is possible to do this with the metronome, so that in the final three patterns of the nine, the four fast notes (notated in The Chart "guide" as 16ths) are equivalent to four of the notes in the notated pattern at tempo. It's a bit tricky to do the mathematical translation in triple meter, but for the Chopin example in Figure 7.21, let us say the target tempo is a conservative dotted half at MM = 92. This means

Chopin, B Minor Sonata, II. Opening

Chopin, B Minor Sonata, II. Opening, The Chart, Rhythm 1

Chopin, B Minor Sonata, II. Opening, The Chart, Rhythm 2

Chopin, B Minor Sonata, II. Opening, The Chart, Rhythm 3

Chopin, B Minor Sonata, II. Opening, The Chart, Rhythm 4

Chopin, B Minor Sonata, II. Opening, The Chart, Rhythm 5

Chopin, B Minor Sonata, II. Opening, The Chart, Rhythm 6

Chopin, B Minor Sonata, II. Opening, The Chart, Rhythm 7

Chopin, B Minor Sonata, II. Opening, The Chart, Rhythm 8

Chopin, B Minor Sonata, II. Opening, The Chart, Rhythm 9

Figure 7.21. Chopin, "Sonata in B minor," II., mm. 1–11, realization of "The Chart."

PRACTICE STRATEGIES FOR SOLVING PHYSICAL PROBLEMS   199

the quarter note tempo is 276 bpm, so two beats would be at MM = 138. With the metronome at MM = 138, perform each of the above rhythms, so that for the final three patterns, the four 16ths of The Chart are equal to the final, goal tempo for four of the 8ths in the passage. If the target tempo is dotted half at 108, you would use MM = 168, etc.[5]

HANDS ALONE

While I have written many times about the importance of practicing hands together as much, and as soon, as possible, there are times when hands separate practice is important and beneficial. It is definitely an important step when working out fingerings (although fingerings should be "tested" hands together), or to work out particularly thorny or complex passages.

Hands separate practice can also be helpful for solving some rhythm problems, especially if these solutions are being worked on with a conscientiously steady pulse, and may include playing one hand while chanting or tapping the rhythm of the other.

For things like two-against-three or three-against-four rhythms, one can use snippets of hands-separate to reinforce the pulse and feel of the division before putting them hands together. If new to these types of rhythms, it is helpful to start with movement and chanting. If you have never done this, it will probably make the most sense to you if you just stand up right now and try it.

1. With feet hip-width apart, keeping feet on the floor, shift weight from side to side (you can lift the opposite heel—this helps us feel the downbeat "landing" a bit better). When your weight lands on your foot, this is the downbeat (Du).
2. With arms at your sides, tap them against the sides of the body in "two," one tap with the weight on the downbeat, one tap in between as you shift. (For young beginners I call this duple, "two beats per foot.") Continue to chant "Du" with each downbeat.
3. Continuing to tap in duple, now chant in triple—"Du-Da-Di," Du's still coinciding with the weight shift to each opposing foot. (This will, of course, be much easier if you have been moving, tapping, and chanting in various meters for a while already.)

To reverse the roles:

1. Maintaining the same pace for the downbeat, switch to tapping in triple, or "three beats per foot."
2. While still shifting (downbeat), tapping (each pulse), chant in duple—"Du-De."

You can then set a metronome to a flowing-paced quarter note[6] and practice the appropriate patterns shown in Figure 7.22, emphasizing the beats with a feeling of dropping or weight at first to reinforce the simultaneities.

Figure 7.22. Two against three, three against two.[7]

In these types of rhythms, the desired musical effect is usually of long, limpid lines rather than a forced, overly conscientious presentation of the rhythmic subdivisions and how they relate mathematically. Finding the common demonimator—in the example in Figure 7.22, the quarter note—and using it as the foundation of the divisions will lead to quicker and more expressive success than chanting things like "Not Dif-fi-cult," which focuses too much on each individual entity to facilitate playing with a sense of line or shape. Moving from feeling the common denominator of the quarter to the common denominator of the half will help generate the line even more once the coordination is established. Fitting rhythms together in minuscule this-to-that mathematical comparisons will not easily translate into musical or at-tempo performance. In cases such as the third *Excursion* by Samuel Barber, learning each hand almost to tempo (with a metronome on the half note, which is the lowest common denominator for most of the piece) and then putting the hands together is one of those rare exceptions to the general goal of avoiding extensive hands-alone practice.

FINGERINGS AND HOW THEY HELP FORM MEANINGFUL UNITS

When I was in high school, my teacher had me write in finger numbers for every note—which I would do, usually under great duress, and then ignore. (In fact, she wrote a LOT of stuff in my scores, which I also ignored. Sorry D. B.)

As a graduate student I was friends with a young woman who was a fabulous pianist, winning lots of competitions. She learned music quickly, and there was never a mark in her scores. When I asked her about it she said that she had an excellent first teacher, who *never let her write anything in her music*. She said, and I quote, that it was her job to observe, and remember.

These two experiences, and observation of the musical benefit of not preordaining every interpretive decision, have led me to be a bit of a minimalist with mark-

PRACTICE STRATEGIES FOR SOLVING PHYSICAL PROBLEMS 201

ing in scores, including in those of my students. Corrections might be made in the margins, so finding what precisely they refer to is a bit more effortful, or on small Post-it notes put right over the notes to which they refer, requiring their removal (to reveal the notes underneath while playing) and replacement[8] (after the practice session) until learned, at which point the Post-it is removed and discarded. Analysis details—chord symbols, etc.—are written in working copies, which are played from for the first week or two and then consulted occasionally or for score study. I encourage writing just a few things: cryptic indications of form, the key followed by a colon at the beginning of any key changes, additional dynamics *if I am sure I am not going to change my mind*, and fingerings *when they are not inherent or implied*. The presence of a finger number should indicate importance, based on a change of position or a choice between competing alternatives; everything else we need is already there. Writing 1-2-3-1-2-3-4-5 for a passage that ascends a one-octave scale is needlessly distracting our attention and/or encouraging us just to ignore *all* of the numbers, including the ones that are crucial to successful execution. That being said, the presence of a 1 or 5 helps us notice a cross or a terminus.

I also discourage adding courtesy accidentals because they discourage thinking in a key. Rather, if a student misses an accidental in the piece that is part of the key signature, s/he gets a second try. If s/he misses it again, I squawk a rubber chicken.[9] If it's missed a third time, we stop and practice all of the technical patterns the student knows in that key, and then we try it again.[10] Watchfulness, observation, and context: most of what we need to know is often already there.

You wouldn't use a crutch if your leg wasn't broken; don't write in the music what is already there

As much as possible, chosen fingerings—whether written into the score or not—should reflect similarity to technical patterns in the musician's vocabulary, with exceptions made based on contour or span such as shown in Figure 7.23.

As much as possible, like patterns should use like fingerings. In Figure 7.24, from Beethoven's *Tempest* Sonata, notice that the editor's suggestion for each ascending four-note group in the left hand is to play using fingerings 4-3-2-1, except for the one at the beginning of m. 71, probably because of the preceding contour change

In C Major, but conceptually "in" E

C Major fingerings until end of the measure – no sense in crossing 1 for the upper 2 notes of either of the above examples

Figure 7.23. C major, but not exactly.

Figure 7.24. Beethoven, "Sonata in D minor," Op. 31 No. 2, *The Tempest*, mm. 67–77, fingerings.

and the prevalence and placement of black keys in that pattern. In many cases, we must choose between two alternatives, each of which may provide a benefit *and* a disadvantage, and our job is to determine which is going to provide more ease and security *in the long run*. This often has a lot to do with how we are grouping into meaningful units and with our own personal facility strengths and/or weaknesses. Another good example of this is in the editor's decision to slide the thumb from the D♯ to the E in m. 74. It may be just as easy, and/or more even, to play this D♯ with finger 2. Again, a comparison of results and consideration of the individual musician's physiology is important.

Planning and playing in groups of three or four is usually more reliable than in groups of two; it allows us to "hold" the pattern in bigger pieces. A good fingering will facilitate thinking in chunks, and help the musician be prepared for whatever comes next. For example, in a passage such as that of Figure 7.25, the fingering at the end of m. 5 leads us back to a similar pattern reminiscent of the beginning of m. 4, and the different fingering for the same notes at the end of m. 6 leads us to the new position of m. 7.

Just a bit later in the movement, the Schenker edition (Figure 7.26) proposes a consistent but quite extended fingering plan. But fingers 1 and 2 spanning a sixth is awkward for many, and strain from an expanded hand may create unevenness or slow down the execution (although it does shift the angle of your hand such as to help lead the ascending sweeping motion).

Figure 7.25. Beethoven, "Sonata in E-flat major," Op. 81a, *Les Adieux*, III., mm. 4–8, fingerings.

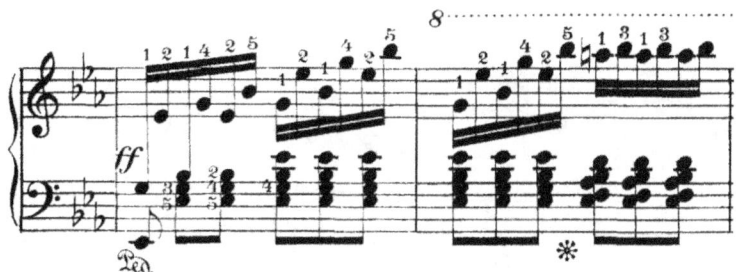

Figure 7.26. Beethoven, Op. 81a, III., mm. 29–30, Schenker edition.

Instead, using 3-4-5 for the upper notes may help preserve the sense of line, and groups of six 16th notes, while avoiding a sense of overextension. Using the thumb on E♭ rather than the Gs connects it to it being an E♭ major four-note chord. It also helps the musician prepare for the transition into the trill at the end of m. 30 and encourages thinking in bigger pieces. This fingering and how it encourages conceptual chunking is shown in Figure 7.27.

Similarly, the passage in Figure 7.28 is going to be more effectively performed thinking of and executing four- or six-note "chunks" that combine into a larger meaningful unit: a G major scale in thirds, spanning three measures. Of course pairs of alternating between fingers 1 and 2 or 1 and 3 over and over again can still combine into the meaningful unit of a scale in thirds, but four subgroups are much easier to keep track of physically and mentally than nine groups of two.

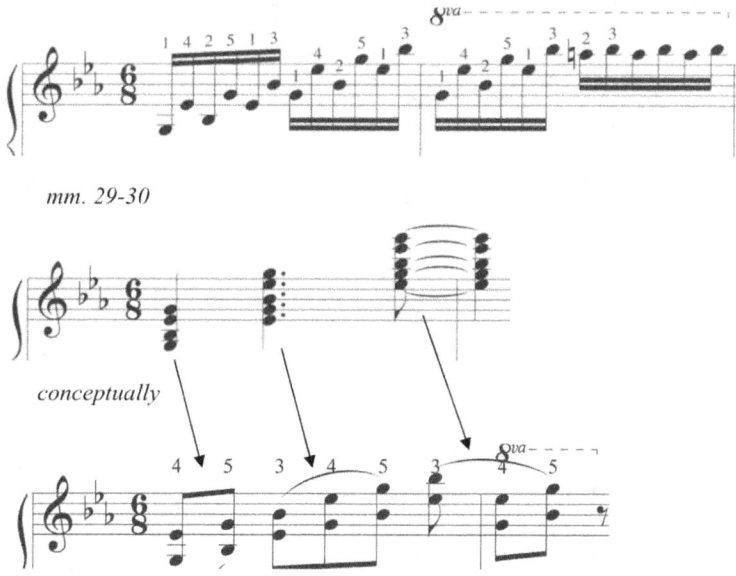

Figure 7.27. Beethoven, Op. 81a, III., mm. 29–30, conceptual chunking.

Figure 7.28. Beethoven, "Sonata in G major," Op. 14 No. 2, III., mm. 225–228, alternating 3rds.

Learning our technical patterns through rule-based learning has established a firm and helpful foundation. Linking fingering choices to related technical patterns as much as possible helps facilitate the transfer of information from established patterns to new paradigms. For example, fingerings for the opening section of the E-flat Major Impromptu by Schubert, shown in Figure 7.29, are based on: (a) the E-flat major scale, (b) facilitating ease in shifting for the relaxed, light touch desired in the flitting passage in mm. 3-4, and (c) accounting for subtle adjustments based

Figure 7.29. Schubert, "Impromptu in E-flat major," Op. 90 No. 2, mm. 1–19.

on a preference for the pinky on the highest note of the pattern such as in mm. 6, 7, 9, etc., which gives us groups of 5 + 3 or 4 + 4.

Likewise, accounting for the entire chord shape relates the passage in Figure 7.30 to known technical patterns and encourages thinking in meaningful units. (Some might balk at the trill figuration using fingers 5 and 4, but a slight bit of hand rotation and developed facility should allow for that with no problem for the advanced musician.)

Chord and inversion fingering patterns, 4 or 3 dependent on relative proximity to 5 and 2.

Beethoven, Sonata Op. 31 No. 2, "The Tempest," mm. 78-82, chord-inversion-influenced fingerings

Figure 7.30. Chord inversion fingerings.

Well-chosen fingerings can also help realize articulations. Ending a slur with a pinky or thumb will help remind the hand that it is moving. Fingerings also forecast changes of direction or configuration, and can impact elements such as tone color and dynamic, which means these elements should be considered and decisions made before making "permanent" fingering decisions.

For example, conversely to the alternating thirds passage discussed above, in the opening of the *Tempest* Sonata, redundant two-note fingering groupings are appropriate, as these facilitate both the physicality and the desired nuance of the two-note slurs. Figure 7.31 shows how we can deconstruct and reconstruct this passage to refine our physical approach. We can start by dropping into the first of each pair/slur (2nd excerpt of 7.31). Then we add the second note of the pair (third excerpt of 7.31) to create a harmonic interval, maintaining the dropping motion into each (this will facilitate the slur/lift to come). After all of the above, review the single quarter notes again (which reestablishes the starting notes in recent working memory), and then the dyads ascending or descending as written, dropping into the first note of each pair, and lifting lightly from the wrist for the second.

mm. 1-17

mm. 1-12, each quarter played tenuto using dropped arm motion

mm. 1-12, each dyad played tenuto using dropped arm motion

Figure 7.31. Beethoven, Op. 31 No. 2, I., mm. 1–17, gesture building and fingerings.

In this next example (Figure 7.32), whether you decide on the top fingering option or the lower one, the change of fingering and therefore change of position initiated on the second of each repeated note facilitates ease while shifting, making the repeated note much easier to execute cleanly.

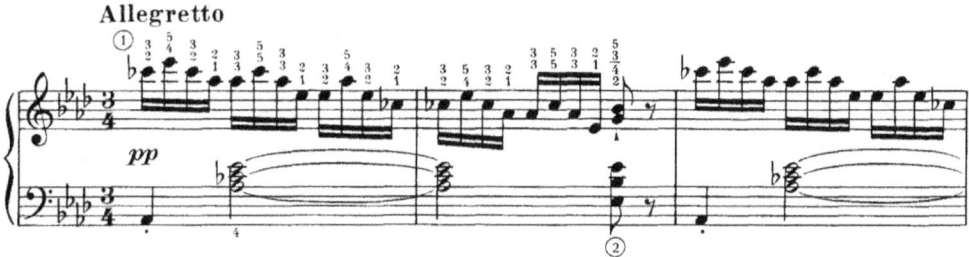

Figure 7.32. Schubert, "Impromptu in A-flat major," Op. 90 No. 4, mm. 1–3, fingerings.

There is a tradition of avoiding thumbs and pinkies on black keys, but quite frankly, this is often unwarranted and can introduce more difficulties than it resolves. Playing with loose arms and wrists and a relaxed technique allows for easy motion into and out of the key bed, making the playing of thumbs on black keys much easier than it may seem. It is maybe not the first option to consider, but should perhaps not be avoided as much as it is.

In all cases, we want fingering decisions to be conducive to the musical demands of the passage, to fit with what we already know as much as possible, and to encourage thinking in chunks rather than isolated minutiae. We also want them, once decided on, to be observed. I had a student working on the E major Invention by J. S. Bach. While she was waiting for her *Urtext* edition to arrive, she was using a highly edited version that had been her mother's, which included a lot of fingerings and articulation marks. Rather than having her erase every mark and start over, I gave her an assignment: to go through the piece carefully and white out *every fingering that was unnecessary*. This forced a deep and conceptual look at, and decisions about, what was already on the page. I had never thought to do this before, but what she sent back to me was spot on—with just numbers as needed at crosses or changes of position. I am hopeful that, since she was the one who decided what was "necessary," she will be much more careful to observe what is included—a good example of the adage "less is more," I think.

ABOVE STRATEGIES IN SEQUENCE AND COMBINATION

You have probably noticed some overlapping of topics in the previous sections, and hopefully also realized how the physical practice strategies I have just outlined help solve the mental challenges in the pieces as discussed in the previous section. Advanced musicians must hone their ability to recognize problems or potential problems, and to identify the best approaches for solving them. The ability to evaluate the success of various attempted strategies, and to store mindfully the solutions that work, is part and parcel of these tasks. Because I have given so many examples, I will try to wrap all this up with just a few more, showing/explaining some of the combinations that might prove beneficial.

A good example of combining layering, to the thumbs, think-it-then-play-it, and gesture first then details comes from a middle section in the "Un Sospiro Etude" already discussed (see Figures 6.15–17). In order: we might practice the left-hand melody first (layering); then practice the right hand "to the thumbs." Then we put the right hand and the melody together, omitting the 16th note pickups, grace notes, and lower chord

mm. 30-35, melody only

mm. 30-31, "to the thumbs"

mm. 30-33, LH leaping gesture

Figure 7.33. Liszt, "Un Sospiro," mm. 30–35, melody, "to the thumbs" » gesture.

PRACTICE STRATEGIES FOR SOLVING PHYSICAL PROBLEMS 209

tones at first. Next, we work on the gesture for the 16th note and grace-note leaps to the chords in the left hand (in the dashed circles), refining as needed, then the right hand and *just* the grace-note gestures. This sequence shown in Figure 7.33.

Lastly, we put the melody and the right hand together in think-it-then-play-it groups of beat to beat, beat one to beat three/beat three to beat one, and then from beat one to beat one, as shown in Figure 7.34.

Liszt, Un Sospiro, think-it-then-play-it beat by beat

Liszt, Un Sospiro, think-it-then-play-it, by the half measure

Liszt, Un Sospiro, think-it-then-play-it, by the measure

Figure 7.34. Liszt, "Un Sospiro," think-it-then-play-it.

The steps and sequencing of strategies will vary depending on the demands of the piece and the challenges or limitations of the musician. Selecting the right strategy is like a carpenter picking the right tool, although an open mind, flexibility to try something different if the strategy you are using doesn't seem to be helping, and remembering that we don't necessarily learn in a nice, evenly ascending line goes a long way toward preserving interest and motivation. I often tell students that we want progress to look like this,

but it usually looks more like this,

and that's ok.

Many of these practice strategies involve some kind of chunking. This acts in support of the need to identify and store meaningful units, and to manage larger pieces of the music physically through a combination of large-scale motions/gestures and build-up of smaller details. Think-it-then-play-it is its own form of chunking, helping us to be prepared mentally and thinking ahead at an optimal buffering speed for the passage at hand. Practicing scaffolding, through playing what is on downbeats only, or beats only, helps establish the long-term harmonic foundation, which informs our memory as well as our musical decisions and helps establish a constant underlying pulse. Attention to musical elements early in the process and linking them directly to the physical actions by which we play results in musically-saturated learning, so that our interpretive elements are incorporated into our learning of the notes themselves, rather than "painted on" at the end and therefore something extra to be remembered separately when we have plenty to remember already. Taking things apart into layers and reassembling them by voice provides insight into the myriad voicings and melodic lines and helps us move more quickly to hands-together practice, which is much more valuable to our learning in every respect. Learning to *feel* our rhythms and meters leads to a more vibrant performance, enabling us to play with nuance, appropriate inflection, and rhythmic vitality. Writing in just the fingerings that we need, and practicing according to shifts of position (i.e., "to the thumbs") or breath facilitates mental grouping of melodic motions, and using The Chart for increasing speed and facility moves the groupings around so that we can identify areas of difficulty and think ahead in groups of varying size and duration. Building this mindful security through awareness of our thought process as well as deep familiarity with the physical motions involved allow us to maintain focus on the appropriate elements and perform with flexibility and expression. Rule learning teaches us the bigger picture, helping us be better able to solve the next problem we encounter with awareness and confidence. All these strategies break down what may feel like insurmountable problems and turn them into a series of steps that we understand and execute freely and with ease.

The subject, and ourselves.

NOTES

1. So often a mistake that seems completely random is due to exactly this scenario—either the pattern is being predicted, based on its similarity to some other pattern(s) in the piece, to be something it is not, or how we are getting to or leaving that pattern is being influenced by a similar occurrence elsewhere. A bit of detective work that reveals these deceptive comparisons is worth every second it takes.

2. William Westney (2003) calls this a *feelmage*; I refer to it as physically audiating, or tell students to "take a picture of how it *felt*." Remember, to *audiate* means to hear and understand music either from a score or from memory; I'm using the term *physically audiate* to refer to mental imagery practice, in planning/predicting, and observing in retrospect.

3. Start here: https://www.youtube.com/watch?v=CdlHspcaKcU

4. I often write this in gothic-style letters because the execution of it is quite arduous. Students seem to find this amusing, and do it anyway.

5. This is actually far easier to compute if you are dealing with a passage in duple and the passagework is in 16ths, but I have already written out all nine of those Chopin patterns so I'm sticking with it.

6. You can use the metronome for the five steps above, actually. I highly recommend it. Learning to MOVE to the metronome is an important first step before you ask someone to PLAY with one. And don't go too slowly—too slow causes subdividing, which interferes with the feel of the spanning of the beat necessary to a proper and musical interpretation of these types of rhythms and will often result in uneven divisions in one or both parts.

7. If the shared thumb on middle C is causing problems, drop your left hand an octave.

8. Every time you take the Post-it out and then have to remember where to put it back reinforces that correction in your mind.

9. I do, seriously. I had a student once who, after a second accidental mistake would cry plaintively, "Not the chicken!"

10. There are perhaps appropriate times for exceptions to this, such as if you have one or two run-throughs before you need to perform something and you miss them. But for the sake of *learning*, when you are working on repertoire that you plan to polish, memorize, etc. it will reinforce cognitively sound learning better if you work on thinking in a key. My favored practice as a teacher, for more urgent and/or desperate situations, is to write the # or ♭ on a small Post-it note, put it directly over the note to which it applies, and when the student is not forgetting anymore we take the Post-it out. Obviously there are extremely chromatic passages where courtesy accidentals are also more appropriate, and they are definitely indicated when there is not a lot of time for preparation before a performance.

PART 4

8

HOW INTENTIONAL PRACTICE BENEFITS PERFORMANCE

Something new is going to happen and we don't [always] know what. (Westney, 2003, p. 140)

A performer who responds with his entire self, not just his thinking mind, can create an art of transcendent spirituality. Not only is the artist as open as a child is, but the constraints of individual ego and personality seem to dissolve in the act of performance. (Westney, 2003, p. 27)

If we don't find the truth in practice . . . [we'll find it in] performance. (Westney, 2003, p. 82)

I have defined cognitively sound, efficient, beneficial practice as *time spent in mindful, focused, observant activities, carefully constructed so as to meet specific goals, to problem-solve, and/or to reinforce previously discovered appropriate solutions.*

During this time, the intentional, effective practicer is:

- choosing appropriate strategies for problem solving based on age, level of achievement, previous experience, knowledge, and awareness of the nature of the challenges being faced;
- focusing on pattern-based reading and physical awareness of the body in space and how it relates to tempo, pulse, and technique;
- striving to anticipate, process, and execute information in chunks based on identifiable and relevant meaningful units; and
- maintaining awareness of how the current state compares to the final goal state and incorporating that awareness as much as possible into the chosen solution strategies.

This results in a constant loop of prediction, enaction, and observation.

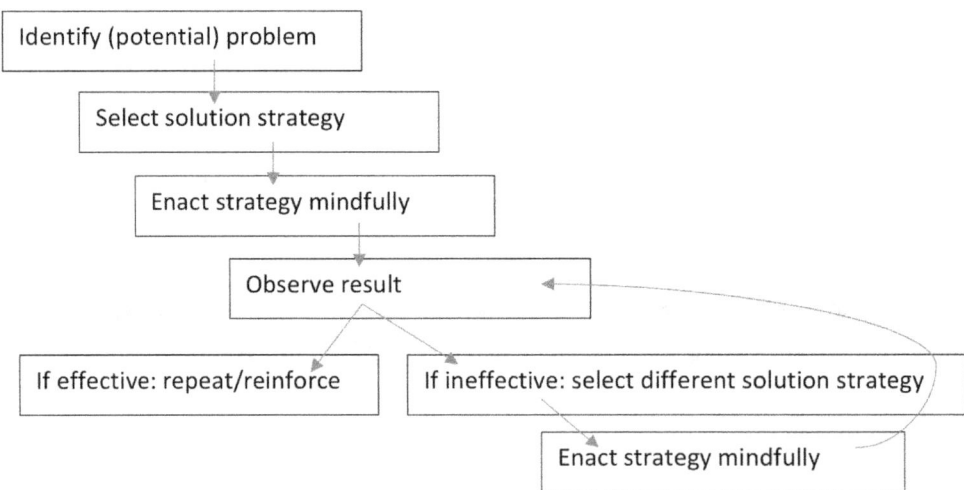

Figure 8.1. Mindful practicing loop.

Of course, all of this assumes established audiation skills, beneficial pacing of difficulties and tasks, a solid and thorough mechanical foundation, and a lot of encouragement and enjoyment of not only the process itself, but of each and every challenge being surmounted. There might be a long way still to go, but you can also see how far you have come and remain optimistic about your chances of achieving your goals.

If done well, everything we learn helps us learn the next thing better, faster. And *knowing*, with depth of understanding and multiple routes to both information and motor signals, gives us the cognitive space to perform with conviction, facility, and creative, personal expression. This knowing consists of fluency in the vocabulary of music; recognition of the melodic, harmonic, and rhythmic patterns that make up our pieces; understanding of stylistic norms; and the physical comfort of mindful action and familiarity with the response of the instrument.

Practicing so as to think ahead, to observe larger- and smaller-scale patterns, to link actions directly to those patterns in response to thought, and to understand how our piece works mentally, physically, and audiationally facilitates reliability and security in our performance in a way that playing something a thousand times a day does not. Observing our actions and the results provides a reliable foundation for performance as well as the flexibility and mental space to make adjustments as needed. You can test that flexibility in practice; you may have a better handle on it than you think you do![1]

This flexibility is, ironically, a hallmark of effective performance, and one of the most important things that intentional practice can help us prepare for. An inherent creativity of approach—of trying different things and observing results, of listening to and responding to the instrument, the room, your own mood or the mood or timing of your collaborators, of making predictions and testing whether they were true—opens us up to the freedom we so need for dynamic, vibrant, personal performance.

There is also a high degree of musical interactivity, so that dynamics, tempo, and articulation, voicing, phrasing, the infinite varieties and types of musical inflection, each affects the others. I have played in very "live" rooms that required slower tempos, a clearer touch, and much less pedal, and which sounded completely different with an audience as compared to the rehearsal. *We must be able to adapt to whatever situation presents itself in that moment.*

> Chaos theory is an open-systems theory. Thus it takes the view that various processes in life are not self-contained, but in fact affect each other in a dynamic, moment-to-moment way. Our physical well-being, for example, is an open system responding in an ongoing way to other systems. . . . Open-systems theories embrace the complexity, dynamism, and wholeness of life, and give up the idea that the world is predictable or that we are in control. . . . Nature, as an open system, operates on "feedback loops"—momentary information from one system that immediately affects another system. . . . Feedback processes are not regular and steady; rather they have moments of stillness followed by bursts of activity, in a pattern that at first glance may appear to be random.
>
> Mastering musical performance skills . . . is a dynamic, natural, open-systems process. . . . The various systems are in constant flux and interact differently from one moment to the next. This is reality. (Westney, 2003, pp. 72–73)

If we practice like it's a closed system, meaning we just do the exact same thing every time and nothing will ever change the sequence of events (like starting a car), we lack the ability to make adjustments for acoustics, audience noise, an unfamiliar instrument (particularly important if you are a pianist), a slight difference or error from one of your collaborators, etc. But musical performance is not a closed system. If we have paid attention to what we did when it sounded like this, that, or the other, we are able to make sometimes tiny incremental adjustments almost instantly, and if we keep our minds and our ears open, in practice as well as in performance, what comes out at any point should be perfectly satisfying, and may, in fact, be better than it has ever been before.

> There are no universal recipes to follow, because only in each moment does a good pathway emerge, based on immediate perceptions. You try something and get a specific result, and only then do you know what to do next. . . . This flowing, nonjudgmental openness to events, this acceptance of how things really are (regardless of prior intentions), is called by Gestalt psychologists the "continuum of awareness." It's quite a refreshing and peaceful state for humans to be in, and it leads to maximum productivity as well. Finding that observant state on a daily basis may not always be easy, but it's certainly worth the effort. (Westney, 2003, p. 77)

In other words, if we know what we are doing, how, and why, when we are doing it, we are that much more likely to be able to do it again, in a way that will feel always authentic, reliable, yet of the moment. Thus, any performance adrenaline serves to heighten focus and energy, making the performance that much better instead of so much worse. If we don't know what we are doing or how we are doing it, when it is time to perform and we get that rush of adrenaline, all we know is that we are nervous. This is of no help. To anyone. Ever.

As Michael Jordan wrote in his book (now, regrettably, out of print) *I Can't Accept Not Trying*, when he is shooting that crucial three-pointer at the final buzzer, he is not thinking about how important it is to the game or his team that he make the shot, he is thinking about how it felt all the other times he made a three-pointer from that position. This is our goal as performers, and if our focus when *practicing* is on whatever we are going to be thinking and doing, and how it feels while we are doing it, we will find a lot more success in performance.

One thing we need to remember is that "nerves" are not necessarily a bad thing. We can help ourselves by using different terminology. We aren't "nervous," we are excited, energized, enthusiastic, eager. We must also realize that the adrenaline is, believe it or not, our friend—it not only gives us energy, but helps foster focus and eliminate distractions. My worst mistakes have been when I wasn't nervous. On the other hand . . .

I burned my palm quite badly one afternoon a few hours before a flute recital I was accompanying—a challenging piece by Lukas Foss, the flutist's senior recital. It couldn't be rescheduled, and nobody was going to fill in for me with that piece on such short notice. I drove to the recital with a bag of ice in my hand, stood backstage with the bag of ice in my hand, wondering how on earth I was going to pull this off. The pain was excruciating. The moment came, I put the ice down, and stepped out on stage. And my hand stopped hurting. It didn't hurt through the entire piece, not even during the bow. As I stepped off stage, the pain returned with a vengeance, and I grabbed up the bag of ice, thinking: "Well *that* was interesting." At that moment I stopped being "afraid" of the nerves, and recognized them for what they were worth. I had an opposite experience a few years later, when I was taking beta blockers for a heart arrhythmia (since diagnosed as a symptom of acute hypothyroidism and treated with thyroid medication), and played an entire recital with only manufactured energy and an overwhelming desire for it just to be over so I could go home and go to bed. This is *not what we want to feel when we are performing*.

Effective practice also seems to help us move more easily through errors, an important skill for convincing performance. Practicing with this in mind may include playing just a bit past a mistake, so as to rehearse recovering, before stopping and going back to fix and reinforce any correction. It is also a good idea to rehearse performing—ideally at the beginning of a practice session rather than the end, as this more closely imitates the performance experience—where all mistakes are ignored. I like to joke that effective performance has no nobility in it—if there's a man down, you leave him in the dirt and don't think about him again. Stopping midperformance to try to fix something is like jumping off a moving train and then trying to jump back *onto the same car*.

Of course this must be in careful balance with practicing so as to find difficulties and fix them. If all we ever do is play through, it is more and more likely that the problem will persist.

Perhaps one of the most significant challenges of performance is finding and staying right on that line between objective observation and expressive freedom. Highly regimented systems of execution have been rehearsed to the point of seeming automaticity, but for musical performance to be vibrant, "alive," it must also have spontaneity and immediacy. If it sounds like this is how you have done it the last hundred times, it may come across as tired, stale, uninspired. You have all heard when a musician holds a rest for long enough *because they are counting it* as compared to when the rest lingers there, like a held breath, leading us all—musician and audience alike—to the next moment with musical suspense. And while some cognitive scientists claim that a true indicator of expertise is when a performer can execute a piece over and over, virtually identically every time, including nuances of phrasing and rubato, I would argue that a true expert would be able to execute a piece effectively, powerfully, successfully, time and time again, yet *never exactly the same*. It should never sound like you are playing it in a certain way because someone told you to, but rather because that is just how it must be, *at that moment in time*. And it might "must be" different next time. Say your *mf* comes out a little louder than expected; the subsequent *f* might then be louder, or maybe start softer and crescendo more. *You might even decide that you like that better.*

Westney (2003) recommends keeping interpretive questions open for longer in the rehearsal process (p. 95). I actually encourage keeping some of them open even until the performance itself, especially for advanced musicians who have more experience keeping more and more information in "process" at the same time. This can actually help encourage, if not actively implement, our staying in the moment, and on that line of focus, awareness, and trust.

Our attention is, in effect, a pie. In practice we rehearse allotting it out, this "slice" to these notes, that one to those fingerings, these to phrasing and balance and timing and tone. As we do so, we observe what works and what does not, and adjust accordingly. And then in performance, we strive to mete out those slices in the same way as that of our most successful rendition, always reserving at least one extra slice for that unexpected guest such as that dynamic that didn't come out exactly how we intended it, a sticky key or flickering stage light or COUGH COUGH COUGH from the audience. I was performing once with a fabulous musician who happened to play the trumpet.[2] I arrived at the top of a spectacular flourish, followed in the score by a short rest, when the cell phone of someone in the audience began to ring. I waited there, arms and breath and mind, for the phone to stop, and then I continued, and he was right there with me. I trusted him, he trusted me, and everyone thought that long pause was rehearsed, planned, and seemingly a complete coincidence with the ringtone. Someone actually asked, "Did you hear that cell phone during that grand pause?"

Why yes, yes we did. :-)

I think that, even after a perfectly lovely and well-received performance, many performers often feel they did not do exactly what they intended. But the audience does not know what you intended; it only knows what it heard. And if what you *do* accounts for the differences, and presents an interpretation that is personal and convincing, is this not still an "effective" performance? Even if we want the same result, sometimes we do actually have to do some thing(s) differently.

The thing is, if we know we know it, we also know we can trust it.

What more could we want?

NOTES

1. I sometimes watch a student working on something that I am quite confident they can do with facility and ease, and they are laboring to the point where I can both see and hear them thinking. At this point I say, "Do it again, but pretend it's easy." It often works, and the student realizes how much they are in their own way.

2. SB, you know who you are. It was a fabulous moment. I can only hope to work with you again.

APPENDIX A: SAMPLE LESSON PLAN AND PRACTICE SHEET

Beginning Musician

Rhythm: Move, tap, and chant triple meter rhythm patterns.

Tonal: Tonic patterns in D major; sing "Ring Around the Rosy" (and all fall down!); tonic and dominant patterns in C♯ minor.

Creativity: Teach I-V-I cadence patterns and tonic arpeggio in G major, assign student to improvise using these patterns, to use for Cotton Candy transposition (below) and also to improvise animal sounds for Old MacDonald (suggest quack, moo, oink, meow; and explore one or two in lesson to find appropriate register for each animal).

REVIEW

- Peter, Peter Pumpkin Eater: slow and "heavy," and fast and "light" (Figure App.1a)
- Falling Leaves: have students replace "leaves" with other items that might fall: marbles, snow, books, etc. to experiment with different sounds, and select a few for practice (Figure App.1b)
- Cotton Candy: also practice starting/ending on G (point out how the student part alone sounds like major, but the accompaniment changes it to Dorian; Figure App.1c)

NEW

- Twin Kangaroos

1. Play Do-Re-Do patterns on D♭—Do up and down the keyboard using the graphic notation as shown on Practice Page (Figure App.1d; use left hand [LH] going up and right hand [RH] going down for this step)
2. Student play two Do-Re-Do patterns, teacher "echo"
3. Teach student ending measure by rote—then play song, have them play the ending
4. Teach student whole song

Unit 2

Music Information
For the Teacher
Duple Meter
Major Tonality
DO is F♯
Connected Style

Check List

Lesson		Home
____	Solo	____
____	Connected Style	____
____	Separated Style	____
____	Played Loudly	____
____	Played Softly	____
____	Chant RP	____
____	Perform RP	____
____	Create with RP	____

Peter, Peter, Pumpkin Eater

Student Solo
Up Stems (RH)
Down Stems (LH)

Track 5

Student Part
Fingers and Hands

Hand Does Not Move — S²
Moving Hand — S¹

8

Figure App.1a. "Peter, Peter Pumpkin Eater."
Used by Permission, Music Moves for Piano.

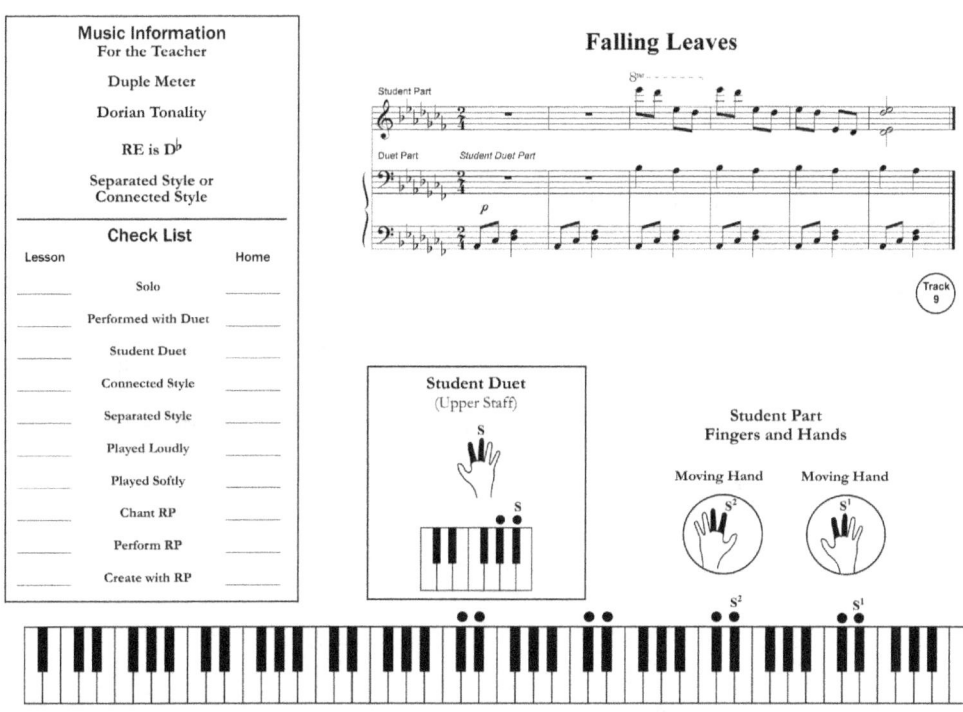

Figure App.1b. "Falling Leaves."
Used by Permission, Music Moves for Piano.

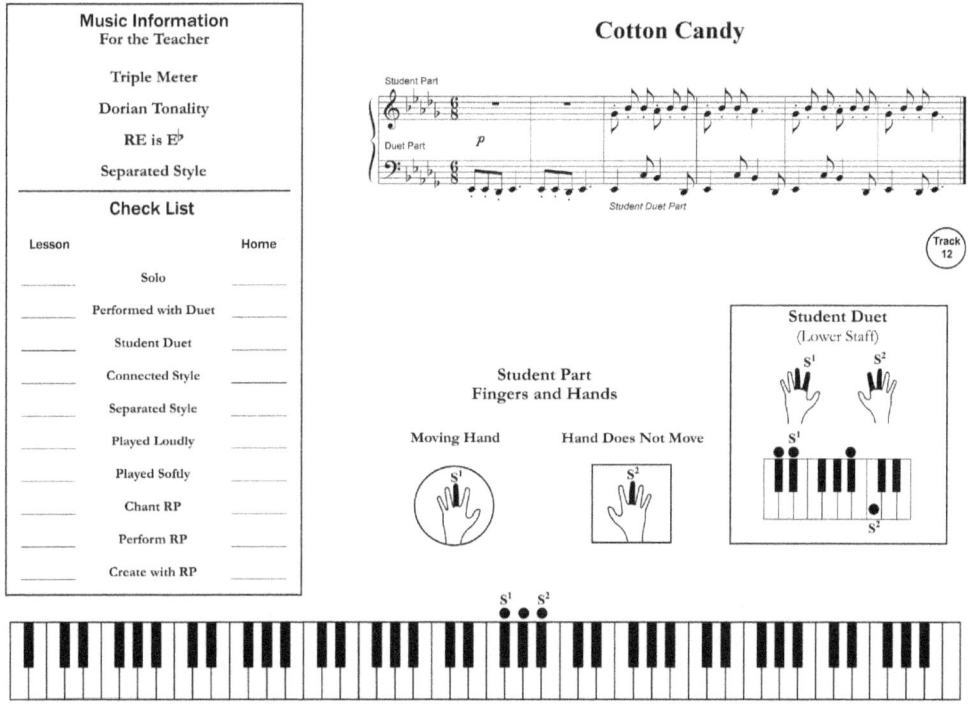

Figure App.1c. "Cotton Candy."
Used by Permission, Music Moves for Piano.

Listen to: Track 21-27
Includes: Folk Song from Wales, Route 76, Latvian Folk Song, Old MacDonald, Big Ben

Songs to Sing Tracks: 13 Ring Around the Rosy; 21 Folk Song from Wales; 23 Latvian Folk Song

Chant: Three triple meter rhythm patterns from *Pattern CD* (GIA)

Creativity/Improvisation: Sing Old MacDonald and design various sounds for various animals in the appropriate microbeat rhythm. Experiment with different registers and dynamics to find the one that sounds most like each animal.

Review Songs:
- Peter, Peter Pumpkin Eater: practice slow and "heavy" and fast and "light"
- Falling Leaves, Marbles, etc.
- Cotton Candy: also practice starting/ending on G.

New Songs:
- Twin Kangaroos

Draw the animals on your farm:

Figure App.1d.   Sample lesson assignment.
Used by Permission, Music Moves for Piano.

APPENDIX B: SAMPLE PRACTICE ASSIGNMENTS

Intermediate Musician

1. **"Gigue a l'Angloise," Georg Philipp Telemann (Figure App.4)**
   Preparatory technique:
   Triads and inversions, broken, in G, C, D, and A major

Figure App.2. Triads and inversions.

Cadence pattern in G major

Figure App.3. Cadence pattern.

SCORE STUDY

(In copy) mark each occurrence of I, IV, V, and V⁷ in G major, find and show D major section with D: Then mark I and V in D.

Look for recurrence of any motives or phrases. Should find a, a', and b, while noting mm. 1–2 slightly varied in mm. 9–10 and mm. 11–12. This can be done from listening to the recording, or in the lesson with the teacher playing it through a few times.

The copy should look something like what's seen in Figure App.4.

PRACTICE

Days 1–3

LH alone, tapping pulse in RH
RH: find and block each chord pattern
RH alone, tapping pulse in LH

Days 4–7

LH alone, tap RH part
RH alone, tap LH part
Working backward from end, practice 4 measures at a time LH/RH/HT; then RH/LH/HT

Subsequent Weeks

Practice by dynamic, so the *mp* sections practiced together, then the *mf* sections. Experiment with articulations and come up with a plan that conveys the phrasing and keeps the texture clear. Apply decisions to parallel phrases.

2. "Ballade," Op 100 No 15, Johann Friedrich Burgmüller (Figure App.5)

Preparatory

Practice cadence and then triads and inversions of tonic, subdominant, and dominant 7ths, in C minor and C major.

Practice measure 3, LH motive in C major, parallel motion in both hands, focusing on loose wrist and attention to arm rotation.

Listen to a recording and write a story that conveys the characters of the ABA sections.

APPENDIX B

Figure App.4. Telemann, "Gigue a l'Angloise."

SCORE STUDY

Mark i, iv, V, V^7 and I, IV, V, V^7 for both sections.

Tap the rhythms of the B section, using a "legato" tap for melody and "staccato" taps for the LH chords.

PRACTICE

1. Practice B section with LH on-beat dotted half chords accompanying RH melody.
2. Play RH tap LH rhythm.
3. Practice hands together.
4. Practice A sections with RH playing downbeat chord (staccato) only, LH as written.

228 SAMPLE PRACTICE ASSIGNMENTS

5. Practice RH accompanying pattern by moving back and forth from C minor triad to the intervening C–E♭–F♯ chord first as long dotted-quarters (by rote), then in recurrent 8th note/staccato pattern (from score).
6. Practice A sections hands together.
7. Put it all together: coda first, then from B to the end, then from the beginning.

Figure App.5. Burgmüller, "Ballade," from *100 Easy Etudes*, mm. 1–46.

3. "Dance," No. 8 from *For Children*, Vol. 2, Béla Bartok (Figure App.6)

PREPARATION

Practice cadence pattern in E minor.
Practice E natural minor scales in various articulation patterns, focusing on staccatos and 2-note slurs.

SCORE STUDY

Find and mark a and a', putting a ° at the moment that is different the second time.

Mark i, iv and V or V^7 chords in E minor with roman numerals.

Write in letter name symbols for chords outside of E minor, such as the $CMaj^7$, m. 18; Em^7, m15.

Find change to relative major, mark with bracket, label chords in G major.

For some students I might have them rewrite the LH part, using as-long-as-possible durations to indicate harmonic rhythm and notice voice-leading chords (shown with dashed arrows, Figure App.7).

PRACTICE

Days 1–3

Practice LH alone, downbeat chords only, played as half notes.

Practice hands together, LH as above, focusing on RH articulation and a conscious drop/lift wrist motion in 2-note slurs (almost exaggerated at this point).

Tap both parts hands together, showing staccatos and accents with the tap.

Days 4–7

In all cases, exaggerate noted articulations, a bit under tempo until coordination of articulations is comfortable.

Practice LH as written, again with tapping the RH part.
Tap the LH part, play the RH.
Try at least 3 times slowly hands together.

Figure App.6. Bartok, "Dance," from *For Children*, vol. 2.

APPENDIX B

Figure App.7. Bartok, "Dance," chord progression map.

APPENDIX C

The Integrated Lesson

One of the challenges of teaching that often comes up in any pedagogy course I've taught or facilitated is how to fit everything into the lesson. As we all know, there is only so much time. My argument would always be that if you do more, and do it thoroughly and well, in the lesson, the student can do even more, better, on their own in the week in between. (The "teach the man to fish" approach.) Aural skills, sightreading, theory, technique—these are not separate entities. If you incorporate these elements into the introduction and study of the repertoire, and combine them with beneficial, intentional practice strategies, the learning is comprehensive and the value of each element reinforced. While it does "front-load" our efforts, ultimately we accomplish more in less time and establish multiple routes to information and solutions, lending depth and security to the endeavor as a whole. We can design an integrated lesson, or presentation of a new piece, so that we invest a bit of time in laying the foundation, and the work done after is that much more secure.

I will use the teaching of Haydn's "Sonata in F major," Hob. XVI/23 as an example, with a timeline of sorts. I am *not* going to outline specific practice strategies from the book in this case.

Two weeks before the piece is going to be introduced (10 minutes):

The student assigned to review sonata form analysis from previous sonatinas studied and to make a map of Sonata-Allegro form. *(Theory/analysis)*

Czerny Etudes from Czerny-Germer Part I #11 (trills, RH part played in the LH), Part II #21, 24 (32nds passagework), and Op 299 No 17 (layered writing). The Czerny-Germer are simple enough for a student at this level they can first be sight-read in the lesson, and maybe even transposed if the student is experienced with this activity. *(Technique, sight-reading, functional skills)*

Aural practice of singing and identifying dominant and diminished 7ths practiced. *(Aural awareness)*

One week before the piece is going to be introduced (5-10 minutes):

The student is assigned to review all known technical patterns in F major, D minor, C major, and G minor. These should include scales, tonic and domiant 7th arpeggios, tonic triads, dominant 7ths, and diminished 7ths in blocked and broken inversion patterns, and the i-VI-iv-V_4^6-V^7-i (I-vi-IV-V_4^6-V^7-I in Major) cadence. The student is also assigned to practice blocked diminished 7th chords ascending chromatically, and then again, resolving each to the minor triad a half step above the played root. *(Technique, Theory)*

The student's map of Sonata-Allegro form is reviewed and checked for accuracy. It should contain the following, in some similar fashion:

First tonal area: FTA
Second tonal area: STA

EXPOSITION			**DEVELOPMENT**	**RECAPITULATION**		
FTA	*	STA	:‖ *anything goes, as long as*	FTA	*	STA ‖
I	modulation	V	*it ends on a V chord...usually*	I	*something's different*	I

Figure App.8. Map of Sonata-Allegro form, major key movement.
(Theory/Analysis)

The student is to listen to the movement once every day while following the score, tapping 8th note (first few days) and then quarter-note pulse. This acquaints the student with the rhythm and details of notation, informing early playing experiences especially given the details of small notes and the off-beat groupings in the Development. *(Rhythm/movement/Aural awareness)*

The student is to find (at home, not at the lesson) the occurrences of each aspect of Sonata-Allegro form, marking each in pencil or with a Post-it. *(Theory/Analysis)*

At the lesson (5-10 minutes):
1. The sonata form sections are confirmed to be correctly labeled.
2. Recurrences of opening motive found.
3. Key areas and cadences found and labeled.

PRACTICE ASSIGNMENT

Continuing to review assigned technical patterns and Czerny etudes, each of which are reviewed before sections below practiced.

Week One

1. Practice from Recapitulation to end, writing in necessary fingerings and putting hands together at least once per day. Make special note of *.
2. Practice Development mm. 68–77, blocking chords and writing in roman numeral or chord analysis.
3. Practice from beginning, playing only downbeat notes/chords; can do in conjunction with a recording if suitable.

Week Two

1. Practice all of Development to end, adding fingerings to Development as necessary.
2. Practice from beginning, playing notes/chords on beats 1 and 2.

Week Three

Practice whole piece as written.

Further research for cultivating a personal, stylistic, effective interpretation:
Multiple recordings upon recommendation of teacher. Photocopy of score made, with individual performer's interpretation specifics indicated in different colored pencil. Preferred recordings practiced a few times, student playing only on beats, to explore timing and rubato.

APPENDIX D

Practice Strategies by Category and Figure Numbers

Table D.1. Practice Strategies and Examples

Practice Strategy	Recommended Situations for Utilization	Examples Within Demonstrating Approach
Preparatory Patterns	Linking technical patterns to repertoire	Figures 4.3, 4.4
Physical chunking	Alberti-based accompaniment figures Broken chord/arpeggiated figures Alternating dyad or chord structures Improves pattern reading According to meaningful units, identified based on musical structures and/or technical demands Comparison of similar patterns, structure for gesture	Figures: 2.9, 4.20, 6.5, 7.1, 7.2, 7.6, 7.7, 7.8, 7.9, 7.10, 7.27
Rhythm movement and chanting	Learning/correct new duration patterns	Figures 4.7, 4.13, 6.26, 7.22
Layering	Overtly contrapuntal works Pieces with multiple voices moving at distinctive rates	Figures 6.1, 6.2, 6.6, 6.8, 7.5
Scaffolding	Pieces or passages with underlying harmonic structures perhaps disguised through surface figuration Pieces in triple meter, especially if the goal is a fast tempo To help establish the harmonic underpinning for the sake of secure memorization	Figures 6.11, 6.19, 6.20, 6.21, 6.22, 6.23, 6.24, 6.27, 7.31

(continued)

Table D.1. *(continued)*

Practice Strategy	Recommended Situations for Utilization	Examples Within Demonstrating Approach
Think it Then Play it (Measure + x)	Passages with disjunct motion, large leaps Passages that require taking in a lot of information in a short time Memorization of short passages, possibly in succession Practicing the seams to eliminate gaps	Figures 4.1, 4.2, 4.9, 4.15, 4.18, 6.12, 6.13, 6.14, 6.15, 6.16, 7.11, 7.12, 7.13, 7.16, 7.17, 7.18
Zoom Out/Zoom In	Identifying source of errors/comparing similar structures that may lead to errors	Figures 4.10, 5.13, 7.4
The Chart	Passagework	Figures 7.19, 7.20, 7.21
Mental practice Score Study	Memory work/check Evaluation of errors and potential adjustments to solve problems Conceptual chunking/mapping Finding structural lines in long-term phrasing structures	Figures 4.6, 4.8, 4.11, 4.12, 4.14, 4.16, 4.17, 4.19, 5.3, 6.3, 6.4, 6.7, 6.9, 6.10, 6.18, 6.19, 6.28, 7.27, 7.28, 7.29
Mapping	Memory work	Figures: 2.10, 6.28, 6.29, 6.30, 6.31, 6.32, 6.33, 6.34, 6.35

EXAMPLES ACCORDING TO STYLE PERIOD

Table D.2. Examples According to Style Period

Baroque	Figures 4.13, 4.14, 4.15, 4.16, 4.17, 4.18, 4.19, 4.20, 5.13, 6.1, 6.2, 6.3, 6.4, 6.19, 6.20, 6.21, 6.28, 6.34, 6.35, 7.16, App.4
Classical	Figures 2.1, 2.9, 4.5, 4.6, 4.7, 4.8, 4.9, 4.10, 4.11, 4.12, 5.3, 6.5, 6.9, 6.10, 6.22, 6.23, 6.24, 7.24, 7.25, 7.26, 7.27, 7.28, 7.31
Romantic	Figures 4.1, 4.2, 4.3, 6.6, 6.7, 6.8, 6.11, 6.12, 6.14, 6.15, 6.16, 6.17, 6.18, 6.30, 6.32, 6.33, 7.12, 7.13, 7.17, 7.18, 7.21, 7.24, 7.25, 7.26, 7.27, 7.29, 7.31, 7.32, 7.33, 7.34, App.5
Contemporary (20th–21st centuries)	Figures 5.12, 6.25, 6.26, 6.27, 7.1, 7.2, 7.3, 7.4, 7.5, 7.6, 7.7, 7.8, 7.9, 7.10, 7.11, 7.14, 7.16, App. 6, App. 7
Folk/Rote/Pedagogical Literature	Figures 1.10, 2.10, 5.4, 5.5, App.1a, App.1b, App.1c
Technical Patterns	Figures 5.6, 5.7, 5.8, 5.9, App.2, App.3

INSTRUMENTAL EXAMPLES

Table D.3. Instrumental Examples

Strings	Figures 1.10, 4.16, 4.17, 4.18, 5.12
Clarinet	Figures 6.17, 6.18
Trumpet	Figures 6.25, 6.26, 6.27

APPENDIX E

Areas of the Brain Involved in Language and Music Production and Comprehension

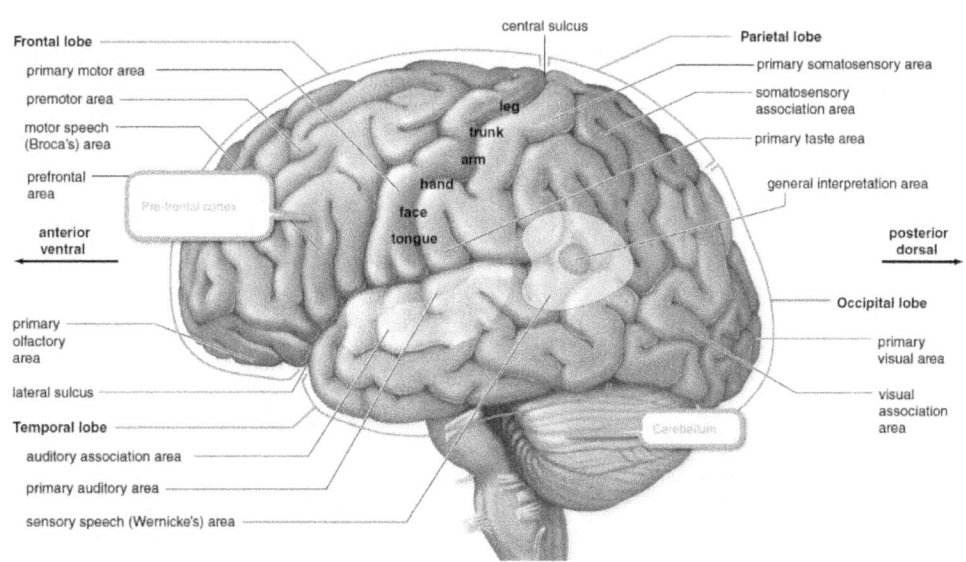

The Limbic System

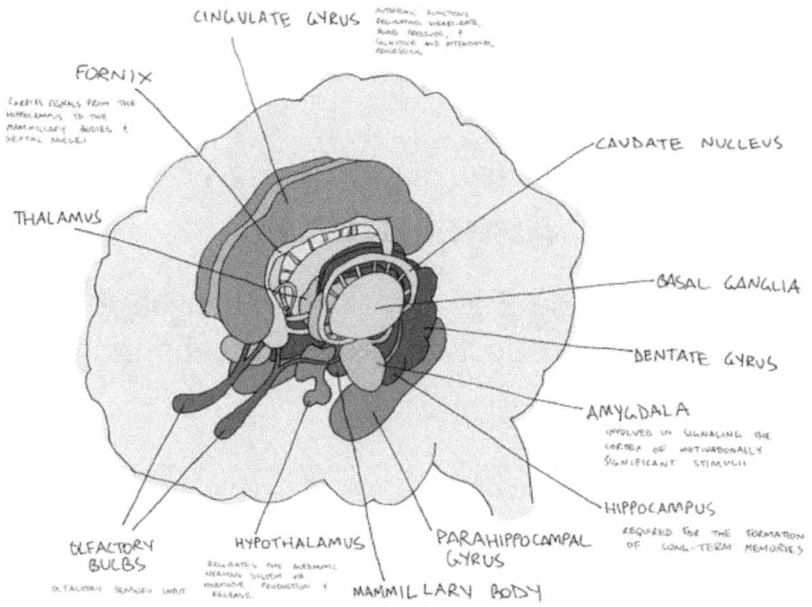

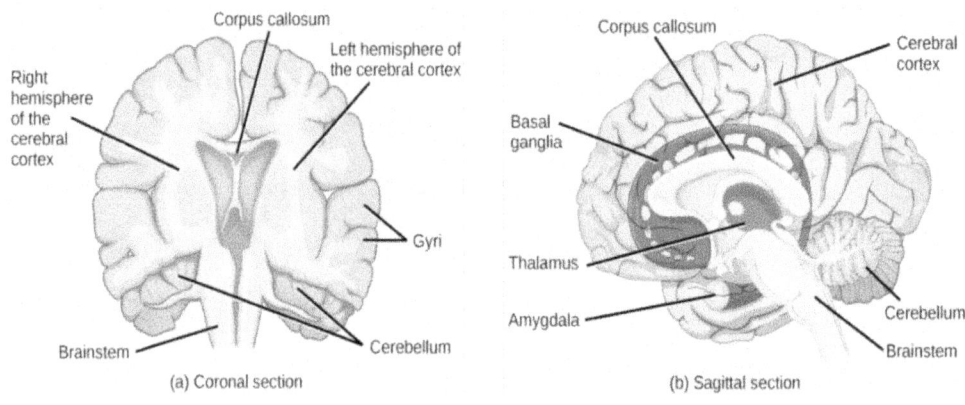

(a) Coronal section

(b) Sagittal section

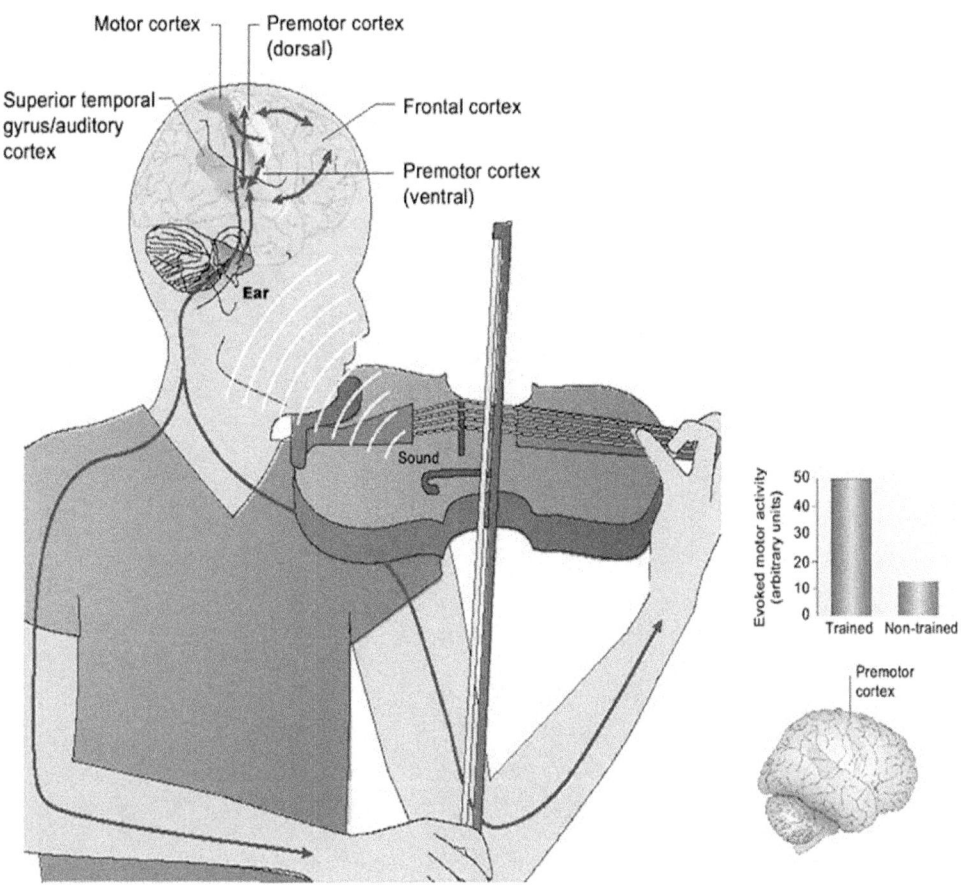

APPENDIX F

Workshop Templates

Beginning Musician: Practice is Play	Music and the Brain Aural Cognition, Language Acquisition, and Musical Processing Music Perception and Preparatory Audiation Optimal Teaching Strategies for the Young Beginner—Sample Activities
Exploratory Lessons for Beginners	Beginning lessons should feel like play, with singing, movement and chanting, improvisation, and rote songs that then serve as fodder for transposition, further improvisation, making up bass line duets, etc. so as to deepen the musician's understanding and stimulate a sense of joy and exploration. Would feature a short talk and then demonstration with a small group of young beginners and/or individual students.
The Intermediate Musician: Fluent Music Reading and Early Problem Solving	Visual Processing, Music Reading, and Bringing Meaning to the Score Theory, When, How, and Why Personality, Character, and Motivation Attention, Working Memory, and Early Problem Solving
Intermediate Practice Philosophies	What to Think About When Know Why You're Doing it Again Audiation Pause Hands Together Sooner, Patterns and Chunking Take a Picture
Teaching an Integrated Lesson—Intermediate	A cognitively sound approach can be fostered and encouraged from the first moment a concept, skill, or piece is introduced to the intermediate-level musician. Teaching in an integrated way, so that audiation, competent (pattern-based) reading, technical patterns, and stylistic awareness contribute to a comprehensive education and approach to new challenges. Workshop would outline an integrated lesson, presenting a couple of broad examples, and then perhaps work with one or two students to introduce a piece of their teacher's choosing.

(continued)

Practice Strategies for Intermediates	Using a set of examples from the intermediate repertoire, a comparison of common practice strategies with those outlined in the book that would prove to be more beneficial. Focusing at this level on guiding the student with detailed preparatory and practice activities and discussing problem-solving strategies appropriate for this level. Rule learning, chunking, (conceptual) mapping, linking technical patterns to music through rhythm, touch, tone, and gesture, structural lines, and learning in the pause specific examples. Importance of hands together sooner, incorporation of musical ideas earlier in the process, and distribution/interleaving of practice of general importance. Having teachers or students there with excerpts of something they are working on and feel stuck with would be very helpful to demonstration.
Advanced Musician: Expertise and Problem Solving	What Makes Someone an "Expert"? Mindful Practice and Non-Automatization Long-Term Memory, Retention, and Retrieval Multiple Intelligences and Rule Learning Avoiding the Risks of Excessive Automaticity Multimodal Imagery and Musical Memorization The Importance of Self-Monitoring and Self-Evaluation Impact of Mood on Problem Solving and Success
Teaching an Integrated Lesson— Advanced	Students who have been well taught can often transition almost seamlessly into advanced repertoire. The comprehensive approach continues to be important, as musicians who approach new repertoire with a developed ear, appropriate sight-reading abilities, and a sound theory foundation with which to analyze and map their pieces early in the process will learn more quickly and with more security. At this stage, *if they don't understand it, they shouldn't be playing it*. Of continuing importance is maintaining the right levels of awareness, discipline, problem-solving curiosity, and willingness to persist through increasing challenges. Two or three selections from the Advanced Repertoire will be chosen and used to demonstrate this integrated lesson approach.
Practice Strategies for Advanced Musicians	Using examples from the advanced repertoire, practice strategies that require a higher level of problem solving and discipline, especially working on passages: to the thumbs, The Chart, Harmonic Scaffolding and Hypermeter, and Think-It-Then-Play-It. Mapping strategies could also be addressed if desired and time. General topics to include: Leitner's Boxes, importance of rule learning and linking "topics" into a comprehensive whole, distribution and interleaving of practice, and memory strategies (as a result of comprehensive approach and additional memory work specifically).
General Practice	Deliberate Distributed Interleaved How it evolves as musicians progress What you should find at every level
Un-Master Classes	How to practice. This could be in a usual master class setup with just a few students, or in more of a buffet-type approach, where anyone in the audience can bring something they're stuck on or curious about and we can work together to solve it. Audience involvement throughout.
Practice Coaching	Zoom/Twitch/Facebook/YouTube channel

BIBLIOGRAPHY

Abril, C., & Gault, B. (2016). *Teaching general music: Approaches, issues, and viewpoints.* Oxford University Press.

Ackerman, H., Wildgruber, D., & Riecker, A. Singing in the (b)rain: Cerebral correlates of vocal music performance in humans. In E. Altenmüller, M. Wiesendanger, and J. Kesslring (Eds.), *Music, motor control and the brain.* Oxford University Press.

Altenmüller, E. (2003). Focal dystonia: Advances in brain imaging and understanding of fine motor control in musicians. *Hand Clinic, 19*(3), 523–538.

Altenmüller, E., Wiesendanger, M., & Kesslring, J. (Eds.). (2012). *Music, motor control and the brain.* Oxford University Press.

Arbib, M. (Ed.). (2013). *Language, music and the brain: A mysterious relationship.* MIT Press.

Author unknown. *What happens in the brain to cause dystonia.* https://www.dystonia.org.uk/what-happens-in-the-brain-to-cause-dystonia

Baddeley, A. (1990). *Human memory: Theory and practice.* Lawrence Erlbaum Associates.

Baddeley, A. (2001). The concept of episodic memory. *Philosophical Transactions of the Royal Society of London, Series B* (1413), 1345–1350. http://doi.org/10.1098/rstb.2001.0957

Bamberger, J. (1991). *The mind behind the musical ear: How children develop musical intelligence.* Harvard University Press.

Bangert, M. (2012). Brain activation during piano playing. In E. Altenmüller, M. Wiesendanger, and J. Kesslring (Eds.), *Music, motor control and the brain.* Oxford University Press.

Barry, N., & Hallam, S. (2001). Practice. In R. Parncutt & G. McPherson (Eds.), *Science and psychology of music performance* (pp. 151–166). Oxford University Press.

Barry, S. R. (2010). Do musicians have different brains? *Psychology Today.* https://www.psychologytoday.com/blog/eyes-the-brain/201006/do-musicians-have-different-brains

Bassok, M. (2003). Analogical transfer in problem solving. In J. E. Davidson & R. J. Sternberg (Eds.), *Psychology of problem solving* (pp. 343–372). Cambridge University Press.

Beal, A. L. (1985). The skill of recognizing musical structures. *Memory & Cognition, 13*(5), 405–412.

Bédard, J., & Chi, M. T. H. (1992). Expertise. *Current Directions in Psychological Science, 1*(4), 135–139. http://www.jstor.org/stable/20182156

Besson, M., Chabert, J., & Marie, C. (2011). Transfer of training between music and speech: Common processing, attention, and memory. *Frontiers in Psychology.* http://journal.frontiersin.org/article/10.3389/fpsyg.2011.00094/full

Bluestine, E. (2000). *The ways children learn music.* GIA Publications, Inc.

Boot, W. R., & Ericsson, K. A. (2013). Expertise. In J. D. Lee & A. Kirlik (Eds.), *The Oxford handbook of cognitive engineering* (pp. 143–158). Oxford University Press.

Bower, G. H., Karlin, M. B., & Dueck, A. (1975). Comprehension and memory for pictures. *Memory & Cognition, 3*(2), 216–220.

Branford, J. D., & Franks, J. J. (1971). The abstraction of linguistic ideas. *Cognitive Psychology 2,* 331–350.

Broadbent, D. E., Cooper, P. J., & Broadbent, M. H. P. (1978). A comparison of hierarchical and matrix retrieval schemes in recall. *Human Learning and Memory, 4*(5), 486–497.

Brown, P. C., Roediger, H. L. III, & McDaniel, M. A. (2014). *Make it stick: The science of successful learning.* Belknap Press.

Bruser, M. (1999). *The art of practicing: A guide to making music from the heart.* Three Rivers Press.

Bugs, J. M., McDaniel, M. A., & Einstein, G. O. (2013). Event-based prospective remembering: An integration of prospective memory and cognitive control theories. In D. Reisberg (Ed.), *The Oxford handbook of cognitive psychology.* Oxford University Press.

Burman, D. D., & Booth, J. R. (2009). Music rehearsal increases the perceptual span for notation. *Music Perception, 26*(4) 303–320. http://online.ucpress.edu/mp/article-pdf/26/4/303/190331/mp_2009_26_4_303

Butler, D. (1989). Describing the perception of tonality in music: A critique of the tonal hierarchy theory and a proposal for a theory of intervallic rivalry. *Music Perception, 6*(3), 219–241.

Chaffin, R., & Imreh, G. (1997). Pulling teeth and torture: Musical memory and problem solving. *Thinking and Reasoning, 3*(4), 315–336.

Chaffin, R., Imreh, G., & Crawford, M. (2002). *Practicing perfection: Memory and piano performance.* Lawrence Erlbaum Associates.

Chi, M. T. H., Feltovich, P. J., & Glaser, R. (1981). Categorization and representation of physics problems by experts and novices. *Cognitive Science, 5*(2), 121–152.

Clifton, C., & Pollatsek, A. (1997). The perceptual span and the eye-hand span in sight reading music. *Visual Cognition, 4*(2), 143–161. https://doi.org/10.1080/713756756

Clynes, M., & Walker, J. (1982). Neurobiological functions of rhythm, time and pulse in music. In M. Clynes (Ed.), *Music, mind and brain* (pp. 171–216). Plenum.

Coffman, D. (1990). Effects of mental practice, physical practice, and knowledge of results in piano performance. *Journal of Research in Music Education, 38*(3), 187–196.

Collins, A., & Colman Graham, S. How playing an instrument benefits your brain. Ted Talk. http://ed.ted.com/lessons/how-playing-an-instrument-benefits-your-brain-anita-collins

Colwell, R. (1992). *Handbook of research on music teaching and learning.* Schirmer Books.

Colwell, R. (Ed.). (2006). *MENC handbook of musical cognition and development.* Oxford University Press.

Conway, A., Cowan, N., & Bunting, M. (2001). The cocktail party phenomenon revisited: The importance of working memory capacity. *Psychonomic Bulletin and Review, 8*(2), 331–335.

Crowder, R. G. (1993). Auditory memory. In S. McAdams & E. Bigand (Eds.), *Thinking in sound: The cognitive psychology of human audition.* Oxford University Press.

Csikszenthmihalyi, M. (1990). *Flow: The psychology of optimal experience.* Harper Collins.

Dahl, S. (2012). Movements and analysis of drumming. In E. Altenmüller, M. Wiesendanger, & J. Kesslring (Eds.), *Music, motor control and the brain.* Oxford University Press.

Davidson, J. E. (2003). Insights about insightful problem solving. In J. E. Davidson & R. J. Sternberg (Eds.), *Psychology of problem solving* (pp. 149–175). Cambridge University Press.

Davidson, L., & Scripp, L. (1990). Education and development in music from a cognitive perspective. In D. J. Hargreaves (Ed.), *Children and the arts* (pp. 59–86). Open University Press.

Davidson, L., & Scripp, L. (1992). Surveying the coordinates of cognitive skills in music. In R. Colwell (Ed.), *Handbook of research on music teaching and learning* (pp. 392–413). Schirmer Books.

Davidson-Kelly, K., Schaefer, R. S., Moran, N., & Overy, K. (2015). Total inner memory: Deliberate uses of multimodal musical imagery during performance preparation. *Psychomusicology: Music, mind, and brain, 25*(1), 83–92. https://psycnet.apa.org/doiLanding?doi=10.1037%2Fpmu0000091

Dennis, W. (1966). Creative productivity between the ages of 20 and 80 years. *Journal of Gerontology, 21,* 1–8.

Department of Education. (2007, September). *IES practice guide: Organizing instruction and study to improve student learning.* https://files.eric.ed.gov/fulltext/ED498555.pdf

Deutsch, D. (1999). Grouping mechanisms in music. In *The psychology of music* (2nd ed.). Academic Press.

Dickinson, S. (2009–2010). Multi-level approach to more secure memorization. *College Music Symposium.* https://www.jstor.org/stable/41225253

Dowling, W. J. (1999). The development of music perception and cognition. In D. Deutsch (Ed.), *The psychology of music* (pp. 603–627). Academic Press.

Dowling, W. J., & Harwood, D. (1986). *Music cognition.* Academic Press.

Elliott, D. J. (1991). Music as knowledge. *Journal of Aesthetic Education, 25*(3), 21–40. https://www.jstor.org/stable/3332993

Ericsson, K. A. (1996). Deliberate practice and the acquisition of expert performance: An overview. In H. Jørgensen & A. C. Lehmann (Eds.), *Does practice make perfect? Current theory and research on instrumental music practice.* Norwegian State Academy of Music.

Ericsson, K. A. (2002). Attaining excellence through deliberate practice: Insights from the study of expert performance. In M. Ferrari (Ed.), *The pursuit of excellence through education* (pp. 21–55). Erlbaum.

Ericsson, K. A. (2003). The acquisition of expert performance as problem solving: Construction and modification of mediating mechanisms through deliberate practice. In J. E. Davidson & R. J. Sternberg (Eds.), *Psychology of problem solving* (pp. 31–86). Cambridge University Press.

Ericsson, K. A., & Charness, N. (1994). Expert performance: Its structure and acquisition. *American Psychologist, 49,* 725–747.

Ericsson, K. A., & Kintsch, W. (1995). Long-term working memory. *Psychological Review, 102*(2), 211–245.

Ericsson, K. A., Krampe, R. T., & Tesch-Römer, C. (1993). The role of deliberate practice in the acquisition of expert performance. *Psychological Review, 100*, 363–406.

Ericsson, K. A., & Lehmann, A. C. (1996). Expert and exceptional performance: Evidence of maximal adaptation to task constraints. *Annual Review of Psychology, 47*, 273–305.

Ericsson, K. A., & Smith, J. (1991). *Toward a general theory of expertise*. Cambridge University Press.

Ericsson, K. A., & Towne, T. (2013). Experts and their superior performance. In E. Reisberg (Ed.), *The Oxford handbook of cognitive psychology* (pp. 886–904). Oxford University Press.

Ettlinger, M., Margulis, E. H., & Wong, P. C. (2011). Implicit memory in music and language. *Frontiers in Psychology.* http://journal.frontiersin.org/article/10.3389/fpsyg.2011.00211/full

Flaugnacco, E., Lopez, L., Terribili, C., Montico, M., Zoia, S., & Schön, D. (2015). Music training increases phonological awareness and reading skills in developmental dyslexia. *PLoS ONE 10*(9): e0138715. https://doi.org/10.1371/journal.pone.0138715

Fischler, I., Rundus, D., & Atkinson, R. C. (1970). Effects of overt rehearsal procedures on free recall. *Psychonomic Science 19*(4), 249–250.

Flohr, J., & Hodges, D. A. (2006). Music and neuroscience. In R. Colwell (Ed.), *MENC Handbook of musical cognition and development*. Oxford University Press.

Foley, H., & Matlin, M. (2009). *Sensation and perception*. Psychology Press.

Forde Thompson, W. (2014). *Music, thought and feeling: Understanding the psychology of music*. Oxford University Press.

Forde Thompson, W., & Schellenberg. E. G. (2006). Listening to music. In R. Colwell (Ed.), *MENC handbook of musical cognition and development*. Oxford University Press.

Gaab, N., & Schlaug, G. (2003). The effect of musicianship on pitch memory in performance matched groups. *NeuroReport 14*, 2291–2295.

Gallo, D. A., & Wheeler, M. E. (2013). Episodic memory. In E. Reisberg (Ed.), *Oxford handbook of cognitive psychology* (pp. 189–205). Oxford University Press.

Garder, P. (Ed.). (1990). *The eclectic curriculum in American music education*. Rowman & Littlefield.

Gembris, H. (2006). The development of musical abilities. In R. Colwell (Ed.), *MENC handbook of musical cognition and development*. Oxford University Press.

Gentili, R., Han, C. E., Schwieghofer, N., & Papaxanthis, C. (2010). Motor learning without doing: Trial-by-trial improvement in motor performance during mental training. *Journal of Neurophysiology 104*, 774–783.

Gladwell, M. (2007). *Blink: The power of thinking without thinking*. Little, Brown.

Gobet, F. (1998). Expert memory: A comparison of four theories. *Cognition 66*, 115–152.

Gobet, F., & Clarkson, G. (2004). Chunks in expert memory: Evidence for the magical number four . . . or is it two? *Memory, 12*(6), 732–747. https://doi.org/10.1080/09658210344000530

Gobet, F., Lane, P. C. R., Croker, S., Cheng, P. C. H., Jones, G., Oliver, I., & Pine, J. M. (2001). Chunking mechanisms in human learning. *TRENDS in Cognitive Science 5*(6) 236–243.

Goldstein, E. B. (1984). *Sensation and perception*. Wadsworth.

Gopnik, A. (2004, May 10). Last of the Metrozoids. *New Yorker*. https://www.newyorker.com/magazine/2004/05/10/last-of-the-metrozoids

Gordon, E. (1997). *Learning sequences in music.* GIA Publications.

Gordon, E. (2001). *Rhythm: Contrasting the implications of audiation and notation.* GIA Publications.

Gruhn, W., & Rauscher, F. (2006). The neurobiology of music cognition and learning. In R. Colwell (Ed.), *MENC handbook of musical cognition and development.* Oxford University Press.

Gruson, L. M. (1988). Rehearsal skill and musical competence: Does practice make perfect? In J. A. Sloboda (Ed.), *Generative processes in music: The psychology of performance, improvisation, and composition* (pp. 91–112). Oxford University Press.

Habib, M., Lardy, C., Desiles, T., Commeiras, C., Chobert, J., & Besson, M. (2016). Music and dyslexia: A new musical training method to improve reading and related disorders. *Frontiers in Psychology, 7*(26). https://doi.org/10.3389/fpsyg.2016.00026

Hambrick, D. Z., & Engle, R. W. (2003). The role of working memory in problem solving. In J. E. Davidson & R. J. Sternberg (Eds.), *Psychology of problem solving* (pp. 176–206). Cambridge University Press.

Hambrick, D. Z., Oswald, F. L., Altmann, E. M., Meinz, E. J., Gobet, F., & Campitelli, G. (2014). Deliberate practice: Is that all it takes to become an expert? *Intelligence, 45,* 34–45.

Hargreaves, D. J. (1996). The development of artistic and musical competence. In I. Deliège & J. A. Sloboda (Eds.), *Musical beginnings: Origins and development of musical competence* (pp. 145–170). Oxford University Press.

Heathcote, A., Brown, S., & Mewhort, D. J. K. (2000). The power law repealed: The case for an exponential law of practice. *Psychonomic Bulletin and Review, 7,* 185–207.

Henderson, J. (2013). Eye movements. In D. Reisberg (Ed.), *The Oxford handbook of cognitive psychology.* Oxford University Press.

Highben, Z., & Palmer, M. (2004). Effects of auditory and motor mental practice in memorized piano performance. *Bulletin of the Council for Research in Music Education, 159,* 58–65.

Hoch, L., Poulin-Charronnat, B., & Tillmann, B. (2011). The influence of task-irrelevant music on language processing: Syntactic and semantic structures. *Frontiers in Psychology.* http://journal.frontiersin.org/article/10.3389/fpsyg.2011.00112/full

Horowitz, V. (1928, June 11). Interview with J. Eisenberg, urging piano students to simplify mechanical problems so that thought and energy may be directed to artistic interpretation. *The Musician.*

Howe, M. J. A., Davidson, J. W., Moore, D. G., & Sloboda, J. A. (1995). Are there early childhood signs of musical ability? *Psychology of Music, 23,* 162–176.

Howe, M. J. A., Davidson, J. W., & Sloboda, J. A. (1998). Innate talents: Reality or myth? *Behavioral and Brain Sciences, 21,* 399–442.

Huber, J. (2013). *Applying educational psychology in coaching athletes.* https://us.humankinetics.com/blogs/excerpt/understanding-motor-learning-stages-improves-skill-instruction

Huss, M., Verney, J. P., Fosker, T., Mead, N., & Goswami, U. (2011). Music, rhythm, rise time perception and developmental dyslexia. *Cortex, 47*(6), 674–689.

Hyman, I., Boss, M., Wise, B. M., McKenzie, K. E., & Caggiano, J. M. (2010). Did you see the unicycling clown? Inattention blindness while walking and talking on a cell phone. *Applied Cognitive Psychology, 24,* 597–607.

Iott, S. (2014). Untangling the tangles: Making sense of Bach's first duet (BWV 802). *MTNA e-Journal*. http://www.mtnaejournal.org/publication/?m=7797&i=197394&p=4

Iott Richardson, S. (2004). Music as language: Sight playing through access to a complete musical vocabulary. *American Music Teacher, 53*(6) 21–25.

Jabusch, H.-C. (2012). Movement analysis in pianists. In E. Altenmüller, M. Wiesendanger, & J. Kesslring (Eds.), *Music, motor control and the brain*. Oxford University Press.

Jäncke, L. (2012a). From cognition to action. In E. Altenmüller, M. Wiesendanger, & J. Kesslring (Eds.), *Music, motor control and the brain*. Oxford University Press.

Jäncke, L. (2012b). The motor representation in pianists and string players. In E. Altenmüller, M. Wiesendanger, & J. Kesslring (Eds.), *Music, motor control and the brain*. Oxford University Press.

Jäncke, L. (2012c). The relationship between music and language. *Frontiers in Psychology*. https://www.frontiersin.org/articles/10.3389/fpsyg.2012.00123/full

Jerde, T. E., Santello, M., Flanders, M., & Soechting, J. F. (2012). Hand movements and musical performance. In E. Altenmüller, M. Wiesendanger, & J. Kesslring (Eds.), *Music, motor control and the brain*. Oxford University Press.

Jorgensen, E. R. (2003). *Transforming music education*. Indiana University Press.

Jørgenson, H. (2004). Strategies for individual practice. In A. Williamon (Ed.), *Musical excellence: Strategies and techniques to enhance performance* (pp. 85–104). Oxford University Press.

Jørgenson, H., & Lehmann, A. C. (Eds.). (1997). *Does practice make perfect? Current theory and research on instrumental music practice*. Norwegian State Academy of Music.

Kahneman, D. (2011). *Thinking, fast and slow*. Farrar, Straus and Giroux.

Kellman, P. J., & Massey, C. M. (2013). Perceptual learning, cognition and expertise. *Psychology of Learning and Motivation, 58*, 117–159.

Kimble, G. A. (1961). *Hilgard and Marquis' conditioning and learning*. Appleton-Century-Crofts.

Kivy, P. (2008). Music, language, and cognition: And other essays in the aesthetics of music. *Journal of Aesthetics and Art Criticism, 66*(3), 314–317.

Koelsch, S. (2012). Response to target article: Language, music and the brain, a resource-sharing framework. In P. Rebuschat, M. Rohmeier, J. A. Hawkins, & I. Cross (Eds.), *Language and music as cognitive systems*. Oxford University Press.

Koelsch, S. (2011). Toward a neural basis of music perception—A review and updated model. *Frontiers in Psychology*. http://journal.frontiersin.org/article/10.3389/fpsyg.2011.00110/full

Kolers, P. A. (1975). Memorial consequences of automatized encoding. *Journal of Experimental Psychology: Human Learning and Memory 1*(6), 689–701.

Kotovsky, K. (2003). Problem solving—large/small, hard/easy, conscious/nonconscious, problem-space/problem solver: The issue of dichotomization. In J. E. Davidson & R. J. Sternberg (Eds.), *Psychology of problem solving* (373–384). Cambridge University Press.

Krampe, R. T., & Ericsson, K. A. (1996). Maintaining excellence: Deliberate practice and elite performance in young and older pianists. *Journal of Experimental Psychology: General 125*, 331–359.

Krumhansl, C. L. (1979). The psychological representation of musical pitch in a tonal context. *Cognitive Psychology, 11*, 346–374.

Krumhansl, C. L. (1990). *Cognitive foundations of musical pitch*. Oxford University Press.

Krumhansl, C. L. (1995). Music psychology and music theory: Problems and prospects. *Music Theory Spectrum, 17*(1) 53–80.

Krumhansl, C. L. (2000). Rhythm and pitch in music cognition. *Psychological Bulletin, 126*(1), 159–179.

Krumhansl, C. L., & Keil, F. C. (1982). Acquisition of the hierarchy of tonal functions in music. *Memory & Cognition, 10*(3), 243–251.

Kwalwasser, J. (1955). *Exploring the musical mind*. Coleman-Ross.

Laney, C. (2013). The sources of memory errors. In D. Reisberg (Ed.), *The Oxford handbook of cognitive psychology* (pp. 232–242). Oxford University Press.

Lehmann, A. C. (2012). Historical increases in expert music performance skills: Optimizing instruments, playing techniques, and training. In E. Altenmüller, M. Wiesendanger, & J. Kesslring (Eds.), *Music, motor control and the brain*. Oxford University Press.

Lehmann, A. C., & Davidson, J. W. (2006). Taking an acquired skills perspective on music performance. In R. Colwell (Ed.), *MENC handbook of musical cognition and development*. Oxford University Press.

Lehmann, A. C., & Ericsson, K. A. (1998). Preparation of a public piano performance: The relation between practice and performance. *Musicae Scientiae, 2*, 69–94.

Lerdahl, F., & Jackendoff, R. S. (1996). *A generative theory of tonal music*. MIT Press.

Levitin, D. J. (Ed.). (2002). *Foundations of cognitive psychology*. MIT Press.

Levitin, D. J. (2003). Musical structure is processed in language areas of the brain: A possible role for Brodmann area 47 in temporal coherence. *NeuroImage, 20*, 2142–2152.

Levitin, D. J. (2007a, February 5). *Music and your brain*. MacNeil-Lehrer Newshour, Public Broadcasting Service.

Levitin, D. J. (2007b). *This is your brain on music*. Dutton.

Li, S. C., & Lewandowsky, S. (1995). Forward and backward recall: Different retrieval processes. *Journal of Experimental Psychology: Learning, Memory and Cognition, 21*(4), 837–847.

Limb, C. J. (2019, October 15). Musical creativity and the brain. Talk given at Michigan State University, FRIB, through the Advanced Studies Gateway.

Lubart, T. I., & Mouchiroud, C. (2003). Creativity: A source of difficulty in problem solving. In J. E. Davidson & R. J. Sternberg (Eds.), *Psychology of problem solving* (127–148). Cambridge University Press.

deLuce, I. (2019). Malcolm Gladwell's famous 10,000 hour rule for mastering a skill isn't holding up in new research. *Business Insider*. https://www.pulse.ng/bi/strategy/malcolm-gladwells-famous-10000-hour-rule-for-mastering-a-skill-isnt-holding-up-in-new/zm779ph

Mach, E. (1991). *Great contemporary pianists speak for themselves*. Dover Publications.

Macnamara, B. N., & Maitra, M. (2019). The role of deliberate practice in expert performance: Revisiting Ericsson, Krampe & Tesch-Römer. *Royal Society Open Science*. https://doi.org/10.1098/rsos.190327

Mandler, J. M., & Ritchey, G. H. (1977). Long-term memory for pictures. *Journal of Experimental Psychology: Human Learning and Memory, 3*(4), 386–396.

Markman, A. B., & Rein, J. R. (2013). The nature of mental concepts. In D. Reisberg (Ed.), *The Oxford handbook of cognitive psychology*. Oxford University Press.

Maynard, L. (2006). The role of repetition in the practice sessions of artist teachers and their students. *Bulletin of the Council for Research in Music Education, 167*, 61–72.

McGilchrist, I. (2009). *The master and his emissary*. Yale University Press.

McRae, K., & Jones, M. (2013). Semantic memory. In D. Reisberg (Ed.), *The Oxford handbook of cognitive psychology* (pp. 206–219). Oxford University Press.

Meister, I. G., Krings, T., Foltys, H., Boroojerdi, B., Müller, M., Töpper, R., & Thron, A. (2004). Playing piano in the mind: An fMRI study on music imagery and performance in pianists. *Cognitive Brain Research, 19*, 219–228.

Milovanov, R., & Tervaniemi, M. (2011). The interplay between musical and linguistic aptitudes: A review. *Frontiers in Psychology.* http://journal.frontiersin.org/article/10.3389/fpsyg.2011.00321/full

Mulligan, N. W., & Besken, M. (2013). Implicit memory. In D. Reisberg (Ed.), *The Oxford handbook of cognitive psychology.* Oxford University Press.

Nirkko, A., & Kristeva, R. (2012). Brain activation during string playing. In E. Altenmüller, M. Wiesendanger, & J. Kesslring (Eds.), *Music, motor control and the brain.* Oxford University Press.

Ochsner, K., & Kosslyn, S. (Eds.). (2013). *The Oxford handbook of cognitive neuroscience.* Oxford University Press.

Ortmann, O. (1929). *The physiological mechanics of piano technique.* Facsimile Publisher reprint, 2016.

Palmer, C. (2012). The nature of memory for music performance skills. In E. Altenmüller, M. Wiesendanger, & J. Kesslring (Eds.), *Music, motor control and the brain.* Oxford University Press.

Palmer, C., & Pfordresher, P. (2003). Incremental planning in sequence production. *Psychological Review 110*(4), 683–712.

Parncut, R., & McPherson, G. (Eds). (2002). *The science and psychology of music: Creative strategies for teaching and learning.* Oxford University Press.

Patel, A. (2010) *Music, language, and the brain.* Oxford University Press.

Patel, A. D. (2011). Why would musical training benefit the neural encoding of speech? The OPERA hypothesis. *Frontiers in Psychology.* http://journal.frontiersin.org/article/10.3389/fpsyg.2011.00142/full

Patel, A. D. (2012). Language, music, and the brain: A resource-sharing framework. In P. Rebuschat, M. Rohmeier, J. A. Hawkins, and I. Cross (Eds.), *Language and music as cognitive systems.* Oxford University Press.

Peretz, I. (2013). The biological foundations of music: Insights from congenital amusia. In D. Deutsch (Ed.), *The psychology of music.* Academic Press.

Peretz, I., & Zatorre, R. (Eds.) (2003). *Cognitive neuroscience of music.* Oxford University Press.

Perlovsky, L. (2015). Origin of music and embodied cognition. *Frontiers in Psychology.* https://doi.org/10.3389/fpsyg.2015.00538

Peterson, M. A., & Kimchi, R. (2013). Perceptual organization in vision. In D. Reisberg (Ed.), *The Oxford handbook of cognitive psychology.* Oxford University Press.

Pretz, J. E., Naples, A. J., & Sternberg, R. (2003). Recognizing, defining, and representing problems. In J. E. Davidson & R. J. Sternberg (Eds.), *Psychology of problem solving* (3–30). Cambridge University Press.

Raffman, D. (1993). *Language, music and mind.* MIT Press.

Rayner K. (1998). Eye movements in reading and information processing. *Psychological Bulletin, 124*(3), 372–422.

Rebuschat, P., Rohmeier, M., Hawkins, J., & Cross, I. (2012). *Language and music as cognitive systems.* Oxford University Press.

Repp, B. H. (1991). Reviewed work: Cognitive foundations of musical pitch by Carol L. Krumhansl. *American Journal of Psychology, 104*(4), 612–621.

Repp, B. H. (1996). The art of inaccuracy: Why pianists' errors are difficult to hear. *Music Precept 14*(2), 161–183.

Repp, B. H. (2012). Musical synchronization. In E. Altenmüller, M. Wiesendanger, & J. Kesslring (Eds.), *Music, motor control and the brain*. Oxford, Oxford University Press.

Riesberg, D. (Ed.). (2013). *The Oxford handbook of cognitive psychology*. Oxford University Press.

Ristad, E. (1981). *A soprano on her head*. Real People Press.

Ritter, F. E., Baxter, G. D., Kim, J. W., & Srinivasmurthy, S. (2013). Learning and retention. In J. D. Lee & A. Kirk, A. (Eds.), *The Oxford handbook of cognitive engineering* (pp. 125–142). Oxford University Press.

Rosenbaum, D. R. (1991). *Human motor control*. Academic Press.

Rosenbaum, D. R. (2013). Planning and performing physical actions. In D. Riesberg (Ed.), *The Oxford handbook of cognitive psychology*. Oxford University Press.

Ross, S. (1985). The effectiveness of mental practice in improving the performance of college trombonists. *Journal of Research in Music Education 33*(4), 221–231.

Ruthsatz, J., Detterman, D., Griscom, W. S., & Cirullo, B. A. (2008). Becoming an expert in the musical domain: It takes more than just practice. *Intelligence, 36*, 330–33.

Salvucci, D. D., & Taatgen, N. A. (2008). Threaded cognition: An integrated theory of concurrent multitasking. *Psychological Review, 115*(1), 101–130.

Schellenberg, E. G., & Weiss, M. W. (2013). Music and cognitive abilities. In D. Deutsch (ed.), *The psychology of music* (3rd ed., 499–550). Elsevier.

Schlaug, G. (2001). The brain of musicians: A model for functional and structural adaptation. In R. J. Zatorre & I. Peretz (Eds.), *The biological foundations of music* (pp. 281–299). New York Academy of Sciences.

Schlaug, G. (2012). Brain structures of musicians: Executive functions and morphological implications. In E. Altenmüller, M. Wiesendanger, & J. Kesslring (Eds.), *Music, motor control and the brain*. Oxford University Press.

Schön, D., & François, C. (2011). Musical expertise and statistical learning of musical and linguistic structures. *Frontiers in Psychology*. http://journal.frontiersin.org/article/10.3389/fpsyg.2011.00167/full

Schuster, C., Hilfiker, R., Amfit, O., Scheidhauer, A., Andrews, B., Butler, J., Kischka, U., & Ettlin, T. (2011). Best practice for motor imagery: A systematic literature review on motor imagery training elements in five different disciplines. *BMC Medicine, 9*(75). http://www.biomedcentral.com/1741-7015/9/75

Schwarz, N., & Skurnik, I. (2003). Feeling and thinking: Implications for problem solving. In J. E. Davidson & R. J. Sternberg (Eds.), *Psychology of problem solving* (pp. 263–290). Cambridge University Press.

Seashore, C. (1967). *Psychology of music*. Dover Publications.

Shaffer, L. H. (1981). Performances of Chopin, Bach, and Bartok: Studies in motor programming. *Cognitive Psychology, 13*, 326–376.

Shockley, R. (1997). *Mapping music: For faster learning and secure memory*. A-R Editions.

Shockley, R. (2006). Mapping music: Some simple strategies to help students learn. *American Music Teacher 56*(2), 34–36.

Simon, H. A., & Gobet, F. (2000). Expertise effects in memory recall: Comment on Vicente and Wang (1998). *Psychological Review 107*(3), 593–600.

Sloboda, J. A. (2005). *Exploring the musical mind*. Oxford University Press.

Sloboda, J. A., Davidson, J. W., Howe, M. J. A., & Moore, D. M. (1996). The role of practice in the development of expert musical performance. *British Journal of Psychology, 87*, 287–309.

Sowa, J. F. (2000). *Knowledge representation—Logical, philosophical, and computational foundations*. Brooks/Cole.

Spelke, E., Hirst, W., & Neisser, U. (1976). Skills of divided attention. *Cognition, 4*, 215–230.

Thompson, J. M., & Goswami, U. (2008). Rhythmic processing in children with developmental dyslexia: Auditory and motor rhythms link to reading and spelling. *J. Physiol.* Paris 102, 120–129.

Tillman, B., Bharucha, J., & Bigand, E. (2000). Implicit learning of tonality: A self-organizing approach. *Psychological Review 107*(4), 885–913.

Torff, B. (2006). A comparative review of human ability theory: Context structure and development. *MENC handbook of musical cognition and development*. Oxford University Press.

Trainor, L. J., & Hannon, E. E. (2013). Musical development. In D. Deutsch (Ed.), *The psychology of music*. Academic Press.

Upitis, R. (1987). Children's understanding of rhythm: The relationship between musical development and musical training. *Psychomusicology, 7*(1), 41–60.

Uszler, M., Gordon, S., & McBride-Smith, S. (1999). *The well-tempered keyboard teacher*. Schirmer Editions.

Varela, V. J., Thompson, E., & Rosch, E. (2017). *The embodied mind: Cognitive science and human experience*. MIT Press.

Vicente, K. J., & Wang, J. H. (1998). An ecological theory of expertise effects in memory recall. *Psychological Review, 105*(1), 33–57.

Vinkhuyzen, A. A., van der Sluis, S., Posthuma, D., & Boomsma, D. I. (2009). The heritability of aptitude and exceptional talent across different domains in adolescents and young adults. *Behavior Genetics, 39*, 380–392.

Vredevelt, A., Hitch, G. J., & Baddeley, A. D. (2011). Eyeclosure helps memory by reducing cognitive load and enhancing visualization. *Memory & Cognition, 39*, 1253–1263. https://doi.org/10.3758/s13421-011-0098-8

Walker, M. P., Brakefield, T., Morgan, A., Hobson, J. A., & Stickgold, R. (2002). Practice with sleep makes perfect: Sleep-dependent motor skill learning. *Neuron, 35*, 205–211.

Ward, J. (2015). *The student's guide to cognitive neuroscience*. Psychology Press.

Weisberg, R., & Reeves, L. (2013). *Cognition: from memory to creativity*. Wiley.

Wenke, D., & Frensch, P. A. (2003). Is success or failure at solving complex problems related to intellectual ability? In J. E. Davidson & R. J. Sternberg (Eds.), *Psychology of problem solving* (pp. 87–126). Cambridge University Press.

Westney, W. (2003). *The perfect wrong note: Learning to trust your musical self*. Amadeus Publishing.

Whitten, S., & Graesser, A. C. (2003). Comprehension of text in problem solving. In *Psychology of problem solving* (pp. 207–232). Cambridge University Press.

Williamon, A., & Valentine, E. (2000). Quantity and quality of musical practice as predictors of performance quality. *British Journal of Psychology, 91*, 353–376.

Yágüez, L., Nagel, D., Hoffman, H., Canavan, A. G. M., Wist, E., & Hömberg, V. (1998). A mental route to motor learning: Improving trajectorial kinematics through imagery training. *Behavioural Brain Research, 90*, 95–106.

Zimmerman, B. J., & Campillo, M. (2003). Motivating self-regulated problem solvers. In J. E. Davidson & R. J. Sternberg (Eds.), *Psychology of problem solving* (233–262). Cambridge University Press.

INDEX

abstraction by intersection training, 71
acculturation. *See* audiation
acquisition of skills, stages of, 92; associative stage, 92–93, 159, 179; autonomous stage, 92–93; cognitive stage, 92
Alexander technique, 128
analysis of music, *80*, 83–84, 108, 146, 173, 201, 233–35, 257–59; benefits of, 145–48, 171, 177; linear. *See* structural lines. *See also* mapping of music
anticipation. *See* prediction/anticipation
aptitude, 4, 9, 17, 27, 29, 30n6, 31n28, 32nn32–33, 109, 117, 133
at tempo practice, 86, 157, 159, 192, 197. *See also* think it then play it; the chart
attention, 6, 17, 35, 38, 44, 61, 63, 75, 97, 107, 120, 124, 130, 136–37, 146, 149, 161, 186, 210, 219
attunement. *See* perceptual learning, theory of
audiation, 9–12, 19–23, 30, 35, 39, 42, 52–53, 55, 57–58, 61–62, 67, 75, 216; acculturation, 10–11, 107; development of, 9–12, 15, 17, 19–23, 27, 30n6, 35, 92, 96; pause and learning pause, 21, 62, 65, 128, 156, 243; linking audiation and practice, 51–52, 69, 74–75, 78, 87, 98, 110, 146, 156, 167, 187, 192; loop, *42*; preparatory, 15–16
aural processing. *See* context
automatic systems of learning, 98
automatization, 45, 93, 134; avoidance of excessive, 96, 121, 244

beats-only. *See* scaffolding practice
blocking » gesture. *See* chunking
brain, 26, 52, 60, 124, 128, 148, 158, 178, 181–82, 239–241; Broca's area, 8; imaging, 8, 66, 133, 139n6, 148, 157; language centers of, 8, *239–41*; motor neurons, 68n5, 157; music and the, 5–11; visuospatial 8
buffering. *See* preview

the chart, 160, 183, 196–198, 210, 238, 244
chunking, 47, 51, 56, 59, 67–68, 101, 104, 115, 126, 128, 139n7, 144–45, 210, 237–38, 243–44; chunking » gesture, 183–87, *188*; conceptual, 74, 102, 108, 152–53, 171, 203, 238; strategies, 59, 70, 72–76, 78–79, 82, 84, 133, 148, 151–53, 184–85, 187, 210
chunking theory, 43, 46–47, 102
conceptual mapping. *See* mapping of music

constraint attunement hypothesis. *See* perceptual learning, theory of
context, 7, 14, 17, 19, 24, 44, 51, 53, 58n19, 71, 87, 98, 102, 106–9, 127, 149; and aural processing, 8–10, 12–15, 20, 57n7; rhythmic, 16, 20, 167, 169; tonal, 12, 19
continuation. *See* Gestalt
contrapuntal music, practicing of, 79, 146, 150, 237. *See also* chunking, conceptual; layers
creative problem solving. *See* problem solving

deliberate practice, xxi, 59, 63, 91, 95, 108, 114, 135, 157, 197; benefits of, 92, 97–99, 101, 117, 123; definition of, xxii, 129–30
discouragement, avoidance of. *See* motivation
discrimination learning, 61
distributed practice, 97, 129–30, 138, 178, 244; benefits of, 132–33 140n21, 179; Leitner's boxes, 132–33
downbeats-only. *See* scaffolding practice

effective practice, xxi, 22, 55–56, 63, 71, 85, 117, 126, 129, 132, 135–36, 215, 218
efficiency, xx, 45, 56, 104, 118, 123–24, 127, 192
effortful learning/practice, xxii, 59, 61, 106, 117, 129–30, 133, 138, 141n39, 179, 201
elaborative rehearsal and semantic processing, 134
embodied cognition, 6, 128
encoding, 10, 45, 47, 57n3, 65, 71, 98–102, 104, 108, 127, 143, 148, 157, 187; and anticipation of retrieval demands, 44, 59, 107; and automatic vs. conscious action, 124; implementation intentions, 107, 157, 179, 187; for retention and retrieval, 59, 143, 157, 171, 177

expectations. *See* prediction/anticipation
evaluation. *See* self-observation and self-evaluation

events (musical), 126, 182n21, 217; distinctive vs. similar, 105–6, 179; stable vs. unstable, 13, 106
excessive repetition 24, avoidance of, 66, 96, 156
expertise, 13, 43–44, 46–47, 52, 63, 96–97, 99, 104–5, 118–*19*, 121, 123, 125, 127, 139nn1–6, 219, 244; acquisition of, 4, 91–96, 114; difference between experts and novices 46, 92, 94–95, 99, 102, 105, 115–16, 118
explicit learning, 7, 10, 107, 109
exploration, 4, 15, 18, 28, 50, 56, 114, 117, 121; and creativity, 56, 66, 86
expressive musical performance, xxi, 35, 56, 62, 77, 86–87, 123, 128, 136, 139n12, 145, 210, 216, 219

facility, 26, 35, 56, 69, 72, 76–77, 87n1, 96, 122–23, 144, 148, 164, 196, 205, 210, 216. *See also*, the chart
fingerings, 67, 75, 78, 84, 87, 110–13, 122, 125, 139n9, 141n27, 146, 158–59, 183–84, 199–207, 210, 219
flexibility in performance. *See* musical performance
focal dystonia 24, 65–66; slow practice and, 158
functional fixedness, 115, 117

Gestalt, 26, 57n7, 83, 87, 148, 217; continuation, 8, 37, 57n7, 84; similarity, 37, 57n7; simplicity, 36
gesture, 69, 78, 86, 155, 179, 183–93, 208–10; 237, 244; building, *206*; chunking » gesture. *See* chunking; gesture » detail, 144, 187–193, *206*
ghosting, 138, *194*
goals, (setting, attainment of) 46, 62, 96–97, 99, 116, 121, 123, 130, 134–38, 146, 158, 181n10, 215; the goal state, 114, 118–19
Gordon, Edwin E., 8, 11–12, 14–18, 21, 26, 30–32, 95, 167
graphic notation: *See* notation

hands, 144, 146, 152, 187, 192, *195*; alone and together, 62, 66–67, 68n8, 69–70,

72, 75, 81, 109, 146, 148, 181n3, 187, 199–200, 210, 227–29, 235, 243–44; possible detriments of hands alone, 60, 81, 148
hypermeter, 162, 166, 244. *See also* scaffolding practice

implementation intentions. *See* encoding
implicit learning, 6–8, 10–12, 14, 24, 30, 85, 107, 143
incubation. *See* interleaved practice
inference learning, 14, 18, 21, 30n14, 61
injury, avoidance of, 59, 65–66, 193. *See also* focal dystonia
integrated lesson, 233, 243–44
interaction, 52, 123–24, 139; of processes, 42
interleaved practice, 97, 129–138, 179, 244; benefits of, 132, 140n21; incubation, 117, 130

keyality, 18, 28, 31n21, 53, 108
knowledge representation, 39, 94, 97–99
Kodaly, 8

language acquisition, 8–9, 11, 29n3, 243
layers, 128, 146–51, 172, 210; practice of 56, 145, 149, 162
learning pause. *See* audiation
learning-style theory, 28, 54, 109. *See also* multiple intelligences; personality, role in learning; motivation; and rule learning
Leitner's boxes. *See* distributed practice
levels of processing, 105
long-term memory. *See* memory
long-term working memory. *See* memory

maintenance rehearsal, 133–34
mapping of music, 19, 50, 56, 84–85, 109, 128, 152, 172–78, 187, 233–34, 244; conceptual, 74, 127, 145, 152–53, 171, *231*, 238; role in memory, 145, 171–79, 238. *See also* memorization, mapping as an aid to
massed practice, 132
meaningful units, 43–44, 48, 51, 53, 59–60, 69, 72, 79, 85, 101–4, 107, 128, 151–52, 158, 160–61, 183–87, 193–94, 197, 200–5, 210, 215, 237. *See also* chunking, conceptual
measure +1. *See* think it then play it
memorization, 61, 85, 126–29, 133–35, 157, 171–79, 237–38, 244; mapping as an aid to, 106, 145, 171–79; multimodal imagery as an aid to, 126–29, 172
memory: long-term, xxii, 6, 44–47, 60, 71–72, 80, 82, 94, 98, 100–101, 104–6, 127, 244; long-term working, 43–46, 71, 101–4; short-term/working, 44, 46–47, 60, 68, 71, 100–102
mental chunking. *See* chunking, conceptual
mental (imagery) practice, 51–52, 65, 68n5, 128, 144–45, 155, 157, 171, 179–80, 192, 211, 238
metacognition, 121
metronome, 76, 88nn5–6, 158, 165–66, 169, 197, 199–200, 211n7
mindful practice, xx, 66, 96, 107, 117, 124, 130, 132, 146, 171, 184, 210, 215, 216, 244
mistakes, 60, 62, 66, 87, 96, 115, 130, 146, 218; finding and fixing 59, 62, 136–37, 141
mood, impact of on problem solving. *See* problem solving
motivation, 28, 54–56, 67, 91, 95–96, 114–15, 119, 121, 135–36, 143–44, 243; how to maintain/maximize, 35–36, 55–56, 62, 87, 96, 210; intrinsic, 3, 55, 95, 114–15, 135
motor: command, 40–41, 52, 57, 123; coordination/control, xxii, 24, 39, 61, 102, 116, 122–126; mechanics, 124
multimodal imagery. *See* memorization
multiple intelligences, 35, 54, 108, 244
music and language, 6, 8; areas of processing, 10; similarities between, 10–11, 44
Music Learning Theory, 28, 30n12, 31n21, 255
music reading, 9, 18, 27, 29, 35, 39–43, 48, 51, 67, 243; bringing meaning to the score, 38–39, *43*, 48–51; pattern

recognition and, 35, 46, 50–52, 67–69, 87, 109–10, 187, 216, 237
music theory, 15, 48, 52–54, 85, 233–34, 243–44; from actual to abstract, 87; sound before sight before, 17–18
musical expression. *See* expressive musical performance
musical pattern vocabulary, 9, 11, 17–18, 20, 28, 35, 39, 46, 50–51, 65, 87, 92, 122, 126
musical performance, xxii, 4, 40, 52, 60, 62–64, 91–95, 107–8, 114, 128, 145, 167, 219; anxiety, 36, 102; benefits of intentional practice to, 46, 56, 66, 68, 77, 85–87, 102, 117, 127–30, 132–34, 136–37, 146, 148, 151, 179–80, 187, 210, 215–220; features of expert, 93–100, 105, 115, 122–23, 125, 127; flexibility within, 117, 123, 179, 181n15, 210, 216–17, 219

notation, 10, 15–16, 18, 20, 22, 24, 28, 36, 39, 48–49, 51, 54–55, 57nn4–14, 75, 79, 129, 171–72, 234; and audiation, 167–68; graphic, 22–23, 49, 58n24, 222

Orff, 8

pattern reading. *See* music reading, pattern recognition and
perceptual learning, theory of, 35, 38, 45; and the constraint attunement hypothesis, 57
perceptual processing, 40, 46, 99, 126–27; loop, 39, 42–43, 50, 56, 99, 217. *See also* preview, buffering
perceptual span, 40, 102, 140n14.
personality, role of in learning 54–55, 95, 109, 144, 243
plateaus, and avoidance of, 35, 45, 87, 93, 98, 102, 143
practice. *See* audiation; deliberate practice; distributed practice; effective; effortful learning/practice; exploration; interleaved practice; maintenance rehearsal; massed practice; mindful practice; problem solving; retrieval practice

practice strategies: *See* at-tempo; chunking; gesture; hands, alone and together; ghosting; layers; measure + 1; memorization; mental imagery; preparatory practice strategies; repetition; rhythm, movement, tapping and chanting; rule learning; scaffolding; slow practice; structure building; think it then play it; to the thumbs; variable priority training; what to think about when
prediction/anticipation, 6–7, 19, 26, 38, 52, 59, 61, 94, 108, 115, 185, 216
preparatory audiation. *See* audiation
preparatory practice strategies, 22, 68, 69–72, 144, 225–26, 237, 244
preview/buffering, 39–42, 71, 102, 104, 193, 197, 210
problem solving, xxii, 4, 9, 19, 32n32, 35–36, 51 54–56, 59–60, 62–63, 68–69, 91–92, 95–96, 98–101, 108–9, 114–119, 121–22, 130, 132, 135, 138, 143–45, 157, 207–8, 211, 215, 238, 243–44; characteristics of creative, effective, xxii, 54, 56, 108, 113–17, 121; impact of mood on, 117–121, 216, 244; problem finding, 22, 24, 55–56, 115, 136

reading. *See* music reading
recall, 46–47, 65, 94, 104–6, 108, 118, 127–28, 133–34, 140n21; forward vs. backward, 178–79. *See also* retention and retrieval
repetition, xx, xxiv, 24, 61–62, 64–66, 123–24, 129, 132–33, 156, 179, 193. *See also* mindful practice
retention and retrieval, 41, 44–47, 56, 59, 61, 77, 98–102, 104–8, 127–28, 131, 133–34, 140nn21–22, 141n39, 157, 244; encoding for, 59, 143, 157, 171, 177
retrieval practice, 132, 179–80
rhythm, 10, *20*, 24–25, 30n12, 53, 75–77, 144, 210; beaming, 20, 48, 51, 167; and dyslexia, 30n5; essential, 24, 28–29, 67, 79, 82; hypermeter 162, 166–167, 244; movement, tapping and chanting, 8–9, 14–21, 23–24, 26–29, 31n22, 48, 53,

61, 67–68, 75–76, 79, 81, 83, 85, 110, 148, 165, 167–69, 199, 221, 226–27, 229, 234, 237; patterns and pattern vocabulary, audiation of 16–17, 19, 21, 23–24, 27–29, 31n23, 39, 41, 52–53, 67–68, 79, 82, 87, 216, 244; problem solving of, 22, 24, 28, 31n26, 75, 79, 81, 148, 164–69, 199–200, 211n7; solfège. *See* solfège, rhythm; and tempo, 22, 29, 68n1, 75–77, 83, 85, 166, 215. *See also* the chart

rule learning, 54, 108–13, 131, 211, 244

scaffolding practice, 12, 56, 68, 83, 145, 162–66, 170–71, 187, 210, 237, 244; (down)beats only, 78, 162–166, 169, 210

scales, 60–63, 68, 72–74, 76–77, 82, 105, 110, 122, 130, 229, 234; rule learning of, 110–13

self-observation and self-evaluation, 35, 55–56, 62–63, 86, 119–121, 135–37, 244; learning-strategy based goals/criterion, 55, 60, 62, 96, 115, 181n10; performance-based goals/criterion, 55, 60, 119, 121

short-term memory. *See* memory

slow practice, 60, 62, 68, 86, 133, 135, 158, 192, 197; potential disadvantages/risks of, 158, 192

solfège, 16, 30nn7–12; rhythm, 18, 20, 30n12, 53, 67, 167; tonal, 14–16, 18, 21, 27, 30n7, 31n27

structural lines, 76–79, 83–85, 148–49, 154, 162–64, 181n6, 238, 244; *Urlinie*, 78–79, 83

structure building, 109. *See also* scaffolding practice

stylistic performance, 56, 145, 216, 235, 243

Suzuki, 5, 8, 20, 25

talent, 91–92, 95, 109, 114. *See also* aptitude

tapping and chanting. *See* rhythm

technical facility, development of 35, 56, 63, 67, 72, 76–77, 87, 96, 122–25, 148, 164, 196, 210; and learning of/linking to technical patterns, 52, 68, 72, 79–82, 130, 201, 204–5, 234, 237–38, 243–44

template theory, 46–47

tempo. *See* rhythm

theory. *See* music theory

think it then play it, 68, 68n5, 77–78, 128, 145, 155–162, 172, 187, 192–93, 208–10, 238, 244; measure +1, 70, 77, 83

threaded cognition, theory of, 40, 50, 148

to the thumbs; 164, 193–196, *208*, 210, 244

transfer, 36, 40, 61, 71–72, 97–99, 101, 106, 109, 116, 118, 125, 130, 204

Urlinie. See structural lines

variable priority training, 97, 117

visual processing, 36–43, 83, 87, 97, 102, 243; loop, *43*, 50. *See also* Gestalt

vocabulary. *See* musical pattern vocabulary; rhythm, patterns and pattern vocabulary, audiation of

what to think about when, xxii, 50, 137, 151, 243

whole-part-whole, 26, 121

working memory. *See* memory

ABOUT THE AUTHOR

Sheryl Iott is an active solo and collaborative performer, speaker, and adjudicator. She recently spent a semester on a Fulbright Scholarship, teaching piano pedagogy and coaching collaborative piano/chamber music at the University of Brasilia in Brasilia, Brazil. While there she performed in recital with numerous UnB faculty, often featuring music of myriad South American composers. She has also performed in Italy and throughout the United Kingdom as well as in many cities in the United States. She has studied with Ralph and Albertine Votapek, Ian Hobson, and Joseph Evans, with additional coachings from Lydia Artimiw, Ward Davenny, and Richard Sim.

Dr. Iott is on the faculty of Interlochen Arts Camp and has served on the faculties of Grand Rapids Community College, Hope College, Michigan State University, and Calvin College. Appointments have included teaching piano, piano pedagogy, keyboard skills, music appreciation, and duties as staff accompanist. She is also a member of the College of Examiners for the Royal Conservatory of Music of Toronto, for which she also works as a facilitator for their online pedagogy courses and as a subject matter expert in piano and piano pedagogy.

Frequently published in music education and piano pedagogy books and magazines, including a chapter in *Practical Applications in Music Learning Theory* and articles in peer-reviewed journals including: "Untangling the Tangles: Making Musical Sense of Bach's First Duet," and "Sightplaying Through Access to a Complete Musical Vocabulary"; Dr. Iott has conducted multiple master and "un"-master classes, as well as workshops on fugue analysis, preparing students for the Royal Conservatory of Toronto practical exams, how theoretical analysis informs musical performance, performance practices of the Classical period, and on effective practice strategies as seminar courses and pedagogy programs across the United States.

www.ingramcontent.com/pod-product-compliance
Lightning Source LLC
Chambersburg PA
CBHW080727230426
43665CB00020B/2641